Wisdom, Analytics and Wicked Problems

The challenges faced by 21st-century businesses, organizations and governments are characterized as being fundamentally different in nature, scope and levels of impact from those of the past. As problems become increasingly complex and wicked, conventional reductive approaches and data-based solutions are limited. The authors argue that practical wisdom is required.

This book provides an integral and practical model for incorporating wisdom into management decision making. Based on a cross-disciplinary conceptualization of practical wisdom, the authors distinguish systematically between data, information, knowledge, and wisdom-based decision making. While they suggest that data, analytics, information and knowledge can assist decision-makers to better deal with complex and wicked problems, they argue that data-based systems cannot replace optimized human decision-making capabilities. These capabilities, the authors explain, include a range of qualities and characteristics inherent in philosophical, psychological and organizational conceptions of practical wisdom.

Accordingly, in this book, the authors introduce a model that identifies the specific qualities and processes involved in making wise decisions, especially in management. The model is based on the empirical findings of the authors' studies in the areas of wisdom and management.

This book is a practical resource for professionals, practitioners, and consultants in both the private and public sectors. The theoretical discussions, critical arguments, and practical guidelines provided in the book will be extremely valuable to students at the undergraduate and postgraduate levels, as well as upper-level postdoctoral researchers looking at business management strategies.

Ali Intezari is a Senior Lecturer in the School of Management at Massey University, Auckland, New Zealand. His work has appeared in journals such as the *Decision Sciences Journal*, *Journal of Business Ethics* and *Journal of Knowledge Management*.

David Pauleen is a Professor in Technology Management at Massey University, Auckland, New Zealand. His work has appeared in journals such as the *Journal of Management Information Systems*, *Sloan Management Review* and *Journal of Business Ethics*.

The Practical Wisdom in Leadership and Organization Series

Series Editors:

Wendelin Küpers is Professor of Leadership and Organization Studies at Karlshochschule International University, Germany.

David Pauleen is a Professor of Technology Management at Massey University, New Zealand.

The Practical Wisdom in Leadership and Organization Series provides a platform for authors to articulate wiser ways of managing and leading and of reassessing practice within organizational settings and organizational research. Books in this series focus on the art and practice of inquiry and reflexivity and explicitly connect with challenges and issues of 'praxis' in the field of organization and management, be that academic research or in situ management practice. Rather than offering closure and final answers, contributions to this series invite further critical inquiry, cross-disciplinary conversations and explorations. The aim is to engage authors and readers – students, academics and practitioners alike – in inspiring, reflexive and critical dialogue. By thus engaging readers, we hope that these books play an important role in informing, teaching and learning in educational contexts and public forums as well as among practitioners and in management boardrooms.

A Handbook of Practical Wisdom
Leadership, Organization and Integral Business Practice
Edited by Wendelin Küpersand David Pauleen

Practical Wisdom in the Age of Technology
Insights, Issues and Questions for a New Millennium
Edited by Nikunj Dalal, Ali Intezari and Marty Heitz

Wisdom Learning
Perspectives on Wising-Up Business and Management Education
Edited by Wendelin Küpers and Olen Gunnlaugson

Wisdom, Analytics and Wicked Problems
Integral Decision Making for the Data Age
Ali Intezari and David Pauleen

For more information about this series, please visit: www.routledge.com/The-Practical-Wisdom-in-Leadership-and-Organization-Series/book-series/WISDOM

Wisdom, Analytics and Wicked Problems

Integral Decision Making for the Data Age

Ali Intezari and David Pauleen

LONDON AND NEW YORK

First published 2019 by Routledge

2 Park Square, Milton Park, Abingdon, Oxon, OX14 4RN
605 Third Avenue, New York, NY 10017

Routledge is an imprint of the Taylor & Francis Group, an informa business

First issued in paperback 2020

British Library Cataloguing-in-Publication Data
A catalogue record for this book is available from the British Library

Library of Congress Cataloging-in-Publication Data
A catalog record has been requested for this book

ISBN: 978-1-4724-6378-4 (hbk)
ISBN: 978-0-367-73305-6 (pbk)

Typeset in Times New Roman
by Out of House Publishing

Contents

Figures

Tables

Series Editor Introduction

Wendelin Küpers

Series Editor, The Practical Wisdom in Leadership and
Organization Series

In human history, for a long time, practical wisdom has provided a source and resource for excellence in judgement and prudent action. As the capacity to find and practice for realizing excellent judgement, wisdom can guide and mediate decisions, including day-to-day managerial decision-making processes in organizations.

This book offers a valuable support for this very making of decisions as one of the most influential and important fields of applications of practical wisdom in relation to organization and management. In a certain sense, in making decisions, wisdom crystallizes concretely. Making wise(r) decisions is not only needed in these unwise times that call for wisdom and its learning (Küpers & Gunnlaugson, 2017), but connecting wisdom and decision making offers a practice link to bring idealist and aspirational ideas and agendas of wisdom down to earth.

In addition to being 'applied', the metaphor of a condensed crystallization or refined distillation of wisdom in decision making refers also to a manifestation and testing as well as touchstone of a wise practice for our time and a more sustainable future to come. Both also imply a critique of conventional forms of decision making.

As this book shows, a practically wise making of decisions entails overcoming traditional functionalist and reductive orientations that pursue calculative, 'objectivist' approaches that nowadays increasingly involve maximizing computing mechanisms.

What is required are excellence-oriented ways of ethically 'optimal' deciding and judging. This excellence requires liberation from orthodox one-sided practices and deliberating about what to do while attending to relevant potentially conflicting particularities. Correspondingly, this can then lead to making wiser judgements and thus informed and forming decisions. Moreover, excellence also implies enacting them in practical doing. Such coordinated execution contributes then to 'well-be(com)ing' of all involved, thus transforming the world towards one worth living in.

Importantly, practical wisdom implies exercising and applying good judgement based on 'proper' desires and intentions, embodied dispositions, values, and principles as well as in relation to available evidence along the way. Good judgement recognizes, in an open manner and with circumspection, the risks and benefits of different options or alternatives. Moreover, it considers the means for realizing intended accomplishments, can prioritize them, and then chooses between them for wise decisions and actions. However, to judge wisely is the ability to make careful decisions not in a mechanistic way, but as a comprehensive process.

Practical wisdom and judgement are emerging developmentally, within an unceasing flow of performative activities, in which morally sensible practitioners are inextricably and also emotionally immersed (Shotter & Tsoukas, 2014). According to Shotter and

Tsoukas, both provide means to establish a new orientation for practitioners to move around within a puzzling landscape of possibilities. Moreover in so doing, they are being spontaneously embodied responses to and imaginative explorations of possibilities and consequences of these movements (Shotter & Tsoukas, 2014). As outlined in Chapter 2, wise responses are needed, in particular in the context of uncertain situations. That which makes one capable of judging correctly in untypical and complex situations is a responsive comprehension and discernment, also to solve difficult dilemmas involving a conflict of virtues, strategies, goals, and aspired ends. The embodied dimension and relation to perceptiveness is crucial, for making correct judgements and wise decisions. Complementing rational analytic understanding of differences and reasons, responsive wisdom also is able to adequately sense and interpret emotional states to judge particular expressions, which are considered in this book as 'masterly' capabilities. In order to develop and realize the required capacities, practitioners of practical wisdom in decision making need memory, habits, imagination, exchange of experience, and participating in social intercourse. Therefore, this book emphasizes the link to Social Practical Wisdom (SPW) that considers systemically the circumstances of life, as well as social realities and processes.

Thus, wise judging and decision making is an ongoing, evolving, and evaluative process including embodied, emotional, cognitive, and social dimensions and with all that its practice is – like practically wise leadership – more an 'art' (Küpers, 2013).

In times of information overload, dataism, algorithm-based calculations, and complex problems, forms of wise decision making are needed more and more. The misapplication of data within false premises, biased frameworks, or exploitative situations is perhaps a greater threat to our society than we have been led to believe. What is needed is that big data techniques and algorithms are audited wisely: that is, their assumptions, sources, and techniques are exposed and examined, and then compared to reality and to social concepts (O'Neil, 2016). Big data needs to 'think big' (Baldassarre, 2017; Pauleen, Rooney, & Intezari, 2016) or have a 'big' picture view and 'thick' description in order not to become 'sick'.

Understanding processes of variegated wisdom in general as well as practically wise decision making in particular calls for inter- and transdisciplinary unfolding and synthesizing the main dimensions and features of practical wisdom that can help to facilitate a multi-perspective, self-guided evaluation and reflection process for an optimized decision practice (Bachmann, Sasse, & Habisch, 2018). This book uses such a cross-disciplinary approach and takes various perspectives on its topic, while also offering helpful pathways towards wiser decision-making practices.

Overall, this book teaches us again the post-Socratic realization that to be wise – also in decision making – is to be acutely aware of and learn about our ignorance. This ignorance cannot be filled with more information and knowledge as this would only mean more ignorance of our ignorance. Wise decision making and living 'knows' how to free us from an overwhelming dependence on amounts of empirical knowledge, conceptual categories, and epistemological representations as well as being able to resist surface appearances, quantifications, and knowledge representations. Furthermore, wisdom is something more than simply recognition of the inevitable limits of knowledge and abandoning a priori visions of perfection. It also means being able to embrace knowledge and ignorance in relation to affect, drives, feelings, and the subconscious as the sources of our creativity and developmental unfolding. Such proto-integral wise practice and practitioners 'know' that it is being complicit and inter-involved with all what is happening in an everyday becoming when there is need for decision making. However, this involvement is not fixated on one-sided purpose-driven ends that are limited to utilitarian orientation but cultivates a creative relationship to constraints, while making responsible decisions. "Wise people embrace doubt, ambiguities, consequences, and experiences – the effects of decisions that they need to live with and not just the decisions themselves" (Chia & Holt, 2007, p. 513).

Wise decision making avoids mistaking the map for the territory, that is making decisions on the basis of representations of decontextualized information and abstracted knowledge (including computer-generated statistics, remote-monitoring processes, performance indicators, charts, and trend analyses etc.), while mistaking these for concrete reality.

"Only by wandering around, with intellectual naïveté and learned ignorance, can organizational leaders truly see for themselves what their priorities are or ought to be in decisional terms" (Chia & Holt, 2007, p. 523), thereby becoming ready for unlearning and disclosing new meanings, and relations with others and things, thus generating real surplus value and wiser practices.

If organizations and leadership as we know them today are the expression of our current world-view, our current stage of development, how can we reinvent them (Laloux, 2014) in a way that allows their creative potentials and evolutionary purpose to unfold wisely? With an advice process, in such organizations the right people with proto-integral mind-sets make quality decisions at the right level with the input and inspiration from relevant and knowledgeable colleagues and stakeholders. Importantly, these decisions are informed and processed not only by the rational mind, but also by the wisdom of emotions, intuition, and aesthetics, while being arranged caringly with a meaningful purpose that is not losing sight of the needs of the whole.

In resonance with all these dimensions, this book contributes to a proto-integral wisdom-fostering decision making that takes perspectives, is ethically qualified, and processed by deciders who are aware of themselves and others with emotional-cognitive mastery and internal-external reflection and practice. With its empirical grounding, clarifying elaboration and conceptual frameworks as well as discussion of implications, it offers a very timely valuable reflection and practice-oriented contribution that hopefully finds decisive resonance for future research and practices that search for a 'living' and 'enlivening' practical wisdom.

As an expression of an integral orientation manifest in this book, there is hope that wisdom becomes practical in our time that is and will be more and more in need of wise decisions and a corresponding making and enacting of them.

References

Bachmann, C., Sasse, L., & Habisch, A. (2018). Applying the practical wisdom lenses in decision-making: An integrative approach to humanistic management. *Humanistic Management Journal*, 2(2), 125–150.

Baldassarre, M. (2017). Think big: learning contexts, algorithms and data science. *REM – Research on Education and Media*, 8(2), 20 January. https://doi.org/10.1515/rem-2016-0020.

Chia, R., & Holt, R. (2007). Wisdom as learned ignorance. In E. Kessler & J. Bailey (Eds.), *Handbook of managerial and organizational wisdom* (pp. 505–526). Thousand Oaks, CA: Sage.

Küpers, W. (2013). The art of practical wisdom – phenomenology of an embodied, wise inter-practice in organisation and leadership. In W. Küpers, W. & D. J. Pauleen (Eds.), *A handbook of practical wisdom. leadership, organization and integral business practice* (pp. 19–45). Aldershot, UK: Gower.

Küpers, W., & Gunnlaugson, O. (2017). Introduction: Contexts and complexities of wisdom learning in management and business education. In W. Küpers & O. Gunnlaugson (Eds.), *Wisdom learning: Perspectives on wising-up management & business education* (pp. 1–38). London: Routledge.

Laloux, F. (2014). *Reinventing organizations: A guide to creating organizations inspired by the next stage in human consciousness*. Brussels: Nelson Parker.

O'Neil, C. (2016). *Weapons of math destruction: How big data increases inequality and threatens democracy*. New York: Crown.

Pauleen, D. J., Rooney, D., & Intezari, A. (2016). Big data, little wisdom: Trouble brewing? Ethical implications for the information systems discipline. *Social Epistemology*, 31(4), 9–33.

Shotter, J., & Tsoukas, H. (2014). Performing phronesis: On the way to engaged judgment. *Management Learning*, 45(4), 377–396.

Foreword

In a complex and heterogeneous world, integration is both a holy grail and seemingly impossible to obtain, unless you are wise. Integration is a basic dynamic in wise action. Wisdom has always been the apex of practicality but its value as such only increases in the contemporary world. It is therefore no surprise that the concept of practical wisdom is well over 2,000 years old and developed more or less simultaneously in different cultures and continents. But you might ask, what happened to it? Why is there so little of it in our leaders and decision makers? Will there be a true renaissance that reboots wisdom? From my perspective, the bottom line is that wisdom was reified as a gift given by God by the mediaeval Scholastic philosophers (most notably by Saint Thomas Aquinas, the neo Aristotelian), and then cast as a mystical or romantic impractical indulgence since the instrumentalism of the scientific and industrial revolutions. Western hubris hijacked science and industry to betray wisdom, wisdom's (and science's) original western architect, Aristotle, and the future.

If this commentary seems excessive, consider carbon emissions and global warming. How unwise were we to let that happen, even though we had the knowledge to see it happening decades ago? How much is a disconnected-from-wisdom technology, engineering and scientific apparatus that has given us a monumental capacity to create carbon emissions responsible for climate change? Where were our political and corporate leaders and decision makers, and what were they doing to have taken so long to see what we were heading towards? And why do they still find it hard to make effective responses?

Perhaps we can consider the globalized financial and economic crises that have rattled around the world since 2006, and neo classical economics' stilted and immature understanding of what it is to be human. In this view there is no society, or right and wrong. And what about contemporary politics where people who resemble cartoon characters rather than fully formed adults are given leadership roles that carry with them the potential to ignite warfare on a truly eschatological scale? Wisdom, I think, is missing in much decision making.

The positive story is that a small group of scholars around the world are working to reteach us what wisdom is, why it is important, and how to be wise. David Pauleen and Ali Intezari are key figures in this project and so is this book.

So why would anyone read the book? In a word, the reason is 'excellence'. Or going a step further, you want to consider how to achieve excellent decisions in a messy, mischievous world that seems to always be getting in the way of doing what's best. Practical wisdom is done in the real world and it is done in specific times and places with uniquely difficult social, economic, environmental, and political circumstances. Practical wisdom is excellence despite the real world.

Ethics is indivisible from wisdom. As my colleague, Bernard McKenna, and I have long maintained, if it is not ethical, it is not wise. In saying this, we are referring to virtue ethics, a system in which virtuous action must be characterized by doing the right thing, for the right reasons, in the right way. This, of course, is a tall order, it is excellence, and sits at the very core of practical wisdom. Nevertheless, if you think we should stop using the real world as a convenient excuse for falling well short of excellence and making unwise decisions, then I think you will see the sense of reading this book.

Wisdom and decision making are also linked to knowledge. But wisdom is not done justice when understood as a special kind of knowledge, even as a special kind of tacit knowledge. Knowledge matters a great deal but it has little long-term value for humanity and our planet if it is not carried by sound judgement, ethicality, creativity, insight, and excellent reasoning to create a kind of holistic cognitive integration. Intelligent heart might be the way one of Aristotle's 'contemporaries', the Buddha, might put it. In a context where algorithmic knowledge, dataism, and the new challenges of data analytics and artificial intelligence present themselves, it would be reckless to think these new things can be direct substitutes for wisdom. Let's not make the mistake again of thinking more and more data, information and knowledge is the answer to our problem: we have been making that mistake over and over again, at least since the scientific revolution and then again with the emergence in the 1920s of the Vienna circle's ideology of positivism.

A useful way to think about this book is to understand it as presenting new ways to think, decide and act using an ancient and well-tested concept that contemporary researchers are fast updating. This book is the next edition in this process. I'm sure you will enjoy and benefit from the journey the book is about to take you on.

David Rooney, Sydney, May 2018

Acknowledgements

First and foremost, I would like to thank my wife, Sara, for standing beside me throughout my study and career. I dedicate this book to her. I would like to especially thank my co-author, and good friend, Professor David Pauleen, who has always encouraged me to take on new intellectual challenges by providing great ideas and support over the last ten years. Without him, this book would not have been written.

Professor Pauleen would like to thank his wife, Beatrix, for her long-suffering patience and understanding.

Introduction

Soichiro Honda, the founder of Honda, once compared business decision making with making a joke:

> You have to grasp the atmosphere of the occasion, [...] which exists only for a particular moment. A joke is all in the timing, in understanding what the present evokes. To joke is to understand human emotion and be present for it.
>
> (Pritscher, 2010, p. 173)

As with a good joke, a good decision is about timing, emotion, and awareness.

While humans may have been searching for the perfect joke since 1900 BC (Reuters, 2008), organizational scholars and practitioners have, for the last 80 years, been attempting to answer a simple yet critical question: How can managers make effective and successful decisions?

Consistently effective decision making is an important competitive advantage, and a deep understanding of it is vital in handling the dynamics of organizations (Nutt & Wilson, 2010). The quality of management and the success of organizations primarily depend on the decisions that are made by managers. A bad decision in a highly competitive or uncertain environment can be disastrous for an organization (Dean & Sharfman, 1993).

Fifty years ago environmental factors that were seen as important to the process of making decisions included: (1) customers; (2) suppliers (capital, labour, materials, etc.); (3) competitors; and (4) regulatory bodies (governments, trade unions, employers' organizations, etc.) (Thompson, 1967). Today, however, the environment has changed drastically. Complexity, socio-environmental paradoxes, rapid advances in technology, globalization and interconnectedness, speed and competition are now the inherent characteristics of the 21st century. It has now been more than two decades since organization and management scholars and practitioners came to the realization that Newtonian-based organizational approaches that posit the future as predictable will no longer be applicable to organizations: "The new world is full of unintended consequences and counterintuitive outcomes. In such a world, the map to the future cannot be drawn in advance. We cannot know enough to set forth a meaningful vision or to plan productively" (Tetenbaum, 1998, p. 24).

In such a complex world, the interactions between humans, knowledge, and the environment need to be wisely managed. One of the commonest leadership failures in the 21st century is trying to apply simplified solutions to complex problems (Uhl-Bien, Marion, & McKelvey, 2007). Yet even when the effort is made to understand a complex decision situation, it is always difficult to accurately identify and predict the solution. Complex challenges are usually value-laden and stir up people's emotions. These are situations where challenges strike at the core feelings and thoughts of others.

According to Snowden and Boone (2007), rather than trying to control such situations, it is in the decision maker's best interest to be patient and encourage emergence of a solution. Snowden and Boone (2007, p. 76) provide this advice:

> In the complex environment of the current business world, leaders often will be called upon to act against their instincts. They will need to know when to share power and when to wield it alone, when to look to the wisdom of the group and when to take their own counsel. A deep understanding of context, the ability to embrace complexity and paradox, and a willingness to flexibly change leadership style will be required for leaders who want to make things happen in a time of increasing uncertainty.

In this book we focus on practical wisdom and its capability to both expand our perspectives and focus our efforts when it comes to engaging in decision making in complex environments. We acknowledge the role of traditional approaches to decision making, as well as the emerging influence of big data and analytics tools and techniques in making successful decisions. We, however, emphasize that the complexity of today's business environment requires managers who can effectively manage uncertain and complex decision situations. Such managers are not tethered to linear decision-making processes. They are capable of applying multi-layered, poly-faceted, and highly complex decision-making processes effectively and in a timely manner, without getting interrupted and undermined by the demands of stakeholders. Moreover, while being engaged in this way, they always act while keeping their legal and ethical obligations foremost in mind.

Aim and focus

This book aims to provide an integral and practical framework for incorporating wisdom into business and management practices in both the private and public sectors.

Overall, it offers an understanding of wisdom that confirms and supports approaches that emphasize the multidimensionality of wisdom (Ardelt, 1997; Baltes & Staudinger, 2000; Birren & Fisher, 1990; Clayton & Birren, 1980; Webster, 2003) and aligns with Kodish's (2006, p. 461) definition of practical wisdom:

> Practical wisdom includes a mix of intertwined and equally important layers. It involves knowledge, perception, decision making, purposive action, grasp of the rational and the [non-rational] principles, character, virtue, experience, promotion of one's own personal interests, understanding of others and endorsing their interests, intuition, and transcendence.

This understanding underlines the association and more importantly the integration of multiple qualities such as knowledge, experience, virtue, and action with wisdom in general and with wise management decision making in particular. Moreover, here we are seeking and investigating how to wisely incorporate contemporary emerging developments and realities such as big data and analytics into the decision-making process. When used wisely, algorithms, big data, and analytics have potentially significant applications for individual and organizational performance improvement, as well as the well-being of humanity.

Although wisdom was a major concern in ancient philosophy, researchers point out that it has only been an afterthought in the 20th century (Grimm, 2015). The Western concept of wisdom typically refers back to the work of Aristotle, who identified wise people as those who see what is good for them and for mankind in general (Baden & Higgs, 2015). Interest in wisdom studies gained momentum in psychological research in the 1980s. Only in recent times have organization and management researchers revived an interest in adapting wisdom theory (Küpers & Pauleen, 2013; McKenna, Rooney, & Kenworthy, 2013).

Although wisdom has been central to philosophical discourses since the time of Aristotle, scholars have experienced some difficulty in trying to define wisdom.

From the outset, we must make it clear that while we recognize that wisdom traditions encompass a range of Western and Eastern traditions, including indigenous, Middle Eastern, African, South American, Chinese, Indian, and other East and South Asian philosophical traditions, we focus primarily on a Western approach. Accordingly, we connect mainly to an understanding of wisdom as presented by ancient Greek philosophers such as Plato, Socrates, and Aristotle. We do so because most contemporary Western academic studies of wisdom, linked to management and organization, draw from this literature. We will leave cross-cultural interpretations of wisdom and their relevance to modern business practice to others.

What the book may lack in cross-cultural perspectives of wisdom, we hope it makes up with a cross-disciplinary conceptualization of 'wisdom'.

In first part, we look at ancient philosophical views of wisdom as well as modern psychological conceptual and empirical definitions. Ultimately, we merge these with modern organizational perspectives on wisdom and develop a practical understanding of wisdom that we then apply to management decision making.

As part of our practical approach, we will explore in some depth the conceptual and concrete differences between data, information, and knowledge, and how they can be more effectively incorporated into wisdom-based decision making.

As our world is awash in data and information, and this grows exponentially, ever greater amounts of these become the de facto objective of business, government, and society. When you make data and information acquisition your goal, then of course you must find ways to use it. We fear, as do a number of serious social and business commentators (cf. Dalal & Pauleen, 2018; Maxwell, 2012; Rooney, McKenna, & Liesch, 2010) that this 'dataism' and its information may be used unwisely and to ill effect. Although it not clear yet how the data age will fully manifest, we certainly hope that at the very least it will be tempered with wisdom.

Wicked problems is how we have characterized the challenges faced by 21st-century businesses and governments. These challenges are fundamentally different in nature, scope, and impact from those of the past. They are 'wicked' in nature in the sense that "they are both pernicious and problematic to address" (Marshak, 2009, p. 58), being tied to multiple stakeholders' interests, exacerbated by gaps in established knowledge, and subject to scientific uncertainty and fragmentation (Head & Alford, 2008). Organizations and managers often face these kinds of problems particularly when they engage in strategic decision making which tends to involve decision-making processes that are often novel, complex, and open-ended (Mintzberg, Raisinghani, & Théorêt,

1976). Perhaps it will be possible to more effectively address these wicked problems by using a combination of data, information, knowledge, and wisdom.

We hope that this book will help business education students and teachers, management training experts, and professional practitioners to answer the question: how can we develop our capabilities and competencies for decision making to be able to make wiser decisions while dealing with the growing complexity of the business world?

Why this book now?

As indicated above, the world is growing more complex, resulting in more and deeper challenges for managers and organizations. Once simple decisions grow more complicated as the web of relationships between individuals, organizations, and society become clearer and subject to increasing scrutiny by concerned stakeholders. The effects of organizational operations often extend beyond the here and now of the organization. Competition, globalization, technology, and growing expectations of social responsibility leave many organizations vulnerable to a myriad of forces and factors. More than ever, success requires the critical consideration and management of the interconnectedness of individuals, organizations, and society.

We have identified the following pressing issues that should be of particular concern to managers and organizations, and which we believe can be more effectively and holistically addressed by adopting the integral wisdom decision-making model introduced in this book.

Sustainability: Globalization and the growing awareness of the social and ethical responsibilities of organizations, i.e. the relationship between a business entity and its surrounding environment including society, has become a critical factor in determining the long-term success of organizations. Organizational decisions have to bring into consideration an increasing number of factors and stakeholders' perspectives. Accordingly, management strategic decisions need to take into account more than just the economic interests or just the factors that affect the organization. The decision-making model that is introduced in this book takes into account the interaction between the organization and the environment and highlights the need for considering stakeholders' perspectives in management decision making. The model explains how to understand and approach the interrelationship between managers, organizations, and their surrounding biophysical environment when making strategic decisions.

Globalization, and society's growing awareness of organizations' social responsibilities, further underscore that decision making in the management setting does not occur under laboratory conditions. Strategic decision making involves a dynamic interplay of various factors between the problem, the decision maker, and stakeholders within a defined context. Such decision making is a complex process that requires a decision maker with multiple skills and tools. Managers cannot solely rely on their previous knowledge and information. Success requires innovative knowledge and perspectives.

Balancing knowledge and doubt: If we accept that knowledge is rooted, to at least some degree, in data, experience, and previous knowledge, then dealing with complex, unpredictable, and emergent decision situations may require decision-making processes in which data, experience, and knowledge must be consciously tailored to effectively address the emerging decision situation. This requires a deep understanding of how the use of data, information, or knowledge may change in the decision-making process, depending on the complexity of the decision situation. A manager's previous experiences do not eliminate uncertainty. Their knowledge may fall short in handling the rapid changes in an extremely competitive business world.

To make effective decisions under such conditions, we believe managers will need to be able to integrate a set of rational and non-rational cognitive capabilities along with external information sources. Decision makers need to question and subsequently go beyond conditioned standards of rationality and what is wrong and right. Wisdom, we argue, will allow these perspectives to take root and grow. As Allee (1997, p. 16) put it:

> Any framework of knowledge that does not include wisdom requires us to operate blind. Without wisdom there is no vision. Without vision we are lost in a sea of knowledge and information with no north star to guide us on our way.

Conceptualizing wisdom: In spite of centuries of philosophical debates on the nature of wisdom and its manifestation in practice, providing an agreed-upon definition of wisdom is still and will continue to be a challenging task for scholars. The diversity of disciplines that have recently attempted to conceptualize wisdom has just added to the challenge. Psychological studies of wisdom over the last three decades have endeavoured to conceptualize and operationalize the notion of wisdom. Other disciplines such as neuroscience and leadership have called for the theoretical and practical incorporation of wisdom into their fields. Despite these attempts to understand and integrate wisdom, and possibly due to these multi-disciplinary approaches, there is still no globally agreed-upon definition of wisdom. Understanding how wisdom manifests in practice and reality is even more problematic.

In this book, we offer an understanding of wisdom linked to the field of decision making that can bridge and integrate the rational and naturalistic perspectives on the management decision-making process. This book confirms and expands on recent studies in management (Rooney, 2013) and in neuroscience (Dijksterhuis, Bos, Nordgren, & van Baaren, 2006) on the need for integration of cognition and emotions in decision making. In line with Pauleen, Rooney, and Holden (2010), who argue that decisions and actions taken solely based on reason and facts are too limited, and consistent with Damasio's (2005) findings that show that emotion and cognition complement each other in decision making, we argue that wise management decisions are based on the integration of cognitive and emotional qualities. In addition, the model of wise management decision making (Chapter 8) does not assume that emotion is something opposite to cognition. Consistent with Rooney (2013), we suggest that using such unconscious capabilities as emotions, feelings, and intuition may lead to more satisfying and better choices.

In addition, the success and value of management decisions should not solely rely on the achievement of management and organizational goals and objectives. Consistent with the understanding that wisdom underlies successful human development (Ardelt, 2005; Erikson, 1963; Hart, 1987), the wise management decision-making model suggests that the success of a management decision should be evaluated by the extent to which the decision leads to the well-being of the decision maker, and those who are affected by the decision, as well as the achievement of organizational goals.

The need for more than expertise: While expertise is critical to the success of management decisions and practices, dealing with complex and poly-faceted decision situations, characterized by organizational, social, environmental, and political interconnectedness, requires more than technical knowledge and field expertise. In this book we provide a more comprehensive understanding of the nature of wisdom and its relationship to data, information, and knowledge, and extend the conventional thinking that data, information, and knowledge are critically important factors for achieving success in the business world. The wise management decision-making model we introduce in this book highlights the critical role of other qualities such as intuition and emotion in wisdom, and shows that wisdom is not a mere accumulation of knowledge. The model deepens and broadens the understanding that knowledge management scholars have provided of wisdom. We argue that success in the current ever-changing business world is not easily achievable if companies just rely on the accumulation and management of information and knowledge.

Management training beyond a knowledge-transferring mechanism: Recent financial and management scandals and blunders remind us that it is time to include wisdom development training in management development programmes (Small, 2004). This book can contribute to education in general, and management education in particular, by affirming the differences between data, information, knowledge, and wisdom, and by providing an integrative approach to them. We argue that making appropriate decisions in the business world requires the wise use, rather than just the effective management of, data, information, and knowledge. The management decision-making model introduced in this book emphasizes the necessity of including the study of wisdom in business courses and management development programmes.

Teaching wisdom is also important as it fosters and leads to creativity as well (Sternberg, 2003). This book paves the way for a wisdom-based pedagogical system in management by offering an integrative approach that incorporates analytics-based and wisdom-based teaching systems. The integration of cognition and emotion, awareness of self and others, and internal and external reflection, are qualities that can be easily integrated into conventional business education systems that heretofore put more emphasis on knowledge transmission than wisdom development.

Management and experiential learning: While it has been broadly suggested that wisdom should be taught in schools (cf. Ferrari & Potworowski, 2008; Küpers & Pauleen, 2015; Maxwell, 2012), wisdom is still neglected in educational settings. This may be due to a number of reasons. It could be because of the lack of a consensus on the concept of wisdom and its component parts among scholars. It might be because of the lack of a systematic approach to teaching wisdom. Or it might be because of the ambiguity and lack of consensus surrounding methods and techniques for developing wisdom.

The emphasis in this book on the development of wisdom through a reflective-learning practice of the wisdom principles (Chapter 9) resonates with the much-discussed and approved Experiential Learning Theory (ELT) by Kolb (Kolb, 1984; Kolb & Kolb, 2001, 2005; Vince, 1998).

The wise management decision-making model (see Chapter 8 for the model) supports and expands on current ELT in management learning. Learning from mistakes is an important way to gain wisdom (Liew, 2013). The wise management decision-making model confirms and underscores the importance of experiential learning in management learning and development. The enhancement of multi-perspective consideration (MPC), self-other awareness (SOA), and cognitive-emotional mastery (CEM) is interwoven with the interaction of practice and reflection. Learning and development as suggested by this book, however, engages more than just reflection on practice and experiences.

The model expands on ELT in management development by underlining and integrating the essential role of emotion (Vince, 1998), intuition (Michelson, 1996), social interaction (Beard & Wilson, 2006; Miettinen, 2000), selflessness (humility) (Brown, 2004; Grint, 2007; Hinterhuber, 1996), and virtue and morality (Driver, 2003) in developing wisdom through reflective learning. Furthermore, our model suggests that the development of wisdom requires reflection on individual and community values, beliefs, and interests, as well as questioning the decision maker's core assumptions. This acknowledges the multi-layered nature of learning and the role of second-order-oriented learning (Gergen, 1992; Senge, 1990).

Moreover, the wise management decision-making model takes experiential learning beyond mere post-action learning towards a more processual during- and prior-action learning (Desmond & Jowitt, 2012; Yalom, 1985). Prior-action learning in wise management decision making refers to learning by reflecting on *possible alternative actions*, and *anticipating* possible consequences and reactions.

Wise management decision making is not simply generalizing memories and learning from previous mistakes to enhance future actions. It involves taking learning beyond post-action learning towards a learning that happens before and during action. Such extended reflective learning embracing the Past, Now, and Future respectively, as illustrated by Figure 9.4, is more integrative. It is integrative in that both retrospective and prospective reflection and learning are critically important in management learning. This is even more necessary as post-action learning and solely relying on past experience may lead to ignorance or avoidance of what is in the present (Vince, 1998).

Assessment tool to measure: Despite the critical role of decision making in the success of organizations, measuring the effectiveness of decisions is a challenging task for many organizations (Blenko, Mankins, & Rogers, 2010; Blenko, Rogers, & Mankin, 2010). The decision-making model that we introduce in this book can be used to assess managers' decision-making ability more holistically. It can serve as a comprehensive practical foundation for the development of an integrated assessment tool that can provide a rigorous evaluation of the extent to which a manager is able to make effective decisions in uncertain decision situations. Such an appraisal tool can be designed based on an integrative approach of the key qualities of MPC, SOA, and CEM. Accordingly it can be used to measure the success of a management decision based on the extent to which the decision has led to the achievement of the organizational goals, communal interests, and the development of the decision maker.

Together, the models and frameworks proposed in this book can be incorporated into wisdom-based decision-making guidelines that can help manager and senior practitioners to make better – and this means also wiser – decisions. So far, the most prominent approaches to wisdom in management have relied on psychological studies that are mainly character based. The organizational and management field, therefore, lacks a comprehensive perspective that represents wisdom as a contextually situated business practice that is always relational and social. It might, therefore, be quite difficult to convince information-age, conventionally MBA-educated managers that what they need more than anything else to effectively face modern business challenges is wisdom: to be able to be both analytical and insightful at the same time. They are inevitably engaged in handling a massive volume of data and information when trying to understand situations and make decisions. Figures and numbers give them the illusory sense that they can easily understand what is going on around them, how they can react, and the likely results of a particular decision.

For those managers, who desperately look to simplification to understand the complex world around them, it might be disappointing to realize that these quantitative representations do not necessarily cover and reflect the reality of the complex and inextricably interwoven social, environmental, political, power, and economic dimensions of the (business) world.

Nevertheless, they may often resist entering into wise management decision-making processes, as it is clearly not as simple as managing reality through the lens of facts and figures.

Accordingly, it is important to understand how to bridge a manager's desires for short-term tangible understanding of reality with the more complex requirements that are suggested by the model introduced here. By incorporating the findings of the authors' empirical studies on management, we hope that what we have outlined here, particularly the practical framework can convincingly help managers to be more effective in making strategic and others decisions in uncertain decision-situations which will lead to longer lasting and more positive effects on the organization and community, with its various stakeholder.

The contents of the book

This book comprises three sections and nine chapters. In Part I we provide an introduction to the concept of 'wisdom' and present a review of some of the major studies around wisdom, as well as challenges that organizations are experiencing in the 21st century. In Part II we discuss the role of knowledge, big data, and analytics in dealing with complex decision situations, and explain decision making as the core of what managers do. In Part III we introduce an integral model of decision making, which we suggest is both an effective method of management decision making and a possible path to personal wisdom in today's organizational settings.

Part I: An ancient concept – 21st-century challenges

Part I provides a review of the fundamental concepts of wisdom and organizational problems. We draw on significant traditions and approaches to wisdom to develop an interdisciplinary conceptual framework of wisdom and in relation to complex and wicked problem as encountered by today's organizations.

Chapter 1: Wisdom from ancient philosophy to modern psychology

The book begins with a review of philosophical discourses of wisdom and then moves to contemporary psychological studies of wisdom. Wisdom is defined in terms of being practical and theoretical and in relation to intellectual and moral virtues. We also review the major psychological studies of wisdom in the contemporary literature.

Chapter 2: Understanding practical wisdom in business and management: an inter-disciplinary perspective

A critical comparative analysis of recent business approaches to wisdom is developed. In the chapter we identify and bring to the fore the foundations, aspects, and perceptions of wisdom that are held in common by different approaches and disciplines. The chapter concludes by suggesting an interdisciplinary conceptualization of wisdom.

Chapter 3: Organizational problems: why decision situations can be more wicked *than we think*

This chapter discusses the nature of the decision problems and challenges that today's organizations face. Many management decision situations are fundamentally complex in nature and tend to include 'mash-ups' of technological, economic, environmental, social, and political factors. The problems are 'wicked' and cannot be resolved by information systems alone or even in combination with human knowledge and traditional decision-making processes.

Part II: Knowledge, information, data / analytics, and decision making

Part II provides further discussions about multiple fundamental aspects related to management decision making. These include the relationship between data, information, and knowledge, as well as the role of analytics in management decision making. Part II consists of Chapters 4, 5, and 6.

Chapter 4: Trapped in the past: dealing with the future: the role of knowledge in dealing with decision situations

This chapter argues that knowledge, being past-oriented, may not be sufficient in handling future circumstances. This generally unexamined assumption about knowledge can be a significant vulnerability when decision makers and organizations encounter unforeseen 'wicked' situations that may require more than experience-based knowledge.

Chapter 5: Big data and analytics: is it a game changer for decision making?

Analytics, powerful algorithmic-based software fuelled by huge amounts of relevant data, and its emerging role and limitations in decision making, is critically discussed in this chapter. Big data and analytics are defined and their relationship with knowledge in tactical and strategic decision making is examined.

Chapter 6: Decision making, the core of what managers do

Decision making is central to what managers do. The success and failure of organizations depends to a high degree on the quality of the decisions that the managers make in the organization. In this chapter, management decision making and different approaches to management decision making are discussed.

Part III: Wisdom in management practice

Part III provides discussions around how to deal with wicked and complex problems in management. Part III includes Chapters 7, 8, and 9, and introduces and discusses a set of wisdom principles that managers can apply to make wise decisions in dealing with complex and wicked problems: a model of wisdom development. This model can be used by managers to enhance their personal wisdom as they practise wise management decision making.

Chapter 7: Wisdom aspects in the management context

The chapter discusses specific manifestations of wisdom in the organizational context. Nine wisdom aspects are identified based on the findings of the authors' empirical studies in the area of wisdom and management. Direct quotes from managers interviewed by the authors are used to clarify the discussions and ground the wisdom aspects in the empirical findings.

Chapter 8: Wise management decision making

This chapter draws on the theoretical and conceptual discussion provided in the previous chapters and proposes a practical business-focused framework of wise management decision making. We argue that in order for a decision to be effective and successful, the decision should be made based an integrated implementation of four principles: Multi-Perspective Consideration, Self-Other Awareness, Cognitive-Emotional Mastery, and Internal-External Reflection.

Chapter 9: The path to management wisdom

In the final chapter we turn our attention to the developmental aspect of wisdom in management settings. Wise management decision making is characterized as an embodied management practice. We argue that for wise managers, the wisdom principles are more than a set of principles: they are habituated and embodied skills. A guideline is introduced that will enable managers to develop their wisdom.

Working terms

Throughout the book we frequently use a number of keywords, the meanings of which may not be straightforward if considered outside their context. As the terms are central to many of our arguments we define these terms here in the introduction. The terms will be defined in detail in the various chapters.

Wisdom

Traditionally, wisdom is of two main types: theoretical and practical. Nevertheless, in the contemporary organizational literature, it is clear that the terms 'wisdom' and 'practical wisdom' are used interchangeably. These contemporary studies of wisdom are more concerned with practical wisdom than theoretical wisdom. Accordingly, theoretical wisdom is either omitted or taken as equivalent to practical wisdom, or even represented as a subset of practical wisdom. We do not presume any specific bifurcation of the concept of wisdom in the outset of the book. Each chapter provides a relevant articulation of the concept of wisdom.

Decision making

Decision making refers to a process of defining the problem, identifying the best possible outcome, developing and accessing multiple alternatives, choosing the best alternative, implementing the option, and assessing the outcomes for improvements in the future.

Strategic decision making

Strategic decision making refers to making those decisions that will have significant and often long-term impacts on the organization and affected stakeholders. These decisions are highly significant as they are often vital to the long-term strategy and the success of organizations (Harrison, 1999). Multiple stakeholders from within and outside the organization including employees, managers, stockholders, business community, and society may be engaged in strategic decision making.

Decision situations

Decision situation, or decision-demanding situation, refers to a situation when decision making is inevitable. In the decision situation, the need for a decision is apparent and the decision maker must begin to define the problem and get involved in the decision-making process.

'Manager' and 'decision maker'

The terms 'manager' and 'decision maker' are used interchangeably throughout the book. Depending on the context, either of the terms may be used. The two terms refer to the individual CEO, manager, executive, practitioner or team who is in a decision-making position.

Big data and analytics

While big data and analytics represent two different technologies, it is difficult to discuss one without the other. Big data can be defined as huge amounts of structured or unstructured data generated moment by moment by a wide range of technologies and data sources, including, but not limited to, social media, sensors, mobile devices, Internet of Things, radio frequency identification (RFID), customer transactions, and so forth (Kacfah Emani, Cullot, & Nicolle, 2015).

Analytics is the term specifically used to describe data analysis applications and includes the use of tools to analyse all data, not necessarily big data.

Virtue and excellence

In the philosophical literature, *virtue* and *excellence* are equal in meaning. For the sake of clarity and simplicity, we use the term 'excellence' wherever possible when speaking of either excellence or virtue. We do so because we believe excellence will have more resonance with managers and organizations.

Multi-Perspective Consideration (MPC)

The extent to which the decision short- and long-term outcomes and ramifications are analysed, alternative points of view are represented as well as individual and communal interests and values are reconciled, and ethical codes are considered.

Cognitive-Emotional Mastery (CEM)

The extent to which the decision maker's cognitive abilities and emotional qualities are integrated throughout the decision-making process.

Self-Other Awareness (SOA)

The extent to which the decision maker's self-awareness (awareness of the internal world) is integrated with his/her Other-awareness (awareness of others, and the external world).

Internal-External Reflection (IER)

A detailed consideration and critical (re-)evaluation of the decision-related facts and assumptions in order to gain a better understanding of the decision situation and how to address the decision problem.

Future thinking

The systematic exploration of and reflection on what will happen in the future, especially as a result of present decisions and actions, as well as how these will be perceived.

Perspective taking

Detailed consideration of multiple stakeholders' individual and communal interests, values, and preferences.

Ethical consideration

Considering ethical codes in the organization, business community, and society.

Self-awareness

The intimidate understanding of one's own (in-)abilities, strengths/weaknesses, knowledge (which includes knowing what one knows, and what one does not know), as well as of one's personality (including values, interests and behavioural characteristics).

Other-awareness

Awareness of the surrounding environment. A true understanding of others' strengths and weaknesses, (in-)abilities, knowledge (what others know, and what they do not know), values and interests, as well as situational awareness.

Cognitive mastery

The extent to which the decision maker can effectively handle the intellectual and cognitive aspects of a decision situation. These aspects include possessing appropriate knowledge and expertise; being able and knowing how to acquire the required data and information and enhance his knowledge; being able and knowing how to use knowledge in the decision situation; possessing insight; and being able to think outside the square.

Emotional mastery

Refers to the degree to which one is able to regulate emotions and to resist becoming overwhelmed by them, while remaining confident in his decisions and actions.

Internal reflection

(Re)evaluating one's own core assumptions, values system, interests, knowledge, and abilities, as well as critically assessing one's previous decisions to learn from failures and successes.

External reflection

(Re)evaluating others' (including individuals and society) core assumptions, values system, interests, knowledge, and abilities, as well as critically assessing others' decisions to learn from their failures and successes.

References

Allee, V. (1997). *The knowledge evolution: Expanding organizational intelligence*. London: Butterworth-Heinemann.

Ardelt, M. (2005). How wise people cope with crises and obstacles in life. *Revision*, 28(1), 7–19.

Baden, D., & Higgs, M. (2015). Challenging the perceived wisdom of management theories and practice. *Academy of Management Learning and Education*, 14(4), 539–555.

Baltes, P. B., & Staudinger, U. M. (2000). Wisdom: A metaheuristic (pragmatic) to orchestrate mind and virtue toward excellence. *American Psychologist*, 55(1), 122–136.

Beard, C., & Wilson, J. P. (2006). *Experiential learning: A best practice handbook for educators and trainers* (2nd ed.). London: Kogan Page.

Birren, J. E., & Fisher, L. M. (1990). The elements of wisdom: Overview and integration. In R. J. Sternberg (Ed.), *Wisdom: Its nature, origins, and development* (pp. 317–332). Cambridge, UK: Cambridge University Press.

Blenko, M. W., Mankins, M. C., & Rogers, P. (2010). *Decide and deliver: Five steps to breakthrough performance in your organization*. Boston: Harvard Business School Press.

Blenko, M. W., Rogers, P., & Mankins, M. C. (2010). The decision-driven organization: Forget the org chart – the secret is to focus on decisions, not structure. *Harvard Business Review*, (June), 54–62.

Brown, S. C. (2004). Learning across the campus: How college facilitates the development of wisdom. *Journal of College Student Development*, 45(2), 134–148.

Clayton, V. P., & Birren, J. E. (1980). The development of wisdom across the life span: A reexamination of an ancient topic. In P. B. Baltes & O. G. Brim Jr (Eds.), *Life-span development and behavior* (Vol. 3, pp. 103–135). New York: Academic Press.

Dalal, N., & Pauleen, D. J. (2018). The wisdom nexus: Guiding information systems research, practice, and education. *Information Systems Journal*.

Damasio, A. R. (2005). *Descartes' error: Emotion, reason, and the human brain*. New York: Penguin Books.

Dean, J., & Sharfman, M. (1993). Procedural rationality in the strategic decision-making process. *Journal of Management Studies*, 30(4), 587–610.

Desmond, B., & Jowitt, A. (2012). Stepping into the unknown: Dialogical experiential learning. *Journal of Management Development*, 31(3), 221–230.

Dijksterhuis, A., Bos, M. W., Nordgren, L. F., & van Baaren, R. B. (2006). On making the right choice: The deliberation-without-attention effect. *Science*, 311(5763), 1005–1007.

Driver, J. (2003). The conflation of moral and epistemic virtue. *Metaphilosophy*, 34(3), 367–383.

Erikson, E. H. (1963). *Childhood & society*. New York: Norton.

Ferrari, M., & Potworowski, G. (Eds.). (2008). *Teaching for wisdom: Cross-cultural perspectives on fostering wisdom*. Dordrecht, The Netherlands: Springer.

Gergen, K. J. (1992). Organization theory in the postmodern era. In M. Reed & M. Hughes (Eds.), *Rethinking organization: New directions in organization theory and analysis* (pp. 207–227). London: Sage.

Grimm, S. R. (2015). Wisdom. *Australasian Journal of Philosophy*, 93(1), 139–154.

Grint, K. (2007). Learning to lead: Can Aristotle help us find the road to wisdom? *Leadership*, 3(2), 231–246.

Harrison, F. E. (1999). *The managerial decision-making process* (5th ed.). Boston: Houghton Mifflin Company.

Hart, W. (1987). *The art of living: Vipassana meditation taught by S.N. Goenka*. San Francisco: Harper.

Head, B., & Alford, J. (2008). Wicked problems: The implications for public management. Paper presented at the 12th Annual International Research Society for Public Management, 26–28 March, Brisbane.

Hinterhuber, H. (1996). Oriental wisdom and western leadership. *The International Executive*, 38(3), 287–302.

Kacfah Emani, C., Cullot, N., & Nicolle, C. (2015). Understandable big data: A survey. *Computer Science Review*, 17 (Aug), 70–81.

Kodish, S. (2006). The paradoxes of leadership: The contribution of Aristotle. *Leadership*, 2(4), 451–468.

Kolb, D. A. (1984). *Experiential learning: Experience as the source of learning and development*. Englewood Cliffs, NJ: Prentice Hall.

Kolb, A. Y., & Kolb, D. A. (2001). *Experiential learning theory bibliography*. Boston: McBer and Co.

Kolb, A. Y., & Kolb, D. A. (2005). Learning styles and learning spaces: Enhancing experiential learning in higher education. *Academy of Management Learning & Education*, 4(2), 193–212.

Küpers, W., & Pauleen, D. J. (2013). *A handbook of practical wisdom: Leadership, organization and integral business practice*. Aldershot, UK: Gower.

Küpers, W., & Pauleen, D. J. (2015). Learning wisdom: Embodied and artful approaches to management education. *Scandinavian Journal of Management*, 31(4), 493–500.

Liew, A. (2013). DIKIW: Data, information, knowledge, intelligence, wisdom and their interrelationships. *Business Management Dynamics*, 2(10), 49–62.

Marshak, R. J. (2009). Reflections on wicked problems in organizations. *Journal of Management Inquiry*, 18(1), 58–59.

Maxwell, N. (2012). Arguing for wisdom in the university: An intellectual autobiography. *Philosophia*, 40(4), 663–704.

McKenna, B., Rooney, D., & Kenworthy, A. L. (2013). Introduction: Wisdom and Management – A guest-edited special collection of resource reviews for management education. *Academy of Management Learning & Education*, 12(2), 306–311.

Michelson, E. (1996). Usual suspects: Experience, reflection and the (en)gendering of knowledge. *International Journal of Lifelong Education*, 15(6), 438–454.

Miettinen, R. (2000). The concept of experiential learning and John Dewey's theory of reflective thought and action. *International Journal of Lifelong education*, 19(1), 54–72.

Mintzberg, H., Raisinghani, D., & Théorêt, A. (1976). The structure of "unstructured" decision processes. *Administrative Science Quarterly*, 21(2), 246–275.

Nutt, P. C., & Wilson, D. C. (2010). Crucial trends and issues in strategic decision making. In P. C. Nutt & D. C. Wilson (Eds.), *Handbook of decision making* (pp. 3–29). Chichester, UK: John Wiley and Sons.

Pauleen, D. J., Rooney, D., & Holden, N. (2010). Practical wisdom and the development of cross-cultural knowledge management: A global leadership perspective. *European Journal of International Management*, 4(2), 382–395.

Pritscher, C. P. (2010). *Einstein & Zen: Learning to learn*. New York: Peter Lang.

Rooney, D. (2013). Being a wise organizational researcher: Ontology, epistemology and axioloxy. In W. Küpers & D. J. Pauleen (Eds.), *A handbook of practical wisdom: Leadership, organization and integral business practice* (pp. 79–98). Aldershot, UK: Gower.

Rooney, D., McKenna, B., & Liesch, P. (2010). *Wisdom and management in the knowledge economy*. New York: Routledge.

Senge, P. M. (1990). *The fifth discipline: The art & practice of the learning organization*. New York, NY: Currency Doubleday.

Simon, H. A. (1945). *Administrative behaviour* (2nd ed.). New York: Free Press.

Small, M. W. (2004). Wisdom and now managerial wisdom: Do they have a place in management development programs? *Journal of Management Development*, 23(8), 751–764.

Snowden, D. J., & Boone, M. E. (2007). A leader's framework. *Harvard Business Review*, 85(11), 68–76.

Sternberg, R. J. (2003). *Wisdom, intelligence, and creativity synthesized*. New York: Cambridge University Press.

Thompson, J. D. (1967). *Organizations in action*. New York: McGraw-Hill.

Tetenbaum, T. J. (1998). Shifting paradigms: From Newton to chaos. *Organizational Dynamics*, 26(4), 21–32.

Uhl-Bien, M., Marion, R., & McKelvey, B. (2007). Complexity leadership theory: Shifting leadership from the industrial age to the knowledge era. *The Leadership Quarterly*, 18(4), 298–318.

Reuters (2008). World's oldest joke traced back to 1900 BC. Retrieved from https://uk.reuters.com/article/uk-britain-joke-life/worlds-oldest-joke-traced-back-to-1900-bc-idUKL129052420080731.

Vince, R. (1998). Behind and beyond Kolb's learning cycle. *Journal of Management Education*, 22(3), 304–319.

Webster, J. D. (2003). An exploratory analysis of a self-assessed wisdom scale. *Journal of Adult Development*, 10(1), 13–22.

Yalom, I. D. (1985). *The theory and practice of group psychotherapy* (3rd ed.). New York: Basic Books.

Part I

An ancient concept – 21st-century challenges

1 Wisdom from ancient philosophy to modern psychology

Introduction

Wisdom is an important, universal, age-old concept that has now found its way into a great number of academic and professional fields, including psychological, philosophical, cross-cultural, cross-disciplinary, contemplative, health- and aging-related, developmental, educational, integral, personal, organizational, practical, gender-based, religious, and psychotherapeutic, among many others (Walsh, 2015). These fields have all contributed to our understanding of wisdom.

Wisdom as understood by two of these fields, philosophy and psychology, is of particular interest to us and sets the stage for this book: philosophy because of its long and fundamental association with wisdom – 'philosophy' means 'love of wisdom'; and psychology because it is a relatively new field of academic endeavour, concerned with the human mind, that in the last 30 years has dedicated a great deal of interest and research into wisdom and its qualities and characteristics.

What is wisdom?

Wisdom can perhaps be most easily understood in terms of character, and it can be argued that character is the difference between the wise and unwise (Robinson, 1990). From a character-oriented perspective wisdom is understood as a constellation of personality dispositions and personal characteristics or capabilities (Ardelt, 2003; Holliday & Chandler, 1986). In this sense, understanding wisdom requires a true understanding of the possible answers to such questions as 'what makes a person wise?', 'in what ways are their personal and behavioural characteristics different from others?' or simply asking, 'how can we distinguish wise people from others?' For example, Grint (2007) characterizes wise leaders as pragmatic. Wise people know how to live a good life (Tredget, 2010) endowed with the capacity of thinking about and judging what should be done to live a fulfilled life (Kekes, 1995; Melé, 2010). They follow the adage "know thyself" (Robinson, 1990, p. 17), are able to see circumstance broadly and deeply (Gibson, 2008), and understand that "which is essential to living the best life" (Garrett & College, 1996, p. 221). As these definitions indicate, then, our understanding of the concept of wisdom is inevitably based and inextricably dependent on our perception of the personal and behavioural characteristics that are exhibited by people who are considered to be wise.

This conceptualization of wisdom in both ancient philosophical and modern psychological writings on wisdom seems to be dominant. For example, Socrates pointed to humbleness as a characteristic of wisdom, noting that "the only true wisdom is knowing you know nothing" (Plato, 175d). Throughout *The Nicomachean Ethics*, Aristotle examines the concept of wisdom by explicitly characterizing wise people. For instance, in discussing that practical wisdom is concerned with deliberation, Aristotle states, "this is above all the work of the man of practical wisdom, to deliberate well" (Aristotle, 2009, 1141b 10–15). The action-oriented nature of wisdom is articulated in such explanations as "the man of practical wisdom is one who will *act*" and "a man has practical wisdom not by knowing only but by being able to act" (Aristotle, 2009, 1146a 5–10; 1152a 8–10).

Psychological characterizations of wisdom also focus on character and capability. Ardelt (2003, 2004) defines wisdom as a personality in which cognitive, reflective, and affective traits are integrated. Similarly, Birren and Fisher (1990) argue that wisdom is an integration of cognitive, affective, and conative features of human abilities. Jeannot (1989) emphasizes that wisdom is associated with the traits of character and qualities of mind. Blatner (2005) argues that wisdom includes a large category of capabilities and activities such as the desire to seek wisdom: "discerning the optimal amounts or degrees of various efforts; exercising compassion and interpersonal sensitivity; appreciating; re-evaluating tradition and accepted knowledge; integrating information and skills; ... becoming alert to self-deception and the temptations towards foolishness" and so forth (p. 33). Wise people are also assumed to possess such positive qualities as being mature, having an integrated personality, and superior judgement skills (Ardelt, 2004; Baltes & Smith, 1990; Etheredge, 1992; Kramer, 1990; Rowley, 2006).

Character-oriented conceptualizations of wisdom have also broadly prevailed in other disciplines including management, organization studies, and leadership (McKenna, Rooney, & Liesch, 2006; Nonaka & Takeuchi, 2011; Yang, 2011). For example, McKenna et al. (2006) argue that rational judgement, counter-intuition, vision, and humanity are the required capacities for a wise manager. Bigelow's (1992) proposition that the development of wisdom results from five major changes (i.e. movement to longer-term strategies, ability to learn from experience, expanding practical knowledge, having meta-knowledge, and representing value and orientation shifts) that deepen one's understanding of, and ability to live, life exemplify the approach. The concept of wisdom in the business context will be discussed in more detail in Chapter 2.

In this book, we complement the character-oriented perspective of wisdom with a practice-oriented one. We posit that almost everyone has the potential to become wise through consciously learning how to make wise decisions and take wise actions, as well as reflecting on and learning from unwise decisions. Accordingly, we argue that a personal understanding of the nature of wisdom can be acquired by combining and applying characteristic-oriented and practice-oriented perspectives. This approach is prevalent across the book. Before we move on and look at the concept of wisdom in the business context in Chapter 2, it is worthwhile to review in some depth philosophical and psychological perspectives on wisdom, which have influenced most contemporary studies of wisdom. In the following section we look at the concept of wisdom as it was understood in ancient philosophies and in modern psychology.

Wisdom: a concept from the ancient era

Early Western discussions of wisdom can be traced back to the philosophical discourses of the classic philosophers such as Socrates (469–399 BCE) and Aristotle (384–322 BCE).

Central to wisdom discourses in classical Greece was human conduct in daily life. The Greek philosophers', particularly Aristotle's, conceptions of wisdom were primarily concerned with dealing with daily life matters. Aristotle defines wisdom as contemplation about how one can live a good life. This ancient Western conception of wisdom as living a good life was prevalent around the ancient world as the following brief synopsis shows.

In the non-Western traditions, early documented discussions of wisdom can be found in ancient traditions in the Middle East and East Asia. For example, wisdom, as outlined in the Confucian *Analects*, is based on righteousness: a wise person knows the Way (Tao), and that knowledge is combined with action (Rowley, 2006). Similarly, in Zoroastrianism, wisdom is conceptualized as the harmony between one's mind, utterance, and *practice* in the interest of making the world progress towards perfection (Yang & Intezari, in press). In a cross-cultural study of core virtues in the influential religious and philosophical traditions (including Confucianism, Taoism, Buddhism, and Hinduism), Dahlsgaard, Peterson, and Seligman (2005) identify six core virtues: courage, justice, humanity, temperance, transcendence, and wisdom. They conclude that there is a convergence across the traditions and across time and place about a number of core virtues, including wisdom.

Confucianism and Buddhism, for example, emphasize the practical nature of wisdom with the core aspect of wisdom focusing on individual and communal behaviour (cf. Case, 2013; Harwood, 2011; Rowley & Slack, 2009; Yang, 2011; Yang & Intezari, in press). For example, in the Japanese tradition wisdom is associated with the interrelationship between and among people and context. Four major aspects constitute wisdom in the Japanese tradition: sociability and interpersonal relationships, education and knowledge, introspective attitudes, as well as understanding and judgement (Takahashi & Overton, 2005). Examples of Shinto teachings show that wisdom according to these traditions manifests in people's daily and professional practices: 'do not be sluggish in your work', 'sincerity is the mother of knowledge', or 'in governing, let us govern with true sincerity'.

Fast-forward to the 20th century and we find wisdom re-emerging as an important area of research. In the last three decades, psychology has been leading this renewed focus on wisdom (e.g. Ardelt, 2010; Baltes, Staudinger, Maerker & Smith, 1995; Sternberg, 2004a). From the early studies done by Clayton (1975, 1976) to more recent work, the psychological studies of wisdom represent three major approaches to the nature of wisdom: from the gerontological, intelligence, and spiritual perspectives. In the gerontologist approach, wisdom is associated with age and experience. In the intelligence approach, which is mainly represented by Sternberg's (1990, 1998) work, wisdom is a knowledge-based entity that engages values. The spiritual perspective, as represented by Ardelt's (2004, 2010) work, considers wisdom as a quality that cannot be detached from the wise person, and draws on the wise person's cognitive, reflective, and affective aspects. The major psychological studies of wisdom will be discussed at the end of this chapter.

More recently, the business, management, and organization disciplines have begun to explore how the business world can benefit from the concept of wisdom. In the fields of management and organizations, various scholars have investigated how wisdom may contribute to the business world (e.g. Intezari & Pauleen, 2013, 2014; McKenna & Rooney, 2012; Pauleen, Rooney, & Holden, 2010; Small, 2011). Leadership (Nonaka & Takeuchi, 2011), knowledge management (Pauleen et al., 2010), and public administration (Rooney & McKenna, 2008) are examples of the fields that have recently examined how wisdom can be incorporated into business practices.

The diversity of disciplines that have studied wisdom and their different understandings of it make it difficult to provide a broadly-accepted definition of wisdom (Intezari & Pauleen, 2014; Nonaka & Takeuchi, 2011). Wisdom is believed to be a polysemantic concept that may take a slightly different meaning in different contexts and applications (Rowley & Slack, 2009). We will look at wisdom from three different perspectives: philosophical and psychological (in Chapter 1), and managerial (in Chapter 2). Since most contemporary academic studies of wisdom draw on the philosophical traditions of wisdom as presented by ancient Greek philosophers such as Plato, Socrates, and Aristotle, the philosophical perspective is discussed first.

Philosophical perspective

In the classical era, wisdom was listed among the cardinal virtues: wisdom (*sophia/ sapientia/prudence*), courage (fortitude), moderation or self-control (temperance [*temperantia*]), and justice (*iustitia*) (O'Toole, 1938; Small, 2004). They are called cardinal as they cannot be derived from or reduced to the other three virtues (Carr, 1988; Steutel & Spiecker, 1997). In Plato's last and longest dialogue, *The Laws*, wisdom is the first virtue among other virtues. For Socratics, wisdom is a cardinal virtue, transcending the realm of the merely cognitive (Robinson, 1990). As mentioned above, in the West the philosophical discourses on the concept of wisdom are rooted in the works of the classical philosophers such as Socrates (469–399 BCE) and Aristotle (384–322 BCE). Aristotle holds that each virtue is a disposition toward proper practical reasoning, action, and emotion within a certain sphere.

In *The Nicomachean Ethics*, Aristotle conceptualizes wisdom as a contemplation of what is good for living a good life. Aristotle provides two main conceptions of wisdom: *sophia* and *phronesis*. *Sophia* or theoretical wisdom is more concerned with eternal truth, and *phronesis* is action-oriented (2009, *1143b*, 15–20), i.e. doing the right thing at a given time (Tredget, 2010). Likewise, in Kant's *Critique of Practical Reason* wisdom is concerned with the practical aim of humans' existence on earth (Rowley & Slack, 2009).

Wisdom and excellence in practice

Virtue is the Latin word for the ancient Greek notion of *arête* (Baggini & Fosl, 2007; Begley, 2006), which broadly means excellence in quality and practice. Virtue refers specifically to socially-valued character traits such as patience, humility, and graciousness (Beauchamp, 1991). Virtue(s) is the excellence that enables a person "to attain the furthest potentialities of his nature" (Pieper, 1966, p. xii). In this sense, virtues (*excellence*) are achieved when humans' emotions, desires, and passions are excellently cultivated and come together in an excellent way (Baggini & Fosl, 2007). As Aristotle put it, "the virtue of man is the *state of character* which makes a man good and which makes him do his own work well" (Aristotle, 2009, *1106a*, 20–25). Aristotle's notion of virtue underpins the connection between virtue and practice. In the business context, efficiency, effectiveness, commitment to work, professional courtesy, and dignity are examples of virtues.

Aristotle believed that there are two types of virtues (i.e. human excellence): *moral* and *intellectual* (2009, *1103a*, 15). According to Aristotle, moral virtue is "a settled disposition of the mind determining the choice of actions and emotions, consisting essentially in the observance of the mean relative to us, this being determined by principle, that is, as the prudent man would determine it" (2009, 1107a, 1–5). In other words, moral virtues are personality traits, habits, and states of character that intrinsically motivate a person in a specific situation to act in a certain way in pursuit of good (O'Toole, 1938; Spielthenner, 2004). Intellectual virtues, on the other hand, denote the excellences of the mind, which enable one to deliberate (Deslauriers, 2002) and to act well. Moral virtues facilitate taking good actions (O'Toole, 1938). In contrast, intellectual virtues aim at one's cognitive connection with reality, and from this point of view, a person of intellectual virtue is the one who succeeds in achieving such access (Abraham, 2006).

Some philosophers, such as Karl Popper, R. F. Dearden, and Anthony Quinton, believe that intellectual virtues are a subgroup of moral virtues (Steutel & Spiecker, 1997). Either as a subgroup of moral virtue or as a separate quality, intellectual and moral virtues are inherently interwoven excellences of human beings (MacIntyre, 1985; Polansky, 2000; Urmson, 1998).

From the Aristotelian perspective, prudence is the highest intellectual virtue (Roca, 2007) that is directed by moral virtue. In this sense, practical wisdom (prudence) is referred to as being associated with both intellectual and moral virtues (O'Toole, 1938), as "it is not possible to be good in the true sense without Prudence, nor to be prudent without Moral Virtue" (Aristotle, 2009, *1144b*, 30–32).

The terms 'practical wisdom' and 'wisdom' have been used interchangeably in the literature, in part because both wisdom and practical wisdom refer to excellence. In matters of theory, the term 'wisdom' is used, while in practical matters, the term 'practical wisdom' is used (Urmson, 1998). Aligned with practical wisdom, there is another complementary quality of wisdom which is more related to non-mundane aspects of life: theoretical wisdom (Holliday & Chandler, 1986). To better understand how moral virtues, intellectual virtues, and wisdom are inter-related, we first need to look at the bifurcation of theoretical and practical wisdom.

Theoretical (philosophical) and practical wisdom

The Western philosophical tradition tends to focus on two types of wisdom: theoretical and practical. *Theoretical wisdom* is also known as *divine*, *esoteric*, *metaphysical*, *pure*, *abstract*, or *theoretically-oriented wisdom*, while *practical* is also referred to as *earthly* or *mundane* wisdom (Begley, 2006; Holliday & Chandler, 1986; Nonaka & Takeuchi, 2011; Ryan, 1996; Tredget, 2010). Practical wisdom (prudence or *phronesis*[1]) stands at the foundation of action, while the basis of theoretical wisdom is philosophy itself, devoted to the truth (Robinson, 1990). Moody (1983) stresses that theoretical wisdom is more associated with theology, and provides meaning to life by questioning the nature of humanity. Practical wisdom, on the other hand, is more associated with such fields as "administration, law, or the management of human affairs" (p. 2) and serves the function of governing society.

Theoretical wisdom in the form of divine wisdom was prevalent in the very early literature on wisdom and is thought to be an unattainable ideal that could only be strived for (Adler, 1992). Earthly or practical wisdom, by contrast, is a framework for understanding all other fields, and it can be achieved and developed through human effort (Holliday & Chandler, 1986).

Aristotle suggested that both theoretical and practical wisdom are attainable by people, as people naturally have the capacity to receive virtues, and thus, virtues or excellence can be acquired by humans through habituation; for example, we become brave by doing brave acts (2009, *1103a*, 15–25) (how wisdom can be fostered and developed in the context of management is discussed in Chapter 9). For Aristotle, the distinction provides an explanation of why some knowledgeable (e.g. theoretically wise in a pure or abstract way) people may be incompetent in their actual life (Baggini & Fosl, 2007). Aristotle identifies three states of mind that relate to wisdom (2009, *1141a*, 1–10):

- *episteme* (ἐπιστήμη, scientific knowledge);
- *sophia* (Σοφία, philosophic wisdom); and
- *phronesis* or prudence (φρόνησις, practical wisdom).

Episteme, or "universally valid scientific knowledge" (Nonaka & Takeuchi, 2011, p. 60) is judgement about things that are universal and necessary (Aristotle, 2009, *1140b*, 30–35). *Episteme* is found in those who understand things from a scientific point of view, and know the nature of things and the governing principles of the behaviour of things (Robinson, 1990).

Theoretical wisdom or *sophia* is the combination of scientific knowledge (*episteme*) and intellect or intuitive understanding (*nous*) (Aristotle, 2009, *1141b*, 1–5). It is focused on those "who have devoted themselves to a contemplative life in pursuit of truth" (Robinson, 1990, p. 14). It is the knowledge of the eternal forms or ideas, the ends-in-themselves, and relies on understanding what something factually is (Baggini & Fosl, 2007; Kleimann, 2013). Theoretical wisdom begins from *episteme* which refers to the knowledge of 'what is' (Baggini & Fosl, 2007). However, it is not "merely factual knowledge", but it "puts factual knowledge in proper perspective" (Ryan, 1996, p. 255).

While theoretical wisdom is not based on experience, both experience and maturity are needed for practical wisdom (Baggini & Fosl, 2007; Begley, 2006). Practical wisdom is an action-based entity (Robinson, 1990), while theoretical wisdom is the basis of philosophy itself, and is not concerned with practice (Aristotle, 2009, *1143b*, 15–25). Theoretical wisdom is the knowledge of eternal truths (Tredget, 2010).

The action-oriented nature of practical wisdom makes it crucial to form sound ethical judgements (Begley, 2006). Practical wisdom (*phronesis*) is one's capacity to direct action (Polansky, 2000). It is "a reasoned and true state of capacity to act with regard to human goods" (Aristotle, 2009, *1140b*, 20), and begins from the apprehension of 'what should be' and whether or not a particular action should be done in a particular circumstance (Baggini & Fosl, 2007). Aquinas makes a similar statement: practical wisdom is "right reason in action" and "a prudent man is one who disposes well of the things that have to be done for a good end" (1948, *II-II*, 47, p. 13). Practical wisdom "locates the prudent course of action and resists the urgings of the passions and the deceptions of the senses" (Robinson, 1990, p. 14).

Because practical wisdom as effective deliberation and sound reasoning leads to a morally right course of action (Baggini & Fosl, 2007), it engages ethics and moral virtues; being practically wise is impossible without being good (Roca, 2007). This means theoretical wisdom (knowledge of ethics and moral virtues) is an essential component of practical wisdom. In this sense, excellence is not achieved unless both practical wisdom and theoretical wisdom are regarded as one single quality and practised in

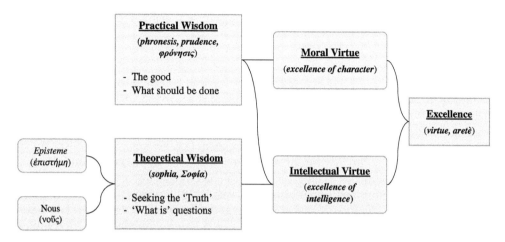

Figure 1.1 Theoretical and practical wisdom (adapted from Intezari, 2014)

an integrated fashion (Figure 1.1). Wisdom, whether explained using the terms 'theoretical wisdom' or 'practical wisdom' and sometimes even 'spiritual wisdom', is regarded as a means to act based on sound judgement and living the good life[2] (Tredget, 2010).

Aristotle asserts that the highest form of human well-being is the life controlled by reason (Beauchamp, 1991). Thus, sound reasoning plays an important role in being wise, and it refers to both theoretical reasoning (the apprehension of what the truth is) and practical reasoning (the apprehension of whether or not a particular action should be done). In this sense, sound reasoning is defined as "the capacity to determine not only the *true* but also *the good* action" (Baggini & Fosl, 2007, p. 17).

Practical wisdom dominates the contemporary academic literature on wisdom. This is probably because it is associated with practice and self-development, which neatly aligns with contemporary Western psychology and management ideals.

In Grimm's discussion of wisdom, he says:

> The wise person not only knows what is good or important for well-being and has effective strategies for achieving these goods, but actually *does* achieve these goods. In other words, she is able to employ these strategies in real life and hence she ends up actually living well.
>
> (2015, p. 153)

Grimm rejects the idea of theoretical wisdom, stating that theoretical wisdom is more like intelligence or insight and it is only a part of wisdom – he regards wisdom in general as practical wisdom. The three types of knowledge needed to achieve wisdom as defined by Grimm are: (1) knowledge of what is good or important for well-being; (2) knowledge of one's standing, relative to what is good or important for well-being; and (3) knowledge of a strategy for obtaining what is good or important for well-being. People who are pointed towards achieving wisdom (who are on the correct path and who have the necessary tools) are called 'incipiently wise'. Because of the notion of incipiently-wise wisdom, Grimm says wisdom comes in various degrees. "Wisdom therefore seems to be essentially an in-process state for human beings at least – more like the 'way' (in Taoism) than a settled destination" (2015, p. 141). However, Grimm does not answer the questions of what wisdom actually is or what this knowledge of well-being is (Grimm, 2015).

Practical wisdom

Contemporary studies of wisdom suggest that wisdom is related to well-being, which conforms to Aristotle's notion of wisdom (Krause & Hayward, 2015). Many modern scholars of wisdom seem to go along with the ancient understanding of different kinds of wisdom: principally *sophia* and *phronesis* (theoretical and practical wisdom). However, opposing views of this division are apparent (e.g. Grimm, 2015; Walsh, 2014). According to Grimm (2015), wisdom should be understood as practical wisdom rather than theoretical wisdom, as practical wisdom refers to the ability to live life well, while the latter is more about intelligence or insight. Walsh (2014) rejects the ancient categorization and instead identifies practical wisdom and *subjective* wisdom as the two types of wisdom, and defines subjective wisdom as a broader view of *sophia*, more complex as it consists of both tacit and explicit knowledge of intuitive and conceptual processes. In practical wisdom, personality, proclivity, time, and attention are factors that account for differences in becoming practically wise (Walsh, 2014).

The bifurcation of practical and theoretical wisdom seems to have been marginalized in contemporary studies of wisdom. The approaches taken by the contemporary gerontologists and intelligence psychologists to examine and measure wisdom offer more practice-oriented conceptions of wisdom. The psychological studies of wisdom have been most influential in the contemporary studies of wisdom. For this reason, before we move on and examine wisdom in the business context (in Chapter 2), it is important to review the major psychological studies of wisdom in the contemporary literature.

Psychological perspective

The concept of wisdom has been extensively studied in psychology over the last three decades. The psychological studies of wisdom were triggered by Erikson's (1963) life-span model as well as the emergence of developmental psychology (Sharma, 2005). Erikson (1963) suggests that the human personality develops over eight psychosocial stages: trust vs. mistrust, autonomy vs. shame, initiative vs. guilt, industry vs. inferiority, ego identity vs. role confusion, intimacy vs. isolation, generativity vs. stagnation, and ego integrity vs. despair. In each stage an individual experiences a psychosocial crisis that must be resolved either positively or negatively. In the last stage, which begins in the later years of life, the aging individual looks back on and evaluates their effect on others and the world in order to provide meaning to their life (Erikson, 1968). Erikson (1959, 1963) argues that those who successfully resolve the earlier stages of psychological crisis achieve a special insight into their existence, meaning of life, and their position in the world. Erikson (1959, 1963) characterizes the achievement of this insight as wisdom.

Wisdom and intelligence can provide positive features of development in the later years of life (Clayton, 1975, 1982), in that, increasingly with age, wisdom leads the person to consider the impacts of her actions on self and on others (Clayton, 1982). Others, such as Brugman (2006), Vaillant (2002), and Meacham (1990), however, suggest that there is no correlation between wisdom and aging. Wisdom has been conceptualized in psychology in different ways and this diversity makes it difficult, if not impossible, to provide a single psychological definition of the concept of wisdom (Bergsma & Ardelt, 2012; Jeste et al., 2010; Kunzmann, 2004). The psychological studies of wisdom can be divided into two main variants: implicit theories and explicit studies (Baltes & Staudinger, 2000; Sternberg, 1990).

Implicit and explicit studies

Implicit studies refer to the theories that are based on common-sense, everyday beliefs, or folk-psychological conceptions of wisdom (Staudinger, 2008; Sternberg, 1998). These are based on the assessment of how wise people are characterized as well as the language-based descriptions of the term wisdom (Baltes & Staudinger, 2000). The studies that have used the implicit theory of wisdom are in principle based on the approach that was first implemented by Clayton (1975). Examples of implicit theories include Clayton (1975, 1976, 1982), Clayton and Birren (1980), Sternberg (1985), Holliday and Chandler (1986), Orwoll and Perlmutter (1990), Bluck and Glück (2005), Webster (2010), Jeste et al. (2010), Glück and Bluck (2011), and König and Glück (2013).

Implicit studies try to understand wisdom by examining people's perception of the concept of wisdom. In this approach a group of people are asked to list the characteristics that they believe to be related to wisdom. Then another group of individuals are asked to rate the characteristics in terms of their wisdom-relatedness or typicality. The rated characteristics are analysed to identify the main dimensions of wisdom (Staudinger, 2008).

Applying this approach, Clayton and Birren (1980) identify three prototypical dimensions of wise people: (1) affective characteristics such as empathy and compassion; (2) reflective processes such as intuition and introspection; and (3) cognitive capacities such as experience and intelligence. In this sense wisdom, which is defined as "the ability to grasp human nature, which is paradoxical, contradictory, and subject to continual change", provides for life-long knowledge acquisitions (Clayton, 1982, p. 315).

Holliday and Chandler (1986) conducted an analysis of prototypical wisdom, studying about 500 participants' descriptions of wise people. To see whether the concept of wisdom was understood as a prototype, they rated the characteristics that the participants attributed to wise people. Based on the ratings, Holliday and Chandler (1986) carried out a principal component analysis, and identified five factors underlying the concept of wisdom: exceptional understanding, judgement and communication skills, general competencies, interpersonal skills, and social unobtrusiveness. Their study indicates that wisdom is perceived as the exhibition of two sets of characteristics: (1) exceptional understanding, and (2) judgement and communication. Wise people learn from their experience and see events and phenomena within the larger context. Moreover, wise people understand life, make thoughtful decisions, and consider multiple points of view.

Glück and Bluck's (2011) study developed a wisdom questionnaire assessing the conceptions of wisdom and how it develops. The questionnaire included eight items collectively asking 'what is wisdom?' and nine items on 'how does one become wise?' Nearly 2,000 lay people rated the importance of the items. The results showed two typical conceptions of wisdom: a 'cognitive conception' and an 'integrative conception'. In the cognitive conception, cognitive and reflective characteristics are rated as central to wisdom. However, people with an integrative conception endorsed all cognitive, reflective, and affective characteristics as important aspects of wisdom. For the participants with a cognitive conception, learning from experience and from wise people were critical in developing wisdom, whilst in an integrative conception, 'experience with life challenges' is added and rated as equally important. Glück and Bluck's (2011) study was later extended by König and Glück (2013), by including a qualitative assessment of people's perception of wisdom and its development. The new findings confirmed both 'cognitive' and 'integrative' conceptions.

Compared with the number of implicit theories, explicit theories of wisdom are less common (Kunzmann & Baltes, 2005; Sternberg, 1990). Explicit studies refer to the studies that collect data from people performing tasks. The tasks are presumed by the researcher to measure wisdom (Sternberg, 1985). The explicit theories of wisdom are tested by scientific methods, and are aimed at the behavioural expressions and manifestations of wisdom (Baltes & Staudinger, 2000). Examples of these approaches include Labouvie-Vief (1990), Baltes and Smith (1990), McAdams and de St. Aubin (1998), Baltes and Staudinger (2000), and Taylor, Bates, and Webster (2011).

Explicit studies of wisdom can be divided into three approaches (Baltes & Staudinger, 2000; Kunzmann, 2004; Pasupathi, Staudinger & Baltes, 2001): (1) personality development: considering wisdom as being related to personality development, and conceptualizing wisdom as personality traits; (2) cognitive development: relating wisdom to the development of cognition, and conceptualizing wisdom in dialectical and post-formal thought; and (3) expertise development: conceptualizing wisdom as an expert knowledge and judgement about the meaning of life. These three approaches to wisdom provide somewhat contradictory conceptualizations of wisdom. First, wisdom involves an integration of cognition and emotion that can be attained by anyone. Second, wisdom is an ideal state of character, and not all people can become wise. Third, wisdom, by setting behavioural standards, guides one's behaviour towards optimizing one's own and others' potentials (Kunzmann, 2004). Among the psychological studies of wisdom, there are three major perspectives that have been most influential in contemporary studies of wisdom: the Berlin School, the Balance Theory, and the 3DW (3-Dimensional Wisdom) model.

The Berlin Wisdom Paradigm

Founded in the early 1980s by Paul Baltes at the Max Planck Institute for Human Development in Berlin, the Berlin School (also known as the Berlin Wisdom Paradigm) offered a ground-breaking and empirical study of wisdom. Wisdom in this school is considered as a utopia of mind and virtue (Baltes & Kunzmann, 2004) that has individual and collective representations (Baltes & Smith, 1990; Baltes & Staudinger, 2000); that is, wisdom development at the individual and collective levels leads to a better world.

In the Berlin Wisdom Paradigm, wisdom is defined as "expert knowledge" (Baltes & Smith, 1990, p. 95; Pasupathi, Staudinger, & Baltes, 2001, p. 351) and "an expertise" (Baltes & Staudinger, 2000, p. 124): "an expert knowledge system in the fundamental pragmatics of life permitting exceptional insight, judgment, and advice involving complex and uncertain matters of the human condition" (Baltes & Staudinger, 1993, p. 76). Wisdom engages five types of knowledge: (1) factual knowledge regarding the fundamental pragmatics of life; (2) procedural knowledge about life problems (e.g. strategies of information searching, decision making, and advice giving); (3) life-span contextualism which refers to the knowledge that considers the contexts of life and societal

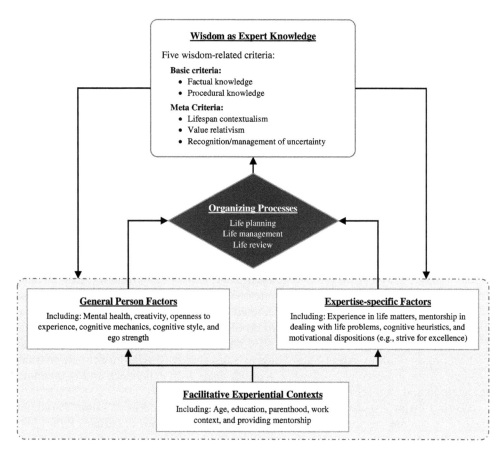

Figure 1.2 The development, structure, and functions of wisdom: a theoretical model (adapted from Baltes & Kunzmann, 2004, p. 295)

change; (4) relativism or the knowledge which considers relativism of values and life goals; and (5) uncertainty (the knowledge which considers the uncertainties of life) (Baltes & Staudinger, 1993).

Figure 1.2 illustrates how the development of wisdom depends on multiple factors including general factors (such as cognitive, cultural, and personal efficiency), specific factors (such as practice with the problems of life), and modifying and facilitative factors (such as professional status and education). Baltes and Kunzmann (2004) argue that wisdom as expert knowledge evolves within life planning, life management, and life review.

Wisdom, therefore, according to the Berlin Wisdom Paradigm, represents a kind of expert knowledge that is not purely cognitive, but rather requires a coalition between experiences and understanding. In addition, wisdom as expert knowledge:

> is not knowledge for knowledge's sake, but rather such expert knowledge is in the service of the fundamental pragmatics of life and plays a central role in the development of one's self and one's contribution to the development of others.
>
> (Baltes & Kunzmann, 2004, p. 295)

The studies by Baltes and colleagues, however, are criticized by others such as Richardson and Pasupathi (2005) and Ardelt (2004). One criticism of the Berlin School is that wisdom-related knowledge might not necessarily result in wise actions (Richardson & Pasupathi, 2005). While the Berlin School emphasizes the use of expert knowledge in taking a course of action to handle life events, or 'the pragmatics of life' (Baltes & Smith, 1990), the school does not give a clear explanation of how that knowledge can be put into action, or how dealing with life events may change depending on context. This linking of knowledge and the consequent actions are, however, as discussed later in this chapter, addressed by the Balance Theory of Wisdom developed by Sternberg (1986, 1998, 2004a). Another significant criticism of the Berlin School has been made by Ardelt (2004), arguing that the definition, operationalization, and measurement of the concept of wisdom that the Berlin School provides assess intellectual knowledge rather than wisdom. Ardelt's (2003, 2004, 2011) approach to wisdom, and her Three-dimensional Wisdom Scale (3D-WS) is discussed next.

The Three-dimensional Wisdom Scale (3D-WS)

Ardelt (2004, 2010) and Bergsma and Ardelt (2012) stress that wisdom, being an integration of cognitive and reflective characteristics, does not exist independently of wise individuals and that it should not be limited to *expertise*. Rather, wisdom must be reserved for wise people, and that wisdom should be characterized as a personal quality. Furthermore, Ardelt (2004) contrasts wisdom and knowledge and emphasizes that considering wisdom as expert knowledge, as suggested by the Berlin School, restricts wisdom to the intellectual level, while wisdom deals with experience and is therefore understood and manifested at the experiential level.

Another major criticism that Ardelt (2004) raises of the Berlin Wisdom Paradigm deals with the measurement of wisdom. In the Berlin Wisdom Paradigm, Baltes and colleagues (Baltes & Smith, 1990; Kunzmann & Baltes, 2005) use the maximal performance approach, which requires participants to solve a challenging problem (Sternberg, 2004b) to measure wisdom. The questions that participants are asked are hypothetical questions about the pragmatics of life. In contrast, Ardelt (2004) uses personality testing, which focuses on one's description of how one typically responds to a given situation (Sternberg, 2004b), and emphasizes that wisdom must be measured on the basis of people's individual assessments of their typical reactions to their own real situations.

Ardelt (2000, 2003) offers a three-dimensional scale that measures three aspects of wisdom: the cognitive, reflective, and affective dimensions. The cognitive dimension refers to one's ability to comprehend a deeper understanding of the events and phenomena in life, in terms of how the phenomena and events have intrapersonal and interpersonal impacts. This dimension underlines the importance of one's knowledge about a particular situation as well as about ambiguity of life and human nature (Ardelt, 2003). The development of the cognitive dimension is based on the reflective dimension. That is, one cannot attain a deeper understanding of life unless one's perception of reality is not distorted. To perceive the reality as it is, Ardelt (2003) suggests that one needs to look at phenomena from different perspectives through reflective thinking. She suggests that reflective thinking can develop one's self-awareness and self-insight, which can also reduce one's self-centredness. The two dimensions can enhance one's affective emotions. The affective dimension refers to the positive emotions and behaviours, such as compassion and sympathy for others. Ardelt (2003) emphasizes that the three dimensions are interdependent, and they all need to be simultaneously present for a person to be considered wise.

The 3D-WS and the Berlin School share commonalities with another influential theory of wisdom, the Balance Theory of Wisdom (Sternberg, 1998). For example, cognition is considered an important dimension of wisdom by both 3D-WS and the Berlin School. The Balance Theory of Wisdom identifies knowledge and intelligence as the foundations of wisdom. This theory is further discussed below.

The Balance Theory of Wisdom

According to the Balance Theory (Sternberg, 1985, 1986, 1998, 2004a; Sternberg & Dobson, 1987), wisdom is the use of intelligence toward the achievement of a common good (Reznitskaya & Sternberg, 2004), that is:

> the use of one's intelligence and experience as mediated by values toward the achievement of a common good through a balance among (1) intrapersonal, (2) interpersonal, and (3) extrapersonal interests, over the (1) short and (2) long terms, to achieve a balance among (1) adaptation to existing environments, (2) shaping of existing environments, and (3) selection of new environment.
>
> (p. 164)

The Balance Theory proposes that the goal of wisdom is achieving the common good. The common good is achieved through a balanced response to the environment. That is, in order to achieve the common good, the wise person may choose to adapt to the existing environmental context, to shape the environmental context, or to select a new environmental context. This aspect of the Balance Theory considers wisdom as embedded in the individual's interaction with the situational context: "the balances proposed by the theory are in the interaction between a person and his or her context, rather than, say, in internal systems of functioning (such as cognitive, conative, and affective)" (Sternberg, 1998, p. 353).

The wise person's balanced responses to the environmental context rely on a balance between stakeholders' interests. The theory suggests that the core of wisdom is tacit knowledge that underlies practical intelligence. The practical intelligence is applied to balancing multiple and often competing interests at three levels: intrapersonal, interpersonal, and extrapersonal. In other words, wisdom is not involved if the practical intelligence is applied to only maximizing self-interest. By the term 'interest', Sternberg (1998) refers to both cognitive (point of view) divergence and motivational (affective) divergence. He points out that "in order to be wise, one must understand not only people's cognitions, but also their motivations and even their affects" (Sternberg, 1998, p. 355).

Sternberg (1998) sees wisdom and values as inherently interwoven, and explains that the balance proposed by the theory is mediated by values: in balancing between multiple interests, balancing responses to the environment, and even the way people define a common good. According to the theory, people may differ in terms of the degree to which they aim for a common good, in their balance of responses and interests, in their level of tacit knowledge in judgemental situations, and in their values. Sternberg, however, does not explain how this balance, whereby the common good is achieved, is accomplished. Wisdom may be located in knowing when and how to balance interests at the intra-, inter-, and extra-personal levels.

The Berlin Wisdom Paradigm, 3D-WS, the Balance Theory, and other psychological studies of wisdom mostly share commonalities with regard to the key aspects of wisdom. The wisdom aspects that the theories have in common include (but are not limited to):

- wisdom is interwoven with values and ethics (Le, 2008; Pasupathi & Staudinger, 2001; Sternberg, 1998);
- it is linked to practice and action (Kunzmann, 2004);
- it is a mixture of cognition and emotion (Ardelt, 2011; Tredget, 2010);
- it engages knowledge and experience (Montgomery, Barber, & McKee, 2002); and
- it goes beyond the personal level, aiming for the common good (Sternberg, 1998).

The psychological interpretations of wisdom by the three schools share much in common, i.e. judgement, action, and achieving goals, and not surprisingly, these characteristics also appear in a wide range of organizational and management studies of wisdom as we shall see in Chapter 2.

Chapter summary

In this chapter, we have reviewed how wisdom was understood by the ancient Western philosophical tradition as well as modern psychological interpretations. In philosophy, wisdom is listed as a cardinal virtue. According to Aristotle, there are two types of wisdom: moral and intellectual wisdom. The two types of wisdom lead to excellence. Aristotle also identifies three states of mind in relation to wisdom including *episteme*, *sophia*, and *phronesis*. Another categorization of wisdom is theoretical vs. practical wisdom. In most contemporary psychological studies of wisdom, wisdom is defined as a practical quality associated with one's daily life.

The common theme through all of the philosophical and psychological conceptions of wisdom is that while wisdom can encompass spiritual and solely cognitive dimensions, it becomes meaningful in the practical matters of life and living well in a community. One prevailing approach to conceptualizing wisdom is the character-oriented perspective. Based on this approach, one conceptualizes wisdom based on the image that one has of examples that one observes in real life.

Psychology is one of the main fields studying wisdom. There are two types of psychological studies: implicit and explicit studies. The implicit studies apply the character-oriented approach. Explicit theories of wisdom are less common than implicit theories. Explicit studies offer three different conceptions of wisdom: personality development, cognitive development, and expertise development. We have also reviewed the three most influential contemporary theories of wisdom: the Berlin Wisdom Paradigm, which defines wisdom as expert knowledge; the Balance Theory, where wisdom involves balancing a number of factors; as well as the 3D-WS model which identifies three dimensions for wisdom, i.e. cognitive, affective, and reflective.

Many disciplines have studied wisdom. The wide range of conceptions has made it difficult to find a globally agreed-upon definition of wisdom. In management, practical matters are of the utmost concern. However, increasingly community and society are also becoming matters of practical concern to management. As such, we believe that the knowledge and practice of practical wisdom could help management cope with the increasing pressures exerted by the environment in which they operate. As discussed in the next chapter, judgement, action, and getting results – the essence of practical wisdom – are essential in management decision making.

Notes

1 While prudence is seen as practical wisdom by some scholars, others may consider '*phronesis*' as practical wisdom. We believe that practical wisdom applies to both *phronesis* and prudence.
2 It might be argued that wisdom is found in Eastern traditions, often, though not always, with a strong theist foundation (Bierly III, Kessler, & Christensen, 2000; Rowley & Slack, 2009; Rowley, 2006). However, a mixture of both mundane/practical and non-mundane/spiritual contemplations of the nature of wisdom can be found in both the Western and Eastern traditions (Yang & Intezari, 2018, in press). In the Eastern tradition wisdom involves leading a good life by establishing harmony with one's environment (Bierly III et al., 2000). As with Western traditions, Eastern traditions look at wisdom as a means to achieving a good life (Yang, 2011). Moreover, the focus of the two traditions is on practicability and everyday use of wisdom (Rowley & Slack, 2009). For example, Confucius in *The Analects* says that "wisdom entails righteousness, and that the wise person studies and knows the Way (Tao), but also that knowledge must be combined with action" (Rowley, 2006, p. 254).

References

Abraham, W. (2006). Education, social transformation, and intellectual virtue. *Christian Higher Education*, 5(1), 3–19.

Aquinas, T. (1948). *Summa theologica*. (Fathers of the English Dominican Province, Trans). New York: Benziger Broders.

Ardelt, M. (2000). Intellectual versus wisdom-related knowledge: The case for a different kind of learning in the later years of life. *Educational Gerontology*, 26(8), 771–789.

Ardelt, M. (2003). Empirical assessment of a three-dimensional wisdom scale. *Research on Aging*, 25(3), 275–324.

Ardelt, M. (2004). Wisdom as expert knowledge system: A critical review of a contemporary operationalization of an ancient concept. *Human Development*, 47(5), 257–285.

Ardelt, M. (2010). Are older adults wiser than college students? A comparison of two age cohorts. *Journal of Adult Development*, 17(4), 193–207.

Ardelt, M. (2011). The measurement of wisdom: A commentary on Taylor, Bates, and Webster's comparison of the saws and 3D-WS. *Experimental Aging Research*, 37(2), 241–255.

Aristotle. (2009). *The Nicomachean Ethics*. (D. Ross, Trans). Oxford, UK: Oxford University Press.

Baggini, J., & Fosl, P. S. (2007). *The ethics toolkit: A compendium of ethical concepts and methods*. Malden, UK: Blackwell Publishing.

Baltes, P. B., & Kunzmann, U. (2004). The two faces of wisdom: Wisdom as a general theory of knowledge and judgment about excellence in mind and virtue vs. wisdom as everyday realization in people and products. *Human Development*, 47(5), 290–299.

Baltes, P. B., & Smith, J. (1990). Toward a psychology of wisdom and its ontogenesis. In R. J. Sternberg (Ed.) *Wisdom: Its nature, origins, and development* (pp. 87–120). New York: Cambridge University Press.

Baltes, P. B., & Staudinger, U. M. (1993). The search for a psychology of wisdom. *Current Directions in Science*, 2(3), 75–80.

Baltes, P. B., & Staudinger, U. M. (2000). Wisdom: A metaheuristic (pragmatic) to orchestrate mind and virtue toward excellence. *American Psychologist*, 55(1), 122–136.

Baltes, P. B., Staudinger, U. M., Maerker, A., & Smith, J. (1995). People nominated as wise: A comparative study of wisdom-related knowledge. *Psychology and Aging*, 10(2), 155–166.

Beauchamp, T. L. (1991). *Philosophical ethics: An introduction to moral philosophy* (2nd ed.). New York: McGraw-Hill.

Begley, A. M. (2006). Facilitating the development of moral insight in practice: Teaching ethics and teaching virtue. *Nursing Philosophy: An International Journal for Healthcare Professionals*, 7(4), 257–265.

Bergsma, A., & Ardelt, M. (2012). Self-reported wisdom and happiness: An empirical investigation. *Journal of Happiness Studies*, 13(3), 481–499.

Bierly III, P. E., Kessler, E. H., & Christensen, E. W. (2000). Organizational learning, knowledge and wisdom. *Journal of Organizational Change Management*, 13(6), 595–618.

Bigelow, J. (1992). Developing managerial wisdom. *Journal of Management Inquiry*, 1(2), 143–153.

Birren, J. E., & Fisher, L. M. (1990). The elements of wisdom: Overview and integration. In R. J. Sternberg (Ed.), *Wisdom: Its nature, origins, and development* (pp. 317–332). New York: Cambridge University Press.

Blatner, A. (2005). Perspectives on Wisdom-ing. *ReVision*, 28(1), 29–33.

Bluck, S., & Glück, J. (2005). From the inside out: People's implicit theories of wisdom. In R. J. Sternberg & J. Jordan (Eds.), *A handbook of wisdom: Psychological perspectives* (pp. 84–109). New York: Cambridge University Press.

Brugman, G. M. (2006). *Wisdom and aging*. Amsterdam: Elsvier.

Case, P. (2013). Cultivation of wisdom in the Theravada Buddhist tradition: Implications for contemporary leadership and organization. In W. Küpers & D. J. Pauleen (Eds.), *A handbook of practical wisdom: Leadership, organization and integral business practice* (pp. 65–78). Aldershot, UK: Gower.

Carr, D. (1988). The cardinal virtues and Plato's moral psychology. *The Philosophical Quarterly*, 38(151), 186–200.

Clayton, V. (1975). Erickson's theory of human development as it applies to the aged: Wisdom as contradictory cognition. *Human Development*, 18(1–2), 119–128.

Clayton, V. (1976). *A multidimensional scaling analysis of the concept of wisdom*. Doctoral dissertation. Los Angeles: University of Southern California.

Clayton, V. (1982). Wisdom and intelligence: The nature and function of knowledge in the later years. *International Journal of Aging and Human Development*, 15(4), 315–320.

Clayton, V., & Birren, J. E. (1980). The development of wisdom across the life-span: A re-examination of an ancient topic. In P. B. Baltes & O. G. Brim Jr (Eds.), *Life-span development and behaviour* (Vol. 3, pp. 103–135). New York: Academic Press.

Dahlsgaard, K., Peterson, C., & Seligman, M. E. P. (2005). Shared virtue: The convergence of valued human strengths across culture and history. *Review of General Psychology*, 9(3), 203–213.

Deslauriers, M. (2002). How to distinguish Aristotle's virtues. *Phronesis*, 47(2), 101–126.

Erikson, E. H. (1959). *Identity in the life cycle*. New York: International Universities Press.

Erikson, E. H. (1963). *Childhood & society*. New York: Norton.

Erikson, E. H. (1968). *Identity: Youth and crisis*. New York: Norton.

Etheredge, L. S. (1992). Wisdom and good judgment in politics. *Political Psychology*, 13(3), 497–516.

Garrett, R., & College, B. (1996). Three definitions of wisdom. In K. Lehrer, B. J. Lum, B. A. Slichta, & N. D. Smith (Eds.), *Knowledge, teaching and wisdom* (pp. 221–232). Dordrecht, The Netherlands: Kluwer Academic Publishers.

Gibson, P. S. (2008). Developing practical management wisdom. *Journal of Management Development*, 27(5), 528–536.

Glück, J., & Bluck, S. (2011). Laypeople's conceptions of wisdom and its development: Cognitive and integrative views. *Journals of Gerontology – Series B Psychological Sciences and Social Sciences*, 66 B(3), 321–324.

Grimm, S. R. (2015). Wisdom. *Australasian Journal of Philosophy*, 93(1), 139–155.

Grint, K. (2007). Learning to lead: Can Aristotle help us find the road to wisdom? *Leadership*, 3(2), 231–246.

Harwood, L. D. (2011). Sagely wisdom in Confucianism. *Analytic Teaching and Philosophical Praxis*, 31(1), 56–63.

Holliday, S. G., & Chandler, M. J. (1986). *Wisdom: Explorations in adult competence.* Basel, Switzerland: Karger.

Intezari, A., & Pauleen, D. J. (2013). Students of wisdom: An integral Meta-competencies theory of practical wisdom. In W. Küpers & D. J. Pauleen (Eds.), *A handbook of practical wisdom: Leadership, organization and integral business practice* (pp. 155–174). Aldershot, UK: Gower.

Intezari, A., & Pauleen, D. J. (2014). Management wisdom in perspective: Are you virtuous enough to succeed in volatile times? *Journal of Business Ethics,* 120(3), 393–404.

Jeannot, T. M. (1989). Moral leadership and practical wisdom. *International Journal of Social Economics,* 16(6), 14–38.

Jeste, D. V, Ardelt, M., Blazer, D., Kraemer, H. C., Vaillant, G., & Meeks, T. W. (2010). Expert consensus on characteristics of wisdom: A Delphi method study. *The Gerontologist,* 50(5), 668–680.

Kekes, J. (1995). *Moral wisdom and good lives.* Ithaca, NY: Cornell University Press.

Kleimann, B. (2013). University presidents as wise leaders? In W. Küpers & D. J. Pauleen (Eds.), *A handbook of practical wisdom: Leadership, organization and integral business practice* (pp. 175–195). Aldershot, UK: Gower.

Kramer, D. A. (1990). Conceptualizing wisdom: The primacy of affect-cognition relations. In R. J. Sternberg (Ed.) *Wisdom: Its nature, origins, and development* (pp. 279–313). New York: Cambridge University Press.

König, S., & Glück, J. (2013). Individual differences in wisdom conceptions: Relationships to gratitude and wisdom. *International Journal of Aging and Human Development,* 77(2), 127–147.

Krause, N., & Hayward, R. D. (2015). Virtues, practical wisdom and psychological well-being: A Christian perspective. *Social Indicators Research,* 122(3), 735–755.

Kunzmann, U. (2004). Approaches to a good life: The emotional-motivational side to wisdom. In P. A. Linley, & S. Joseph (Eds.), *Positive psychology in practice* (pp. 504–517). Hoboken, NJ: Wiley.

Kunzmann, U., & Baltes, P. B. (2005). The psychology of wisdom: Theoretical and empirical challenges. In R. J. Sternberg & J. Jordan (Eds.), *A handbook of wisdom: Psychological perspectives* (pp. 110–135). New York: Cambridge University Press.

Labouvie-Vief, G. (1990). Wisdom as integrated thought: Historical and developmental perspectives. In R. J. Sternberg (Ed.), *Wisdom: Its nature, origins, and development* (pp. 52–83). New York: Cambridge University Press.

Le, T. N. (2008). Cultural values, life experiences, and wisdom. *The International Journal of Aging and Human Development,* 66(4), 259–281.

MacIntyre, A. (1985). *After virtue: A study in moral theory.* London: Duckworth.

McAdams, D. P., & de St Aubin, E. (Eds.), (1998). *Generativity and adult development: How and why we care for the next generation.* Washington, DC: American Psychological Association.

McKenna, B., & Rooney, D. (2012). Making sense of irrealis in the global financial crisis. *Culture and Organization,* 18(2), 123–137.

McKenna, B., Rooney, D., & Liesch, P. W. (2006). Beyond knowledge to wisdom in international business strategy. *Prometheus,* 24(3), 283–300.

Meacham, J. A. (1983). Wisdom and the context of knowledge: Knowing that one doesn't know. In D. Kuhn & J. A. Meacham (Eds.), *On the development of developmental psychology* (pp. 111–134). Basel, Switzerland: Karger.

Melé, D. (2010). Practical wisdom in managerial decision making. *Journal of Management Development,* 29(7/8), 637–645.

Montgomery, A., Barber, C., & McKee, P. (2002). A phenomenological study of wisdom in later life. *International Journal of Aging & Human Development,* 54(2), 139–157.

Moody, H. R. (1983). Wisdom and the search for meaning. Paper presented at the 36th Annual Meetings of the Gerontological Society of America. November, San Francisco.

Nonaka, I., & Takeuchi, H. (2011). The big idea: The wise leader. *Harvard Business Review,* 89(5), 58–67.

Pauleen, D. J., Rooney, D., & Holden, N. (2010). Practical wisdom and the development of cross-cultural knowledge management: A global leadership perspective. *European Journal of International Management*, 4(2), 382–395.

Orwoll, L., & Perlmutter, M. (1990). The study of wise persons: Integrating a personality perspective. In R. J. Sternberg (Ed.), *Wisdom: Its nature, origins, and development* (pp. 160–177). New York: Cambridge University Press.

O'Toole, C. J. (1938). The teaching of intellectual and moral virtues. *Ethics*, 49(1), 81–84.

Pasupathi, M., & Staudinger, U. M. (2001). Do advanced moral reasoners also show wisdom? Linking moral reasoning and wisdom-related knowledge and judgment. *International Journal of Behavioral Development*, 25(5), 401–415.

Pasupathi, M., Staudinger, U. M., & Baltes, P. B. (2001). Seeds of wisdom: Adolescents' knowledge and judgment about different life problems. *Developmental Psychology*, 37(3), 351–361.

Pieper, J. (1966). *The four cardinal virtues*. Notre Dame, IN: University of Notre Dame Press.

Polansky, R. (2000). Phronesis on tour: Cultural adaptability of Aristotelian ethical notions. *Kennedy Institute of Ethics Journal*, 10(4), 323–336.

Reznitskaya, A., & Sternberg, R. J. (2004). Teaching students to make wise judgments: The "teaching for wisdom" program. In P. A. Linley, & S. Joseph (Ed.), *Positive psychology in practice* (pp. 181–196). New York: Wiley.

Richardson, M. J., & Pasupathi, M. (2005). Young and growing wiser: Wisdom during adolescence and young adulthood. In R. J. Sternberg & J. Jordan (Eds.), *A handbook of wisdom. Psychological perspectives* (pp. 139–159). New York: Cambridge University.

Robinson, D. N. (1990). Wisdom through the ages. In R. J. Sternberg (Ed.), *Wisdom: Its nature, origins, and development* (pp. 13–24). New York: Cambridge University Press.

Roca, E. (2007). Intuitive practical wisdom in organizational life. *Social Epistemology*, 21(2), 195–207.

Rooney, D., & McKenna, B. (2008). Wisdom in public administration: Looking for a sociology of wise practice. *Public Administration Review*, 68(4), 709–721.

Rowley, J. (2006). What do we need to know about wisdom? *Management Decision*, 44(9), 1246–1257.

Rowley, J., & Slack, F. (2009). Conceptions of wisdom. *Journal of Information Science*, 35(1), 110–119.

Ryan, S. (1996). Wisdom. In K. Lehrer, B. J. Lum, B. A. Slichta, & N. D. Smith (Eds.), *Knowledge, Teaching, and Wisdom* (pp. 233–242). Dordrecht, The Netherlands: Kluwer Academic Publishers.

Sharma, R. (2005). Five factors of personality and wisdom. *Gyanodaya*, 2(2), 82–87.

Small, M. W. (2004). Wisdom and now managerial wisdom: Do they have a place in management development programs? *Journal of Management Development*, 23(8), 751–764.

Small, M. W. (2011). Developing wisdom and moral duty in management. *Journal of Management Development*, 30(9), 836–846.

Spielthenner, G. (2004). Moral virtues. *Florianópolis*, 3(1), 27–35.

Staudinger, U. M. (2008). A psychology of wisdom: History and recent developments. *Research in Human Development*, 5(2), 107–120.

Sternberg, R. J. (1985). Implicit theory of intelligence, creativity, and wisdom. *Journal of Personality and Social Psychology*, 49(3), 607–627.

Sternberg, R. J. (1986). Intelligence, wisdom, and creativity: Three is better than one. *Educational Psychologist*, 21(3), 175–190.

Sternberg, R. J. (1990). Wisdom and its relations to intelligence and creativity. In R. J. Sternberg (Ed.), *Wisdom: Its nature, origins, and development* (pp. 142–159). New York: Cambridge University Press.

Sternberg, R. J. (1998). A balance theory of wisdom. *Review of General Psychology*, 2(4), 347–365.

Sternberg, R. J. (2004a). What is wisdom and how can we develop it? *The Annals of the American Academy of Political and Social Science*, 591(1), 164–174.

Sternberg, R. J. (2004b). Words to the wise about wisdom? *Human Development*, 47(5), 286–289.

Sternberg, R. J., & Dobson, D. M. (1987). Resolving interpersonal conflicts: An analysis of stylistic consistency. *Journal of Personality and Social Psychology*, 52(4), 794–812.

Steutel, J., & Spiecker, B. (1997). Rational passions and intellectual virtues: A conceptual analysis. *Studies in Philosophy and Education*, 16(1–2), 59–71.

Takahashi, M., & Overton, W. (2005). Cultural foundations of wisdom: An integrated developmental approach. In R. J. Sternberg & J. Jordan (Eds.), *A handbook of wisdom: Psychological perspectives* (pp. 32–60). New York: Cambridge University Press.

Taylor, M., Bates, G., & Webster, J. D. (2011). Comparing the psychometric properties of two measures of wisdom: Predicting forgiveness and psychological well-being with the self-assessed wisdom scale (SAWS) and the three-dimensional wisdom scale (3D-WS). *Experimental Aging Research*, 37(2), 129–141.

Tredget, D. A. (2010). Practical wisdom and the rule of Benedict. *Journal of Management Development*, 29(7/8), 716–723.

Urmson, J. O. (1998). *Aristotle's Ethics*. Oxford, UK: Basil Blackwell.

Vaillant, G. E. (2002). *Aging well: Surprising guideposts to a happier life from the landmark Harvard study of adult development*. Boston: Little, Brown and Company.

Walsh, R. (2014). *The world's great wisdom: Timeless teachings from religions and philosophies. SUNY Series in Integral Theory*. New York: State University of New York Press.

Walsh, R. (2015). What is wisdom? Cross-cultural and cross-disciplinary syntheses. *Review of General Psychology*, 19(3), 278–293.

Webster, J. D. (2010). Wisdom and positive psychosocial values in young adulthood. *Journal of Adult Development*, 17(2), 70–80.

Yang, S. (2011). East meets West: Cross-cultural perspectives on wisdom and adult education. *New Directions for Adult and Continuing Education*, 131(Fall), 45–54.

Yang, S., & Intezari, A. (in press). Non-Western lay conceptions of wisdom. In R. J. Sternberg & J. Gluck (Eds.), *Cambridge handbook of wisdom*. Cambridge, UK: Cambridge University Press.

2 Understanding practical wisdom in business and management

An inter-disciplinary perspective

Introduction

Wisdom 2.0 is an annual conference that explores the intersection of wisdom and technology. In 2018 the gathering included 3,000 people from 30 countries' events. Google and other companies offer mindfulness classes that are fully booked. These activities suggest the time is ripe for change in business and management practice, a view confirmed by fast-growing academic interest in the role of wisdom in management practice (McKenna, Rooney, & Kenworthy, 2013).

Wisdom studies in the management and organizational fields draw extensively upon philosophical and psychological studies. Accordingly, as with philosophy and psychology, it is difficult to capture a single definition of wisdom in management. However, in concurrence with the psychological understanding of wisdom, managerial perspectives, on the whole, treat wisdom as an integral compound. It integrates both a *unifying quality of rationality* (cognition, knowledge, and reason) *and at the same time a non-rational dimension* (feeling, intuition, and emotions) (McKenna, 2013; Rooney, McKenna, & Liesch, 2010; Rowley, Gibbs, & Gibbs, 2008). Importantly, both qualities can be learnt, developed, and applied (Elkin, Martin-Niemi, & Cathro, 2013; Intezari & Pauleen, 2013; McKenna, 2013a). As wisdom relies on the particular, contextual, and subjective, it goes beyond rational and objective understanding, and what is already known. As such, wisdom is an especially useful quality for managers (Rowley et al., 2008) as they have to deal with various emergent and wicked problems that require effective decisions, while facing uncertainty.

As wisdom is studied in different areas of management and organizational studies, we see correspondingly different interpretations of what it is and how it manifests. For example, wisdom has been defined as the highest level of abstraction, vision, and foresight (Awad & Ghaziri, 2004), knowledge-based action (Bierly III, Kessler, & Christensen, 2000), or a way of thinking and acting (Hays, 2010) that is exhibited through decision making (Rowley & Slack, 2009). In leadership, wisdom has been defined as strategic thinking and visioning, being self-disciplined, as well as being able to communicate and engage with others (Rowley & Slack, 2009). McKenna et al. (2008) argue for wisdom in organizations and in leadership, emphasizing that it is founded on both the wise leader's and the organizational capacity for wise practice which they create. Rowley (2006b) defines wisdom as "the capacity to put into action the most appropriate behavior for an organization, taking into account what is known and the legitimate concerns of its various stakeholders" (p. 262). Rooney et al. (2010, p. xi) stress that "wisdom is the quality that shapes action in ways that are likely to lead to good judgment, good decisions, and good acts".

One very clear way that wisdom can potentially manifest in the business context is in management decision making (Intezari, 2014). However, despite the growing attention to wisdom in management, fundamental questions remain unanswered, such as: what does wisdom look like in a business setting, in particular in decision-making situations? How can it be applied? Can it be learned on the job? The following chapters will respond to some of these important questions. In this chapter, we examine the concept of wisdom from a management perspective based in large part on the philosophical and psychological understandings of wisdom introduced in Chapter 1. This chapter provides a theoretical foundation for the central discussion of the book: how can wisdom be practically incorporated into and improve management decision making?

Management perspectives on wisdom

In more recent studies of wisdom in relation to management and leadership, ancient philosophies, both Western and Eastern, such as Aristotelian, Confucian, and Buddhism have been explored (Case, 2013; Harwood, 2011; Yang, 2011). By studying ancient concepts of wisdom, that once were at the heart of philosophical debate in the classical era, organizational and management scholars investigate how such qualities as 'wisdom' can be applied to management practice today (Small, 2011). This growing attention towards ancient wisdom traditions in modern management theory and practice represents an increasingly important attempt to address a fundamental critique of modern management theory and practice. In particular, classical economic models in general and management theory in particular tend to undervalue the role of individual intentions, by making an assumption about human nature that people's behaviour is only based on self-interest (Baden & Higgs, 2015). The inability of business to clearly distinguish between means and ends results in an organization's or manager's inability to distinguish between profit maximization and the common good. This lack of perspective can result in sacrificing the long-term social welfare of the wider community of stakeholders for short-term profit (Baden & Higgs, 2015). Current models and frameworks represent a conventional management 'wisdom', which is more representative of foolishness than genuine wisdom (Baden & Higgs, 2015).

Not only is wisdom not embodied in business, particularly in business ethics (Solansky, 2014), but unethical behaviour is validated by common practice (Baden & Higgs, 2015). The Academy of Business Society and Yale's Practical Wisdom Initiative conceives of business and management as forces for well-being. The initiative explores the underlying qualities of managerial decision making that lead to wise decisions in a business (Malloch, 2015). Initiatives like this one manifest both the need and growing interest for wisdom-enriched management theories.

As this relates to decision making, Malloch (2015), using in-depth case studies, demonstrated that making wise decisions has been 'unnecessarily unsupported' by business ethics and has hindered managers' capabilities to make decisions that pre-empt abuse in organizations. Not surprisingly, these conventional management views have also hindered realizing the relevance of an understanding of moral responsibilities by management students as well (Solansky, 2014). In response, Baden and Higgs (2015) unequivocally state that enhancing curricula of business schools with wisdom-enriched teachings is a high-demand need.

Wisdom has been examined in many management-related fields, including leadership (McKenna & Rooney, 2008; McKenna, Rooney, & Boal, 2009), and management education (Intezari & Pauleen, 2013; Küpers & Gunnlaugson, 2016; Tredget, 2010), as well as public administration (Rooney & McKenna, 2008), and policy making (Etheredge, 2005). Furthermore, related fields such as organizational learning (Bierly III et al., 2000), the learning organization (Bennet & Bennet, 2008), Management Information Systems (Pauleen, Rooney, & Intezari, 2017; Pauleen, Dalal, Rooney, Intezari, & Wang, 2015), and knowledge management (Rowley, 2006a), as well as business ethics (Intezari & Pauleen, 2014) are increasingly being investigated.

The diversity of the fields has led to different conceptualizations, and various qualities have been attributed to the notion of wisdom. 'Wisdom' has been referred to as a morally-based understanding (Begley, 2006) that leads to moral behaviour. Wisdom can also be defined as the capacity to take the most appropriate actions for the organization by taking into consideration the legitimate concerns of all stakeholders (Rowley, 2006a).

Others have defined wisdom as a knowledge-based action (Ackoff, 1989) and a way of thinking and acting (Holliday & Chandler, 1986). Holliday and Chandler (1986) define wisdom in terms of wise people's characteristics such as being cognitive, interpersonal, and experimental.

Korac-Kakabadse, Korac-Kakabadse, and Kouzmin (2001) take an Aristotelian approach, considering practical wisdom as qualities of mind. Moreover, there are certain traits and characteristics which suggest that moral leadership allows the movement of followers into leadership roles also requiring practical wisdom.

In the leadership field, the main attempts to conceptualize wisdom are focused on the characteristics of wise people. For example, Biloslavo and McKenna (2013) characterize wisdom by identifying the main characteristics of those who are widely regarded as wise, such as Gandhi. These characteristics include being knowledgeable and experienced, having agentive self-control and willpower, being able to deal with uncertainty, showing a high level of affective development in their ability to regulate their own emotions and to understand the emotions of others, and being highly moral.

Biloslavo and McKenna (2013) suggest a developmental model of wisdom that aims to identify human characteristics that indicate wisdom in individuals. The underlying assumption of the model is that the only way to judge wisdom is through actions of individuals, and that individual actions can be predicted by personality traits. The model is based on four inter-dependent dimensions: cognitive, conative, affective, and moral.

Cognitive complexity refers to the capability to consider and discriminate different aspects when thinking about something. Conative complexity includes the capacity to coordinate different systems of motives and relate them to set goals. Affective complexity refers to one's capacity to understand that some emotions conflict, and to reflectively regulate and differentiate one's own emotion. Moral complexity refers to having a desire for human dignity and showing a high level of moral development which can help the wise person to understand human interconnectedness within complex social systems.

According to the model, a wise action comprises these four dimensions synthesized at the meta-systemic level and the development of wisdom requires an integrative development along all four dimensions (Figure 2.1). The development happens through three stages: formal, systematic, and meta-systematic. A person with a high level of moral complexity is aware of his interconnectedness with the wider natural and social systems. A person pursuing the rights of human beings is committed to virtuous outcomes, and

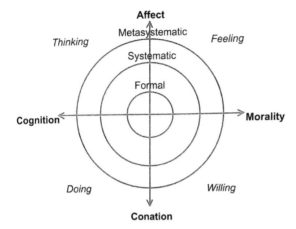

Figure 2.1 Integrated wisdom development model (Biloslavo & McKenna, 2013, p. 117)

recognizes that some legal and peer standards may not be fully moral. Biloslavo and McKenna (2013) claim that the model provides a comprehensive way to assess wisdom in others' actions. They test the model through a textual analysis of the lives of political leaders such as Nelson Mandela, and conclude that he demonstrated a high level of integration of the four dimensions.

The importance of the integration of morality and cognition in wisdom is also highlighted by other studies of wisdom in management. For example, drawing on the premise that knowledge alone is insufficient for solving problems in a complex world, Intezari and Pauleen (2014) suggest that wisdom is a necessary quality for effective management. Specifically, they argue that the fallibility of knowledge, unpredictability of today's world, and inconsistency of human cognition, can result in unintended consequences when organizations and management respond to unpredictable environments. They suggest that wisdom contributes to management through three wisdom-related aspects that help managers and organizations operate wisely (Figure 2.2).

Drawing on Aristotelian principles, Intezari and Pauleen (2014) see wisdom as a *Moral virtue*, which helps set appropriate goals, harmonizing morality at both individual and communal levels. As an *Epistemic virtue*, wisdom embeds 'epistemic responsibility', 'awareness of limitations', and a 'balance between certainty and doubt' into management decisions and actions. Finally, as a *Practical virtue*, the contribution of wisdom to management can be understood in two ways: achieving the desired goals and achieving those goals through appropriate means. The wisdom virtues are critical in order to act wisely in complex, uncertain, and challenging environments (Intezari & Pauleen, 2014) as when facing wicked problems (see Chapter 3).

Highlighting the inextricable link between organizations and their surrounding environment and the interrelationship with wisdom, Edwards (2013) proposes a wisdom typology – comprising transformative, transitive, innovative, conformative, and adaptive wisdom – and argues that depending on the level of environmental turbulence, organizational responses may vary based on these five types of wisdom. According to this model (Figure 2.3), when the environment is highly stable and the conventional modes of managing dominate, organizations may move towards *innovative* (nurturing

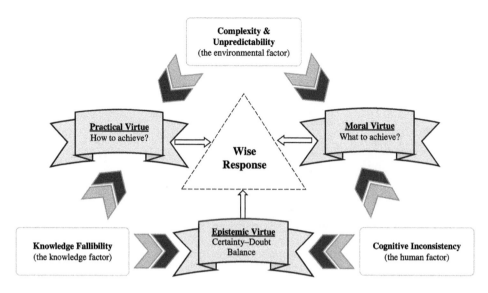

Figure 2.2 Wise responses to uncertain situations (adapted from Intezari & Pauleen, 2014, p. 397)

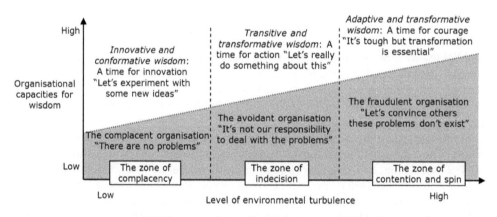

Figure 2.3 Organisational wisdom capacity and environmental turbulence (Edwards, 2013, p. 207)

innovative ideas) and *conformative wisdom* (scanning the environment, and focusing on conventional contingencies that form strategic goals).

As environmental turbulence grows, organizations may call on their capacities of *transitive* or *transformative wisdom* to take decisive action. When the environmental turbulence is at its peak, organizations use their capacities towards qualitative changes and so shift to new systems and values (*adaptive and transformative wisdom*). Transformative wisdom resonates with what Hays (2013) calls 'transformational learning'.

Hays (2013) offers a dynamic model of organizational wisdom that integrates transformational leadership (T[1]), transformational learning (T[2]), and transformational organizational changes (T[3]) in association with transcendence and organizational

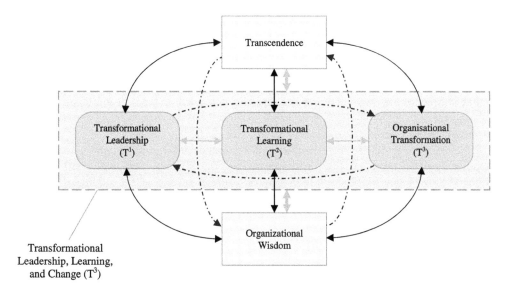

Figure 2.4 Dynamic model of organizational wisdom (adapted from Hays, 2013, p. 135)

wisdom (Figure 2.4). He argues that the integration of the transformation is critical for organizational survival, and that leaders play a key role in all transformational learning and changes.

Hays (2013) differentiates transformational leaders from transactional leaders with regard to their approaches to wisdom development in followers. He emphasizes that transactional leadership, helping others to become wise, promotes organizational wisdom. Transformational change is greater than gradual and incremental change, as it is concerned with both structural and cultural changes. Within an organization, transformational change requires fundamental changes in understandings, attitudes, beliefs, and cultural values. Transformational learning, according to Hays (2013), is an instrumental part of transcendence and transformation, and it plays a vital role in wisdom. Compared to shallow or superficial learning, which is limited to what is already known, transformational learning leads to discovery and development, and fundamentally changes an individual in some way. The transformation influences both *what* and *how* one thinks. Transcendence is a capacity that leads wise leaders to look beyond their own interests.

The transformations are actualized by transcendence. Transcendence contributes to purposeful, conscious, and continuous learning and change, and, therefore, actualizes transformational leadership, learning, and change, and contributes to the development of organizational wisdom through the integration of the transformations.

Social Practice Wisdom (SPW)

A recent and comprehensive theory of wisdom in management and organizational contexts is the theory of Social Practice Wisdom (SPW), introduced by Rooney and McKenna (Rooney et al., 2010). The theory expounds on SPW principles and offers a framework that can enable researchers in social sciences, especially in organizational and management fields, to examine the practical and intellectual nuances of wisdom in situ. Intezari et al. (2016) argue that the outcomes of studies that are designed and conducted based on the SPW framework can more effectively deal with the economic, social, political, and environmental complexities of the contemporary world.

David Rooney and Bernard McKenna are pioneers in organizational and management studies of wisdom.[1] Their main thesis about wisdom and its implication(s) for management is articulated in their book, *Wisdom and management in the knowledge economy* (Rooney et al., 2010).

Their early arguments for the necessity of wisdom in organizational and management studies draw primarily on their criticism of the conventional non-axiological conception of knowledge (axiology is the study of values). In one of their first writings on wisdom, Rooney and McKenna (2005) argued that the inadequate conceptualization of knowledge lacked an axiological dimension and so limited the discourse on knowledge-based economies to ends-based ways of achieving growth without consideration of the means to that growth and the effects on extended stakeholder communities. They then suggest that "a wisdom-based renaissance of humanistic epistemology is needed to avoid increasing social dysfunction and a lack of wisdom in complex technological societies" (Rooney & McKenna, 2005, p. 307). Emphasizing the urgency of wisdom in the contemporary turbulent world, they propose that "wisdom be established as the ideal of organizational practice and that practices be measured against that ideal" (McKenna, Rooney, & ten Bos, 2007, p. 84). Rooney et al. (2010) note that "having good judgment, making good decisions, and acting well do not automatically happen in management, and wisdom is the quality that shapes action in ways that are likely to lead to good judgment, good decisions, and good acts" (p. xi). Therefore, in an uncertain and complex environment wisdom becomes a key resource for management, as it acknowledges the relativity of truth, knowledge, perception, and human cognitive limitations (Rooney et al., 2010).

Taking a neo-Aristotelian approach, Rooney et al. (2010) introduce an interdisciplinary-driven theory of wisdom, which draws on a philosophical-psychological foundation with managerial implications. SPW refers to "the integration of rationality, calculation, intuition, insight, imagination, and creativity while acting in everyday life" (Rooney et al., 2010, p. 63). The core of the theory is:

> a complex, multidimensional integration that creates clarity and decisiveness through equanimity and corresponding dispositions that generate the insight, composure and motivation to deploy the resources needed to act excellently and successfully in the best interests of oneself, others and the planet.
>
> (Rooney, 2013, p. 36)

SPW brings together both knowledge (reason, rational knowing) and intuition (emotions, non-rational knowing). As McKenna (2013a) reiterates, wise thinking is based on rationality, intuition, and ethics. McKenna emphasizes that real-world problems can only be solved through an explicit combination of science and intuition, and truth and values, as well as intuition and transcendent cognitive processes.

More recent iterations of SPW developed by Rooney and various co-authors (Rooney et al., 2010; Rooney, Hearn, & Kastelle, 2012; Pauleen et al., 2015, 2017) describe SPW as the pinnacle of social excellence, distinguishing it from common sense, judgement, and knowledge, which allows for the flexible integration of its particular qualities to produce social excellence dynamically in everyday life (cf. Grossmann, Gerlach, & Denissen, 2016). The most recent revision of SPW adds principles from Buddhist philosophy and contemporary wisdom and mindfulness research in management, psychology, neuroscience, spirituality, and education disciplines (Rooney et al., 2010; Zhu, Rooney, & Phillips, 2016). SPW principles include qualities of mind and spirit, transcendent reasoning, and ethicality, as well as embodied praxis.

Normatively, SPW can and should be practised in everyday social life, including in business and management, with its constantly shifting social relations, resource limitations, power and political asymmetries, and environmental, technological, and economic disruption. As conceived by Pauleen et al. (2017), SPW is a multilevel conceptual framework accounting for features at macro-, meso-, and micro-levels. In brief, the five animating principles of SPW are:

1. *Qualities of mind and spirit*: An aware, equanimous, compassionate, humble, and actively open mind with habituated dispositions creating an integrated mental culture and habitus of interrelated dispositions that drive insightful and virtuous action.
2. *Agile, transcendent, and reflexive reasoning*: Integrating knowledge, information, transcendent ability, different perspectives, and accurate and reflexive insight to create and transform a situation despite uncertainty and ambiguity.
3. *Ethical virtuosity*: This includes pro-social virtues, competence, and the ability to understand and act positively to meet people's emotional, social, and material needs.
4. *Embodiment and praxis (or mastering wise action)*: Drawing from one's habitus of dispositions to creatively and responsively (decisively) embody and enact wise performative skills in a situation, based on experience, understanding, timing, aesthetics, and judgement for responsible application of knowledge, power, and communication as a wise way of being.
5. *Outcomes that improve the conditions of life*: This involves galvanizing, purposeful leadership and artful communication to effect virtuous change with exceptional outcomes. Creating positive cultures and sustainable communities are central to this.

The offered review of management studies of wisdom reveals that, as with the philosophical and psychological studies, there is no consensus among management scholars with respect to the nature of wisdom. Moreover, it is challenging to delineate strictly management-based conceptions of wisdom because of the extensive borrowing of ideas and concepts from philosophy and psychology. Therefore, it makes sense to purposefully incorporate the aforementioned disciplinary perspectives into an inter-disciplinary approach towards the conceptualization of and further research on wisdom. This inter-disciplinary review is based on the supposition that despite the lack of one widely-shared definition of wisdom (Baltes & Staudinger, 2000; Gugerell & Riffert, 2011), management, philosophical, contemporary psychological, and other studies of wisdom share many commonalities (Biloslavo & McKenna, 2013; Rooney et al., 2010).

For this reason, various disciplinary definitions of wisdom are provided and their shared qualities or elements are noted and discussed. The review is important as it provides a comprehensive understanding of wisdom that transcends discipline-bounded conceptualizations.

Wisdom: an inter-disciplinary perspective

In this chapter and in Chapter 1, numerous descriptions of wisdom have been presented. These range from the classical Greek philosophical tradition that sees wisdom as an enlightened and morally-based (rather than knowledge-based) understanding of 'living well', to the most recent psychological approaches defining wisdom as *expert knowledge* (Baltes & Kunzmann, 2004; Baltes & Staudinger, 1993), knowledge-based action (Bierly III et al., 2000), or a way of knowing (Csikszentmihalyi & Rathunde, 1990), which put emphasis on knowledge/intellect or ethics/emotion, or both. We have also reviewed some of the major management studies of wisdom. The conceptions of wisdom that the management discipline offers range from wisdom as a multidimensional quality that engages cognition, conation, affection, and morality (Biloslavo & McKenna, 2013), to shaping behaviour and action towards good judgement, good decisions, and good acts (Rooney et al., 2010). Wisdom is also defined as a moral, epistemic, and practical virtue geared towards achieving appropriate goals through appropriate management decisions and actions (Intezari & Pauleen, 2014).

These divergent approaches to wisdom, however, have considerable overlap in terms of the qualities associated with wisdom. There is a consensus in the disciplines that wisdom is a multidimensional construct that encompasses interrelated qualities. In both modern and historical models of wisdom, wisdom is associated with such concepts as judgement about important matters, knowledge and the implementation of knowledge, achieving well-being of all, and awareness of the social consequences of one's action. For example, in a psychological approach, wisdom is conceptualized as expert knowledge (Baltes & Kunzmann, 2004) and human affairs-related judgement that contains awareness of the ill-structured, contextual, and often contradictory nature of experience (Kramer, 1990). Likewise, from a managerial and leadership perspective, wisdom is considered as experiential knowledge that helps people make ethically-sound judgements (Liew, 2013; Nonaka & Takeuchi, 2011). Many studies have attempted to provide a list of the constructs of wisdom by examining different definitions of wisdom.

Gibson (2008), for example, conducted an interpretive study of the nature of practical management wisdom, and developed a heuristic model of wisdom. In the study, Gibson (2008) reviews the wisdom literature and identifies six constructs on which wisdom relies. The constructs include "a dynamic interaction between perception, experience, character, and an insightful vision of what is proximately and ultimately good for people, organizations, and business" (p. 528). Likewise, Greene and Brown (2009) suggest that wisdom comprises six interconnected elements: self-knowledge, understanding of others, judgement, life knowledge, life skills, and willingness to learn.

An empirical study conducted by Jeste et al. (2010) indicated a consensus among most of the 57 international wisdom experts who participated that wisdom is:

> human; a form of advanced cognitive and emotional development that is experience driven; and a personal quality, albeit a rare one, which can be learned, increases with age, can be measured, and is not likely to be enhanced by taking medication.
>
> (p. 668)

Similarly, Rowley and Slack (2009) identify the key facets of wisdom, by exploring the early Western-Eastern philosophical traditions, as well as the more recent philosophical, psychological, and organizational approaches to wisdom. Rowley and Slack (2009) propose that the key aspects of wisdom can be summarized as: wisdom (a) "is embedded in or exhibited through *action*"; (b) "involves the sophisticated and sensitive use of knowledge"; (c) "is exhibited through decision making"; (d) "involves the exercise of judgement in complex real-life situations"; (e) "requires consideration of ethical and social considerations and the discernment of right and wrong"; and (f) "is an interpersonal phenomenon, requiring exercise of intuition, communication, and trust" (pp. 113–114).

Kok (2009) draws on different philosophical and psychological statements (e.g. Aristotle's and Sternberg's) of wisdom and summarizes the main principles of wisdom:

- using reason and careful observation to make logical deductive explanations;
- evaluating the salience and truth-value of logical propositions by using clear understandings of ontological categories that theoretically describe substance, process and quality through logical argument;
- acknowledging the sensory and visceral as important components of decision making and judgment;
- having a metaphysical and spiritual quality that does not bind one absolutely to the rules of reason thereby enabling vision, insight and foresight;
- respecting and drawing upon tradition as a means of apprehending who and what one is as a form of personal insight enabling them to understand the contingency of life and constructedness of phenomena;
- being humane and producing virtuous and tolerant decisions;
- being practical and oriented towards everyday life;
- being articulate and understanding the aesthetic dimension of one's work and seeking the intrinsic personal and social rewards of contributing to the good life" (p. 55).

In another study, Meeks and Jeste (2009) analyse ten published descriptions and definitions of wisdom and identify six subcomponents of wisdom that the definitions commonly included. The subcomponents include prosocial attitudes/behaviours, social decision making/pragmatic knowledge of life, emotional homeostasis, reflection/self-understanding, value relativism/tolerance, and acknowledgment of and dealing effectively with uncertainty. Table 2.1 outlines the subcomponents.

In Table 2.2 a variety of disciplinary definitions of wisdom are listed. Providing multiple wisdom definitions, conceptions, and statements from diverse approaches in one place may facilitate an inter-disciplinary understanding as to the meaning and nature of wisdom, and the elements researchers have proposed as associated with wisdom. It must be noted that the table includes only some of the numerous wisdom definitions which exist in the vast pool in the literature, and is by no means exhaustive.

One of the main commonalities of all of the definitions in Table 2.2 is that wisdom is highly associated with practice. For example, Strijbos (1995) believes that "wisdom is not just connected with action; it includes action" (p. 363). Table 2.2 indicates that contemporary understandings of wisdom tend toward the conception of 'practical wisdom' rather than 'theoretical wisdom', so that the term 'wisdom' is broadly used interchangeably with 'practical wisdom' (this bifurcation has been discussed earlier in Chapter 1). The pervasiveness of the practice-oriented approach may be because of the great interest among scholars in the implications of wisdom in daily and business life (e.g. Baltes &

Table 2.1 Subcomponents of wisdom (adapted from Meeks & Jeste, 2009, p. 356)

The Subcomponents of Wisdom	Definitions
Prosocial attitudes and behaviors	- Altruism. Achieving the common good - Positive emotion and behaviors toward others - Warmth
Social decision making and pragmatic knowledge of life	- Life knowledge: knowledge regarding human nature and life course. Knowledge about the ways of dealing with life's problems. Life skills - Knowing when, where, how, and why to apply knowledge - Expeditious use of information and expertise in advice giving - Good interpersonal skills and understanding - Judgment
Emotional homeostasis	- Emotional stability and emotional management. - Remaining positive in the face of adversity; and the absence of indifferent or negative emotions toward others.
Reflection/self-understanding	- Reflective abilities and judgement - Self-knowledge and self-understanding
Value relativism and tolerance	- Value relativism and tolerance - Absence of projections. Ability and willingness to examine phenomena from multiple perspectives. - Tolerant and understanding
Acknowledgment of and dealing effectively with uncertainty and ambiguity	- Comprehension of and handling uncertainty, including the limits of knowledge - Emotional stability despite uncertainty and openness to new experience - Ability to make decisions and act in the face of uncertainty

Kunzmann, 2004; Rooney et al., 2010). The key aspects of wisdom that are commonly suggested by the definitions in Table 2.2 are discussed in the following section.

Key aspects of wisdom

Based on these different conceptualizations of wisdom, a set of ten fundamental characteristics or qualities can be identified that have been attributed to wisdom. These are summarized in Table 2.3 and briefly discussed below.

Concerned with fundamental matters of life, including living a good life

Wisdom is concerned with the fundamental aspects and uncertainty of human life (Baltes & Kunzmann, 2004; Baltes & Smith, 1990; Etheredge, 1992; Pasupathi & Staudinger, 2001). Maxwell (1984) explains that wisdom includes the desire for and the ability to see *what is of value* in the circumstances of life. In philosophy, wisdom is understood as being associated with knowledge and sound judgement in order to *live a good life* (Small, 2004). Wise people understand the importance of commonplace truths for living the good life, and know how to construct a pattern that leads to a good life

Table 2.2 Wisdom definitions

Definitions	Disciplines
Aristotle's definition: "a reasoned and true state of capacity to act with regard to human goods" (Aristotle, 2009, Trans. the Nicomachean Ethics 1140b, 20).	Philosophy
"Wisdom is the way in which knowledge is held. It concerns the handling of knowledge, its selection for the determination of relevant issues, its employment to add value to our immediate experience. This mastery of knowledge, which is wisdom, is the most intimate freedom obtainable" (Whitehead, 1967, p. 30).	Philosophy
Practical wisdom is "the sense of governance we have in directing our free and voluntary choices to ends befitting us as human beings" (Hakim, 2006, p. 97).	Philosophy
"Knowledge about certain principles and causes" (Hakim, 2006, p. 99).	Philosophy
"The ability to make right use of knowledge, or the capacity to judge rightly in matters relating to life and conduct" (Ostenfeld, 2003; as cited in Rowley, 2006a, p. 1248).	Philosophy
Practical wisdom is "sound reasoning and effective deliberation that leads to morally right practice" (Baggini & Fosl, 2007, p. 153).	Philosophy
"The competence in, intention to, and application of, critical life experiences to facilitate the optimal development of self and others" (Webster, 2007, p. 164).	Psychology
"Wisdom can be defined as the ability to grasp human nature, which is paradoxical, contradictory, and subject to continual change" (Clayton, 1982, p. 315).	Psychology
"A blending of the intellectual perception of truth and the moral sentiment of right is wisdom" (Emerson, 1929, p. 45, as cited in Csikszentmihalyi & Rathunde, 1990, p. 31).	Psychology
"Wisdom is an attitude taken by persons toward the beliefs, values, knowledge, information, abilities, and skills that are held, a tendency to doubt that these are necessarily true or valid and to doubt that they are an exhaustive set of those things that could be known" (Meacham, 1990, p. 187).	Psychology
Wisdom is "expert knowledge and judgement about important, difficult and uncertain questions associated with the meaning and conduct of life" (Baltes & Kunzmann, 2003, p. 131).	Psychology
"Wisdom is a form of judgment pertaining to some domain of human affairs that involves an awareness of the ill-structured, contextual, and often contradictory nature of experience" (Kramer, 1990, p. 291).	Psychology
"The ability to recognize the limits of one's knowledge" (Holliday & Chandler, 1986, p. 15).	Psychology
"A set of attributes assumed to be correlated with advanced age and not usually covered under the umbrella of intelligence" (Labouvie-Vief, 1990, p. 52).	Psychology
"Wisdom is the use of one's intelligence and experience as mediated by values toward the achievement of a common good through a balance among (1) intrapersonal, (2) interpersonal, and (3) extrapersonal interests, over the (1) short and (2) long terms, to achieve a balance among (1) adaptation to existing environments, (2) shaping of existing environments, and (3) selection of new environments" (Sternberg, 2004, p. 164).	Psychology
"Wisdom is conceptualized as the personal philosophy (perspective on life), sense of balance and understanding of the complexities of inter-actions within a landscape" (Korac-Kakabadse, Korac-Kakabadse, & Kouzmin, 2001, p. 213).	Psychology

(Continued)

Table 2.2 (Continued)

Definitions	Disciplines
"Wisdom is the continually evolving understanding of and fascination with the big picture of life and what is important, ethical, and meaningful; it includes the desire and ability to apply this understanding to enhance the well-being of life, both for oneself and for others" (Lombardo, 2010, p. 34).	Psychology
"The optimum, ultimate expression of a blend of human qualities" (Birren & Fisher, 1990, p. 323).	Psychology
"An integration of cognitive, reflection, and affective dimensions" (Ardelt, 2003, p. 277).	Psychology
"Wisdom is both correct insight and action consistent with it" (Strijbos, 1995, p. 363).	Psychology
"A perfect, perhaps utopian, integration of knowledge and character, of mind and virtue" (Kunzmann, 2004, p. 504).	Psychology
Wisdom comprises "critical thinking skills (or strategies), the disposition to use these skills, and metacognitive monitoring of the critical thinking process" as well as "a way for deciding which goals should be desired, a way that is based on a balance among self and other interests and short- and long-term goals" (Halpern, 2001, p. 255).	Psychology
"The capacity to put into action the most appropriate behaviour, taking into account what is known (knowledge) and what does the most good (ethical and social considerations)" (Rowley, 2006b, p. 257).	Management
"Wisdom is the critical ability to use knowledge in a constructive way. Equally, wisdom has in it the critical ability to discern ways in which new ideas can be created" (Matthews, 1998, p. 209).	Management
"A capacity to perceive, deliberate, decide, and act effectively" (Gibson, 2008, p. 528).	Management
"Wisdom is the highest level of abstraction, with vision, foresight, and the ability to see beyond the horizon" (Awad & Ghaziri, 2004, p. 40).	Management
"Wisdom is the ability to act critically or practically in a given situation. It is based on ethical judgement related to an individual's belief system" (Jashapara, 2004, p. 17).	Management
"Wisdom consists of the ability to move away from absolute truths, to be reflective, to make sound judgments related to our daily existence, whatever our circumstances" (Merriam & Caffarella, 1999, p. 165).	Management
"Practical wisdom is experiential knowledge that enables people to make ethically sound judgments" (Nonaka & Takeuchi, 2011, p. 60).	Management
"The ability to best use knowledge for establishing and achieving desired goals and learning about wisdom as the process of discerning judgments and action based on knowledge" (Bierly III et al., 2000, p. 601).	Management
"Wisdom is the quality that shapes action in ways that are likely to lead to good judgment, good decisions, and good acts" (Rooney et al., 2010, p. xi).	Management
"Practical wisdom refers to a habituated pattern of actions that are normatively positive both in terms of their process and in terms of their outcome" (Statler & Roos, 2007, p. 88).	Management
"Wisdom is socially accepted or experience-validated explication of purpose" (Zeleny, 2006, p. 7).	Management Systems

Definitions	Disciplines
"Wisdom is the proper use of knowledge that has been applied in a way that takes into account all its pertinent relationships and that is consistent with universal laws" (Walker, 2005, p. 33).	Leadership
"A disposition toward cleverness in crafting morally excellent responses to, or in anticipation of, challenging particularities" (Moberg, 2007, p. 536).	Business Ethics
"Wisdom means to choose one's behaviour based on knowledge and shared values, in order to enhance the well-being of all and awareness that personal actions have social consequences" (Blasi, 2006, p. 407).	Education
"A positive process that encompasses three core components: 1) cognitive integration of what are ordinarily considered separate ideas or conflicting ideals to form a vision promoting the good life, 2) actions that embody the integrated thought or vision, and 3) positive effects of the actions on the actor and others" (Yang, 2011, p. 49).	Management & Education
Wisdom is "assessing self and others (wider community), in a specific time and place where a particular set of interactions between people and their situation occurs. The wise person integrates their general and abstract knowledge, values and understandings into decisions and actions for that situation and the well-being of all involved, over both the short and long term." (Intezari et al., 2016, p. 2).	Education & Research
"Wisdom is knowledge plus ingredients that resist easy characterization but typically are based in the long experience of communities. If you must have an equation; wisdom = knowledge + accumulated experience of communities" (Pantzar, 2000, p. 234).	Education & Learning
"Wisdom is a process that brings together the rational and the transcendent, the prosaic and higher virtues, the short- and long-terms, the contingent and the absolute, and the self and the collective rather than being only concerned with rational processing of knowledge" (Kok, 2009, p. 56).	Education & Learning
"The power to choose well", which involves the qualities or abilities of 'epistemic discernment', 'awareness of the limits of one's own knowledge', 'the quality of desiring well', and 'self-knowledge' (Gayle, 2011, p. 72).	Education & Learning
"The capacity (and perhaps the active desire) to realize what is of value in life, for oneself and others" (Maxwell, 2012, p. 165).	Education & Learning
"The ability to base sound judgements on deep understandings in conditions of uncertainty" (O'Sullivan, 2005, p. 222).	Health and Social Care
"Wisdom is a practice that reflects the developmental process by which individuals increase in self-knowledge, self-integration, nonattachment, self-transcendence, and compassion, as well as a deeper understanding of life. This practice involves better self-regulation and ethical choices, resulting in greater good for oneself and others" (Aldwin, 2009, p. 3).	Human Development and Family Science
"Something highly personal involving the integration of theory, religion/philosophy and subjective experience" (Krill, 1990, p. 14).	Human Services
"Wisdom is good judgment about important matters" (Etheredge, 1992, p. 497).	Politics

Table 2.3 Key aspects of wisdom

Wisdom aspects	Description
Concerned with fundamental matters of life	Wisdom is related to fundamental and pragmatic aspects of life.
Knowledge	Knowledge is important in making wise decisions and taking wise actions. However, wisdom is more than a mere accumulation of knowledge. Wisdom is also associated with one's ability to use knowledge.
Experience	Experience is a critical subcomponent of wisdom. Experience, however, in and of itself, does not necessarily lead to wisdom.
Practice-oriented	Wisdom is prone to act. Wisdom is a way of being and doing. Wise people are defined as being "the sort of person who acts". Wisdom is not just about the achievement of good ends, but it is also about how to achieve desired goals.
Ethics	Wisdom and morality are interwoven. Ethics is a substantial aspect of wisdom.
Self-transcendence	Wisdom is not restricted to the individual level, but it manifests at both individual and social levels. Wisdom is concerned with well-being of self and others.
Judgment	Wisdom enables people to make good pragmatic judgments about important matters of life.
Non-rationality	Wisdom engages non-rationality, and goes beyond rational and objective understanding, and what is already known.
Emotions	Wisdom is not a purely cognitive quality. Wise decisions, however, are not overly affected by emotions. Wisdom helps to keep a balance between emotions and logic.
Awareness of the limits of knowledge	Wisdom is about being aware of what is not known. Wise people are aware of the limitations of their knowledge.

(Kekes, 1995). Similarly, Garrett and College (1996, p. 221) state that wise people understand that "which is essential to living the best life".

"Wisdom is the truth seeker and pattern finder that penetrates to the core of what really matters" (Allee, 1997, p. 44). Wisdom pursues the fundamental meaning of existence (Kramer, 1990), and helps people consider the world and life as a whole: "having practical wisdom is to be endowed with a capacity which makes one good at thinking about what one should do, not to achieve particular goals but to live a fulfilled and worthwhile life as a whole" (Melé, 2010, p. 641). Kramer (1990) says that wisdom is associated with the pragmatics of life, i.e. the extrapersonal, intrapersonal, and interpersonal situations that are personally meaningful to the individual.

Knowledge

Wisdom, as represented by the disciplinary literature, is broadly associated with knowledge (Garrett & College, 1996; Kekes, 1995; Lehrer & Smith, 1996; Ryan, 1996). This refers to both possessing knowledge (Maxwell, 1984) and the ability to make use of knowledge and experience (Birren & Fisher, 1990; Matthews, 1998;

Walker, 2005). According to Bierly III et al. (2000), wisdom, being associated with choosing and applying the appropriate knowledge effectively in a given situation, "is the ability to best use knowledge for establishing and achieving desired goals" (p. 601). Wisdom, therefore, is not a simple accumulation of knowledge (Maxwell, 2007, 2013; Nunamaker, Romano, & Briggs, 2002); rather it relies on character and mind, and is more concerned with how one apprehends and deploys knowledge than with how much one knows (McKenna et al., 2008). Ardelt (2004) asserts that the accumulation and *quantity* of knowledge cannot be an indicator of wisdom, as knowledge is believed to exist only at the intellectual level, whilst wisdom is seen at the experiential level.

Experience

Although experience, in and of itself, does not necessarily lead to wisdom (Holliday & Chandler, 1986), it is essential and required for practical wisdom (Baggini & Fosl, 2007; Grint, 2007; Kodish, 2006; Urmson, 1998). Knowledge accumulation does not lead to knowledge; as the Roman lyric poet, Horace (65–8 BCE), says, "wisdom is not wisdom when it is derived from books alone". Experience can progressively lead one to become wise and wiser (Birren & Fisher, 1990). Aristotle (2009, *1142a,* 10–15) emphasizes the role of experience in the development of wisdom, by saying:

> While young men [can] become geometricians and mathematicians and wise in matters like these, it is thought that a young man of practical wisdom cannot be found. The cause is that such wisdom is concerned not only with universals but with particulars, which become familiar from experience, but a young man has no experience, for it is length of time that gives experience.

Practice-oriented

In the disciplinary literature, wisdom is characterized as being *prone to act* (Birren & Fisher, 1990), and as excellence, leads things to perform their function well (Aristotle, 2009). Wisdom is a way of being and doing (Bierly III et al., 2000; McKenna et al., 2008; Nichols, 1996; Rooney et al., 2010). Wisdom does not undervalue the importance of achieving business goals. Wisdom in the business context is about achieving business goals, while making sure that the goals are good ends in terms of ethics and the impacts that the goals will have on various stakeholders (Intezari & Pauleen, 2013). Gibson (2008) defines wisdom as "a capacity to perceive, deliberate, decide, and *act* effectively" (p. 528). Wise people are defined as being "the sort of person who acts" (Telfer, 1990), and they try to act wisely every time they make a decision or take an action. According to Küpers and Pauleen (2015), wisdom is an embodied and habitual quality. That is, wise people act wisely out of habit. This implies that one can become wise by continuously practising wise actions (we shall further discuss wisdom development in Chapter 9). Beck (1999) asserts that wisdom encompasses both action and knowledge, which are related to doing what is good and to understanding the truth, respectively. Wise people not only *know how* to live, but they also live well (Nozick, 1989; Ryan, 1996). As Garrett and College (1996) put it, "living well, living better or living the best life is what lies behind our interest in wisdom" (p. 226).

Ethics

Ethical action is central to wise practice (Rooney & McKenna, 2008). In this sense, morality is considered a necessary feature of wisdom, as achieving the peak levels of wise performance is not possible without having the capacity of moral reasoning (Pasupathi & Staudinger, 2001). Aristotle (in *The Nicomachean Ethics*) points out that nothing could lead to good ends without being good, as "a good person will naturally do the right thing, whereas someone who has intellectual insight alone may possess neither the motivation nor the requisite skills and habits to carry out the right action" (2009, as cited in LeBon, 2001, p. 58). From a practical wisdom perspective, understanding the ethical dimension of one's action is important to fully understand the action (Melé, 2010). In this sense, practical wisdom brings together ethics, knowledge, and practice. Distinguishing between wisdom and knowledge, Courtney (2001) says that "knowledge involves the ability to act intelligently and to learn", and "wisdom guides knowledge actions on the basis of moral and ethical values" (p. 23). Wise managers are experienced and intelligent enough to know what is right, and they always try to do the right thing to enhance social well-being.

Self-transcendence

Self-transcendence is a critical element of wisdom (Curnow, 1999). Self-transcendence underlines that one's understanding of the self should be focused more on spirituality and interiority (rather than reliance on externals), as well as a greater understanding of connectedness with the surrounding environment and others including past and future generations (Levenson, Jennings, Aldwin, & Shiraishi, 2005). Wisdom has a multidimensional nature and is associated with both individual and communal levels (Baltes & Kunzmann, 2004; Intezari & Pauleen, 2014; Pasupathi & Staudinger, 2001). Levenson et al. (2001) argue that transcending the ego is a developmental process that leads to wisdom. Küpers (2007) considers wisdom as a socio-cultural process, which refers to development in two dimensions: individuality and communality. Maxwell (1984) writes: "wisdom can be conceived of, not only in personal terms, but also in institutional or social terms" (p. 66).

According to Staudinger (1996), wisdom has a three-faceted social-interactive nature, and can manifest on both individual and cultural levels. The three facets of the social-interactive nature of wisdom include the development of wisdom over time, the application of wisdom in social situations, and identifying a given written, verbal, or behavioural product as wise (Staudinger, 1996). Personal, interpersonal, and societal factors are involved in the developmental origins of wisdom. Thus, practical wisdom is not limited to the individual level – only helping its possessors to act well – but also allowing them to advise others about appropriate action (Polansky, 2000). Wisdom therefore is associated with choosing "one's behaviour based on knowledge and shared values, in order to enhance the well-being of all and awareness that personal action has social consequences" (Blasi, 2006, p. 407).

Judgement

In the disciplinary literature wisdom is associated with judgement. Wisdom enables people to make good pragmatic judgements about important matters of life (Baltes &

Smith, 1990; Holliday & Chandler, 1986; Rooney et al., 2010). Being able to make sound judgements regarding the conduct of life is one of the factors which differentiate wise people from those who are merely knowledgeable (Bierly III et al., 2000). This implies that good judgement is one of the important characteristics of wisdom (Etheredge, 1992; Roca, 2007). Kramer (1990) even defines wisdom as "a form of judgement" that pertains to the domain of human affairs (p. 291). Gibson (2008) asserts that to make wise decisions and take wise actions, experience, character, and judgement are of great importance.

Non-rationality

Wisdom is a unifying quality of rationality (cognition, reason) and non-rationality (feeling, intuition) (McKenna, 2013b; Rooney et al., 2010; Rowley & Gibbs, 2008). Wisdom goes beyond rational and objective understanding, and what is already known (Rowley et al., 2008), in that it incorporates subjective and non-rational elements into judgement (Rooney et al., 2010). For example, McKenna, Rooney, and Liesch (2006) assert that wisdom in management is based on reason, but it coalesces a humane and virtuous teleology of non-rational and practical wisdom. Pauleen, Rooney, and Holden (2010, p. 392) expressed this unity of the rational and non-rational as it relates to leadership "as being logical and analytical, sensitive and intuitive, clear and articulate, creative, practical, empathetic and ethical".

Emotions

Wisdom, as conceptualized in the disciplinary literature, is not a purely cognitive quality (Intezari & Pauleen, 2013). Wisdom involves emotional characteristics (Baltes & Kunzmann, 2003; Tredget, 2010). Wise people acknowledge the emotional component of all stakeholders including themselves when making decisions (Baltes & Kunzmann, 2004; Birren & Fisher, 1990; Roos, 2006; Tredget, 2010). A person of practical wisdom knows how to account for emotions while choosing from a range of possible options in order to achieve the good end in particular circumstances (Beauchamp, 1991). Emphasizing the emotional dimension of *phronesis*, Roos (2006) asserts that "our emotional reactions manifest, or indicate also the moral dimensions of the situation at hand" (p. 215). For this reason, the achievement of virtues happens when one's emotions, desires, and passions are excellently cultivated (Baggini & Fosl, 2007). In this sense, emotions cause a person of intellectual virtue to abhor intellectual vice and to be quite careful about the truth (Abraham, 2006).

Awareness of the limits of knowledge

According to Aristotle (2009), wise people are aware of the limitations of their knowledge. Wisdom does not connote knowing specific facts; rather it is 'knowing' while keeping a balance between excessive confidence and excessive cautiousness (Meacham, 1990). Wise people are aware of their own knowledge limitations (Baltes & Kunzmann, 2004; Holliday & Chandler, 1986; Kitchener & Brenner, 1990; Meacham, 1990). Awareness of unknowns and their applications in judgement and problem solving are the main characteristics of wise people (Kitchener & Brenner, 1990), as unlike unwise people, who believe that they are wise, wise people are those who do not consider themselves wise. Wise people's awareness of their own limitations leads them to learn from mistakes through evaluative and reflective skills (Sternberg, 1985).

From the different perspectives on wisdom found in the disciplinary literature, we see the primary elements associated with wisdom, and understand that possession of any single quality does not necessarily lead to wisdom. The diversity of opinions makes it a challenging task to conceptualize wisdom in a way that takes account of all of these elements, but Birren and Fisher (1990) and Kodish (2006) tried and as a result developed the following conceptualizations of wisdom as "the optimum, ultimate expression of a blend of human qualities" (Birren & Fisher, 1990, p. 323) that involves various elements including perception, experience, knowledge, rationality and non-rationality, decision making, purposive action, virtue, character, transcendence, understanding one's own and others' interests, and promotion of self and others (Kodish, 2006). Although the combined definition does not explain how the qualities are related to one another, or which qualities and to what extent may make a greater contribution to wisdom, it does identify the many important qualities associated with wisdom.

As outlined in Table 2.3, the multidisciplinary review of the wisdom literature in this chapter identifies the main aspects of wisdom that are commonly identified by the disciplinary literature. These aspects include self-transcendence, knowledge, experience-based, ethics, practice-oriented, judgement, non-rationality, emotions, and awareness of the limits of knowledge.

We, therefore, define wisdom in the business context as the professional manager's capacity to:

(1) critically and accurately assess self, others, and the decision situation, and to:
(2) integrate personal and communal knowledge and values into decisions and actions, in order to:
(3) achieve the well-being of all involved, over both the short and long term.

We will refine and further extend the definition of wisdom as we progress through the chapters and in Chapters 7 and 8 provide a practical definition of the wise management decision-making process.

Chapter summary

In ancient times, wisdom was deeply connected to an ethically guided practice of leadership that focused on excellence and the common good. Modern management and leadership theory and practice has lost this orientation while focusing on maximizing profit for the shareholders or other self-interest (Solansky, 2014). While profit maximization was, and still is, seen as a benefit to society (Adam Smith's *Wealth of Nations*, 1776/ 1976, as cited in Baden & Higgs, 2015), as a means to reach the end of social well-being, it is clear that an overemphasis on profit in modern businesses confuses the means with the ends (Baden & Higgs, 2015). By returning to its ancient roots, wisdom theory and practice is regaining attention and is being studied and applied in management and leadership contexts.

Following a review of the philosophical and psychological literature of wisdom in Chapter 1, in this chapter we focused on its connection to management studies. Considering numerous definitions of wisdom offered by multiple disciplines including philosophy, psychology, management, and education, we developed an understanding of wisdom in the business context as the professional manager's capacity to critically and accurately assess self, others, and the decision situation, and to integrate personal and communal knowledge and values into decisions and actions, in order to achieve the well-being of all involved, over both the short and long term.

The definition sets the stage for the rest of the book as we discuss a practical framework of the incorporation of wisdom in management decision making. As discussed in the next chapter, the complexity of the issues that managers and leaders deal with in the business world requires them to have the capacity to make the 'best' decisions, which optimizes the chances of achieving excellent outcomes, within limited time frames and resource constraints. Wise managers have such a capacity when dealing with complex and wicked problems and use it towards achieving the well-being of self and others.

Note

1 See for example: McKenna et al., 2006, 2007, 2009, 2013; McKenna, Rooney, & Hays, 2011; McKenna & Rooney, 2007, 2009; Rooney & McKenna, 2005; Rooney, Hearn, & Ninan, 2005; Rooney et al., 2010, 2012.

References

Abraham, W. (2006). Education, social transformation, and intellectual virtue. *Christian Higher Education*, 5(1), 3–19.

Ackoff, R. L. (1989). From data to wisdom. *Journal of Applied Systems Analysis*, 16, 3–9.

Aldwin, C. M. (2009). Gender and wisdom: A brief overview. *Research in Human Development*, 6(1), 1–8.

Allee, V. (1997). *The knowledge evolution: Expanding organizational intelligence*. London: Butterworth-Heinemann.

Ardelt, M. (2003). Empirical assessment of a three-dimensional wisdom scale. *Research on Aging*, 25(3), 275–324.

Ardelt, M. (2004). Wisdom as expert knowledge system: A critical review of a contemporary operationalization of an ancient concept. *Human Development*, 47(5), 257–285.

Aristotle. (2009). *The Nicomachean ethics*. (D. Ross, Trans.). Oxford, UK: Oxford University Press.

Awad, E. M., & Ghaziri, H. M. (2004). *Knowledge management*. Upper Saddle River, NJ: Prentice Hall.

Baden, D., & Higgs, M. (2015). Challenging the perceived wisdom of management theories and practice. *Academy of Management Learning and Education*, 14(4), 539–555.

Baggini, J., & Fosl, P. S. (2007). *The ethics toolkit: A compendium of ethical concepts and methods*. Malden, UK: Blackwell Publishing.

Baltes, P. B., & Kunzmann, U. (2003). Wisdom: The peak of human excellence in the orchestration of mind and virtue. *The Psychologist*, 16(3), 131–133.

Baltes, P. B., & Kunzmann, U. (2004). The two faces of wisdom: Wisdom as a general theory of knowledge and judgment about excellence in mind and virtue vs. wisdom as everyday realization in people and products. *Human Development*, 47(5), 290–299.

Baltes, P. B., & Smith, J. (1990). Toward a psychology of wisdom and its ontogenesis. In R. J. Sternberg (Ed.), *Toward a psychology of wisdom and its ontogenesis* (pp. 87–120). New York: Cambridge University Press.

Baltes, P. B., & Staudinger, U. M. (1993). The search for a psychology of wisdom. *Current Directions in Psychology Science*, 2(3), 75–80.

Baltes, P. B., & Staudinger, U. M. (2000). Wisdom: A metaheuristic (pragmatic) to orchestrate mind and virtue toward excellence. *American Psychologist*, 55(1), 122–136.

Beauchamp, T. L. (1991). *Philosophical ethics: An introduction to moral philosophy* (2nd ed.). New York: McGraw-Hill.

Beck, S. (1999). Confucius and Socrates: The teaching of wisdom. Retrieved from www.san.beck. org

Begley, A. M. (2006). Facilitating the development of moral insight in practice: Teaching ethics and teaching virtue. *Nursing Philosophy: An International Journal for Healthcare Professionals,* 7(4), 257–265.

Bennet, A., & Bennet, D. (2008). Moving from knowledge to wisdom, from ordinary consciousness to extraordinary consciousness. *VINE: The Journal of Information and Knowledge Management Systems,* 38(1), 7–15.

Bierly III, P. E., Kessler, E. H., & Christensen, E. W. (2000). Organizational learning, knowledge and wisdom. *Journal of Organizational Change Management,* 13(6), 595–618.

Biloslavo, R., & McKenna, B. (2013). Evaluating the process of wisdom in wise political leaders using a developmental wisdom model. In W. Küpers & D. J. Pauleen (Eds.), *A handbook of practical wisdom: Leadership, organization and integral business practice* (pp. 111–132. Aldershot, UK: Gower.

Birren, J. E., & Fisher, L. M. (1990). The elements of wisdom: Overview and integration. In R. J. Sternberg (Ed.), *Wisdom: Its nature, origins, and development* (pp. 317–332). Cambridge, UK: Cambridge University Press.

Blasi, P. (2006). The European university – Towards a wisdom-based society. *Higher Education in Europe,* 31(4), 403–407.

Case, P. (2013). Cultivation of wisdom in the Theravada Buddhist tradition: Implications for contemporary leadership and organization. In W. Küpers & D. J. Pauleen (Eds.), *A handbook of practical wisdom: Leadership, organization and integral business practice* (pp. 65–78). Aldershot, UK: Gower.

Clayton, V. (1982). Wisdom and Intelligence: The nature and function of knowledge in the later years. *International Journal of Aging and Human Development,* 15(4), 315–320.

Courtney, J. F. (2001). Decision making and knowledge management in inquiring organizations: Towards a new decision-making paradigm for DSS. *Decision Support Systems,* 31(1), 17–38.

Csikszentmihalyi, M., & Rathunde, K. (1990). The psychology of wisdom: An evolutionary interpretation. In R. J. Sternberg (Ed.), *Wisdom: Its nature, origins, and development* (pp. 25–51). New York: Cambridge University Press.

Curnow, T. (1999). *Wisdom, intuition, and ethics.* Aldershot, UK: Ashgate.

Edwards, M. G. (2013). Wisdom and integrity: Metatheoretical perspectives on integrative change in an age of turbulence. In W. Küpers & D. J. Pauleen (Eds.), *A handbook of practical wisdom: Leadership, organization and integral business practice* (pp. 197–216). Aldershot, UK: Gower.

Elkin, G., Martin-Niemi, F., & Cathro, V. (2013). Developing wisdom in future managers: Encouraging practical wisdom via voluntary engagement during undergraduate business education. *International Journal of Economics and Business Research,* 5(2), 214–225.

Etheredge, L. S. (2005). Wisdom in public policy. In R. J. Sternberg & J. Jordan (Eds.) (pp. 297–328). Cambridge: Cambridge University Press.

Etheredge, L. S. (1992). Wisdom and good judgment in politics. *Political Psychology,* 13(3), 497–516.

Garrett, R., & College, B. (1996). Three definitions of wisdom. In K. Lehrer, B. J. Lum, B. A. Slichta, & N. D. Smith (Eds.), *Knowledge, teaching, and wisdom* (pp. 221–232). Dordrecht, The Netherlands: Kluwer Academic Publishers.

Gibson, P. S. (2008). Developing practical management wisdom. *Journal of Management Development,* 27(5), 528–536.

Greene, J. A., & Brown, S. C. (2009). The wisdom development scale: Further validity investigations. *International Journal of Aging and Human Development,* 68(4), 289–320.

Grimm, S. R. (2015). Wisdom. *Australasian Journal of Philosophy,* 93(1), 139–154.

Grint, K. (2007). Learning to lead: Can Aristotle help us find the road to wisdom? *Leadership*, 3(2), 231–246.

Grossmann, I., Gerlach, T. M., & Denissen, J. J. A. (2016). Wise reasoning in the face of everyday life challenges. *Social Psychological and Personality Science*, 7(7), 611–622.

Gugerell, S. H., & Riffert, F. (2011). On defining "wisdom": Baltes, Ardelt, Ryan, and Whitehead. *Interchange*, 42(3), 225–259.

Hacker-Wright, J. (2015). Skill, practical wisdom, and ethical naturalism. *Ethical Theory and Moral Practice*, 18(5), 983–993.

Hakim, A. B. (2006). *Historical introduction to philosophy* (5th ed.). Upper Saddle River, NJ: Prentice Hall.

Halpern, D. F. (2001). Why wisdom? *Educational Psychologist*, 36(4), 253–256.

Harwood, L. D. (2011). Sagely wisdom in Confucianism. *Analytic Teaching and Philosophical Praxis*, 31(1), 56–63.

Hays, J. M. (2010). The ecology of wisdom. *Management & Marketing*, 5(1), 71–92.

Hays, J. M. (2013). Transformation and transcendence: The emergence and sustainment of wise leaders and organizations. In W. Küpers & D. J. Pauleen (Eds.), *A handbook of practical wisdom: Leadership, organization and integral business practice* (pp. 133–154). Aldershot, UK: Gower.

Holliday, S. G., & Chandler, M. J. (1986). *Wisdom: Explorations in adult competence*. Basel, Switzerland: Karger.

Intezari, A. (2014). *Wisdom and decision making: Grounding theory in management practice*. School of Management, Massey University, Auckland, New Zealand.

Intezari, A., & Pauleen, D. J. (2013). Students of wisdom: An integral meta-competencies theory of practical wisdom. In W. Küpers & D. J. Pauleen (Eds.), *A handbook of practical wisdom: Leadership, organization and integral business practice* (pp. 155–174). Aldershot, UK: Gower.

Intezari, A., & Pauleen, D. (2014). Management wisdom in perspective: Are you virtuous enough to succeed in volatile times? *Journal of Business Ethics*, 120(3), 393–404.

Intezari, A., Pauleen, D. J., & Rooney, D. (2016). Rediscovering philosophia: The PhD as a path to enhancing knowledge, wisdom and creating a better world. *Journal of Business Ethics Education*, 13, 147–168.

Jashapara, A. (2004). *Knowledge management: An integrated approach*. Harlow, UK: FT/Prentice Hall.

Jeste, D. V, Ardelt, M., Blazer, D., Kraemer, H. C., Vaillant, G., & Meeks, T. W. (2010). Expert consensus on characteristics of wisdom: A Delphi method study. *The Gerontologist*, 50(5), 668–680.

Kekes, J. (1995). *Moral wisdom and good lives*. Ithaca, NY: Cornell University Press.

Kitchener, K. S., & Brenner, H. G. (1990). Wisdom and reflective judgment: Knowing in the face of uncertainty. In R. J. Sternberg (Ed.), *Wisdom: Its nature, origins, and development* (pp. 212–229). New York: Cambridge University Press.

Kodish, S. (2006). The paradoxes of leadership: The contribution of Aristotle. *Leadership*, 2(4), 451–468.

Kok, A. (2009). Realizing wisdom theory in complex learning networks. *Electronic Journal of e-Learning*, 7(1), 53–60.

Korac-Kakabadse, N., Korac-Kakabadse, A., & Kouzmin, A. (2001). Leadership renewal: Towards the philosophy of wisdom. *International Review of Administrative Sciences*, 67(2), 207–227.

Kramer, D. A. (1990). Conceptualizing wisdom: The primacy of affect-cognition relations. In R. J. Sternberg (Ed.), *Wisdom: Its nature, origins, and development* (pp. 279–313). New York: Cambridge University Press.

Krause, N., & Hayward, R. D. (2015). Virtues, practical wisdom and psychological well-being: A Christian perspective. *Social Indicators Research*, 122(3), 735–755.

Krill, D. F. (1990). *Practice wisdom: A guide for helping professionals*. Newbury Park, CA: Sage.

Kunzmann, U. (2004). Approaches to a good life: The emotional-motivational side of wisdom. In P. A. Linley, S. Joseph, & M. E. P. Seligman (Eds.), *Positive psychology in practice* (pp. 504–517). Hoboken, NJ: Wiley.

Küpers, W. (2007). Phenomenology and integral pheno-practice of wisdom in leadership and organization. *Social Epistemology: A Journal of Knowledge, Culture, and Policy*, 21(2), 169–193.

Küpers, W., & Gunnlaugson, O. (2016). *Wisdom learning: Perspectives on wising-up business and management education.* London: Routledge.

Küpers, W., & Pauleen, D. J. (2015). Learning wisdom: Embodied and artful approaches to management education. *Scandinavian Journal of Management*, 31(4), 493–500.

Labouvie-Vief, G. (1990). Wisdom as integrated thought: Historical and developmental perspectives. In R. J. Sternberg (Ed.), *Wisdom: Its nature, origins, and development* (pp. 52–83). New York: Cambridge University Press.

LeBon, T. (2001). Wise therapy: Philosophy for counsellors. *Practical Philosophy*, 4(3), 24–32.

Lehrer, K., & Smith, N. D. (1996). Introduction. In K. Lehrer, B. J. Lum, B. A. Slichta, & N. D. Smith (Eds.), *Knowledge, teaching, and wisdom* (pp. 3–17). Dordrecht, The Netherlands: Kluwer Academic Publishers.

Levenson, M. R., Jennings, P. A., Aldwin, C. M., & Shiraishi, R. W. (2005). Self-transcendence: Conceptualization and measurement. *International Journal of Aging & Human Development*, 60(2), 127–143.

Liew, A. (2013). DIKIW: Data, information, knowledge, intelligence, wisdom and their interrelationships. *Business Management Dynamics*, 2(10), 49–62.

Lombardo, T. (2010). Wisdom facing forward: What it means to have heightened future consciousness. *The Futurist*, September/October, 34–42.

Malloch, T. R. (2015). *Practical wisdom in management: Business across spiritual traditions.* Sheffield, UK: Greenleaf/Academy of Business in Society.

Matthews, P. (1998). What lies beyond knowledge management: Wisdom creation and versatility. *Journal of Knowledge Management*, 1(3), 207–214.

Maxwell, N. (1984). *From knowledge to wisdom: A revolution in the aims and methods of science.* Oxford, UK: Basil Blackwell.

Maxwell, N. (2007). Can the world learn wisdom? *The E-Newsletter of Solidarity, Sustainability, and Non-Violence*, 3(4).

Maxwell, N. (2012). How universities can help humanity learn how to resolve the crises of our times – from knowledge to wisdom: The University College London experience. In D. Rooney, G. Hearn, & T. Kastelle (Eds.), *Handbook on the knowledge economy, Volume two* (pp. 158–180). Cheltenham, UK: Edward Elgar.

Maxwell, N. (2013). From knowledge to wisdom: Assessment and prospects after three decades. *Integral Review*, 9(2), 76–112.

McKenna, B. (2013a). Teaching for wisdom: Cross cultural perspectives on fostering wisdom. *Academy of Management Learning and Education*, 12(2), 319–320.

McKenna, B. (2013b). The multi-dimensional character of wisdom. In M. J. Thompson & D. Bevan (Eds.), *Wise Management in organizational complexity* (pp. 13–33). London: Palgrave Macmillan.

McKenna, B., & Rooney, D. (2007). Wisdom in organizations: Whence and whither. *Social Epistemology*, 21(2), 113–138.

McKenna, B., & Rooney, D. (2008). Wise leadership and the capacity for ontological acuity. *Management Communication Quarterly*, 21(4), 537–546.

McKenna, B., & Rooney, D. (2009). Book review: Kessler, E. H. & Bailey, J. R. (Eds.), Handbook of organizational and managerial wisdom, 2007 Sage. *Organization Studies*, 30(4), 447–449.

McKenna, B., Rooney, D., & Boal, K. B. (2009). Wisdom principles as a meta-theoretical basis for evaluating leadership. *The Leadership Quarterly*, 20(2), 177–190.

McKenna, B., Rooney, D., & Hays, J. M. (2011). Wisdom and the good life. *Philosophy of Management*, 10(1), 1–8.

McKenna, B., Rooney, D., & Kenworthy, A. L. (2013). Introduction: Wisdom and management – A guest-edited special collection of resource reviews for management education. *Academy of Management Learning & Education*, 12(2), 306–311.

McKenna, B., Rooney, D., & Liesch, P. W. (2006). Beyond knowledge to wisdom in international business strategy. *Prometheus*, 24(3), 283–300.

McKenna, B., Rooney, D., & ten Bos, R. (2007). Wisdom as the old dog… with new tricks. *Social Epistemology*, 21(2), 83–86.

McKenna, B., Rooney, D., Liesch, P. W., & Boal, K. (2008). Snapshot: Knowledge in the absence of wisdom. In D. Barry & H. Hansen (Eds.), *The Sage handbook of new approaches in management and organization* (pp. 344–345). London: Sage Publications.

Meacham, J. A. (1990). The loss of wisdom. In R. J. Sternberg (Ed.), *Wisdom: Its nature, origins, and development* (pp. 181–211). New York: Cambridge University Press.

Meeks, T. W., & Jeste, D. V. (2009). Neurobiology of wisdom: A literature overview. *Archives of General Psychiatry*, 66(4), 355–365.

Melé, D. (2010). Practical wisdom in managerial decision making. *Journal of Management Development*, 29(7/8), 637–645.

Merriam, S. B., & Caffarella, R. S. (1999). *Learning in adulthood: A comprehensive guide* (2nd ed.). San Francisco: Jossey-Bass.

Moberg, D. J. (2007). Practical wisdom and business ethics: Presidential Address to the Society for Business Ethics. *Business Ethics Quarterly*, 17(3), 535–561.

Nichols, R. (1996). Maxims, "Practical wisdom," and the language of action: Beyond grand theory. *Political Theory: An International Journal of Political Philosophy*, 24(4), 687–705.

Nonaka, I., & Takeuchi, H. (2011). The big idea: The wise leader. *Harvard Business Review*, 89(5), 58–67.

Nozick, R. (1989). What is wisdom and why do philosophers love it so? In R. Nozick (Ed.), *The examined life* (pp. 267–278). New York: Touchstone.

Nunamaker Jr., J. F., Romano Jr., N. C., & Briggs, R. O. (2002). Increasing intellectual bandwidth: Generating value from intellectual capital with information technology. *Group Decision and Negotiation*, 11(2), 69–86.

O'Sullivan, T. (2005). Some theoretical propositions on the nature of practice wisdom. *Journal of Social Work*, 5(2), 221–242.

Pasupathi, M., & Staudinger, U. M. (2001). Do advanced moral reasoners also show wisdom? Linking moral reasoning and wisdom-related knowledge and judgement. *International Journal of Behavioral Development*, 25(5), 401–415.

Pantzar, E. (2000). Knowledge and wisdom in the information society. *Foresight, The Journal of Future Studies, Strategic Thinking and Policy*, 2(2), 230–236.

Pauleen, D. J., Rooney, D., & Holden, N. (2010). Practical wisdom and the development of cross-cultural knowledge management: A global leadership perspective. *European Journal of International Management*, 4(2), 382–395.

Pauleen, D. J., Rooney, D., & Intezari, A. (2017). Big data, little wisdom: trouble brewing? Ethical implications for the information systems discipline. *Social Epistemology*, 31(4), 9–33.

Pauleen, D. J., Dalal, N., Rooney, D., Intezari, A., & Wang, W. (2015). In bed with technology? Peril, promise, and prudence. *Communications of the Association for Information Systems*, 37(1), 783–796.

Polansky, R. (2000). Phronesis on tour: Cultural adaptability of Aristotelian ethical notions. *Kennedy Institute of Ethics Journal*, 10(4), 323–336.

Roca, E. (2007). Intuitive practical wisdom in organizational life. *Social Epistemology*, 21(2), 195–207.

Rooney, D. (2013). Empirical wisdom research: A community approach. In M. J. Thompson & D. Bevan (Eds.), *Wise management in organizational complexity* (pp. 34–52). London: Palgrave Macmillan.

Rooney, D., & McKenna, B. (2005). Should the knowledge-based economy be a savant or a sage? Wisdom and socially intelligent innovation. *Prometheus*, 23(3), 307–323.

Rooney, D., & McKenna, B. (2008). Wisdom in public administration: Looking for a sociology of wise practice. *Public Administration Review*, 68(4), 709–721.

Rooney, D., Hearn, G., & Kastelle, T. (Eds.) (2012). *Handbook on the knowledge economy, Volume 2*. Cheltenham: Edward Elgar.

Rooney, D., Hearn, G., & Ninan, A. (2005). *Handbook on the knowledge economy*. Cheltenham, UK: Edward Elgar.

Rooney, D., McKenna, B., & Liesch, P. (2010). *Wisdom and management in the knowledge economy*. New York: Routledge.

Roos, J. (2006). *Thinking from within: A hands-on strategy practice*. Basingstoke, UK: Palgrave Macmillan.

Rowley, J. (2006a). What do we need to know about wisdom? *Management Decision*, 44(9), 1246–1257.

Rowley, J. (2006b). Where is the wisdom that we have lost in knowledge? *Journal of Documentation*, 62(2), 251–270.

Rowley, J., & Slack, F. (2009). Conceptions of wisdom. *Journal of Information Science*, 35(1), 110–119.

Rowley, J., Gibbs, J., & Gibbs, P. (2008). From learning organization to practically wise organization. *The Learning Organization*, 15(5), 356–372.

Ryan, S. (1996). Wisdom. In K. Lehrer, B. J. Lum, B. A. Slichta, & N. D. Smith (Eds.), *Knowledge, teaching, and wisdom* (pp. 233–242). Dordrecht, The Netherlands: Kluwer Academic Publishers.

Small, M. W. (2004). Wisdom and now managerial wisdom: Do they have a place in management development programs? *Journal of Management Development*, 23(8), 751–764.

Small, M. W. (2011). Developing wisdom and moral duty in management. *Journal of Management Development*, 30(9), 836–846.

Solansky, S. (2014). To fear foolishness for the sake of wisdom: A message to leaders. *Journal of Business Ethics*, 122(1), 39–51.

Statler, M., & Roos, J. (2007). *Everyday strategic preparedness: The role of practical wisdom in organizations*. New York: Palgrave Macmillan.

Staudinger, U. M. (1996). Wisdom and the social-interactive foundation of the mind. In P. B. Baltes & U. M. Staudinger (Eds.), *Interactive Mind: Life-span perspectives on the social foundation of cognition* (pp. 276–315). New York: Cambridge University Press.

Sternberg, R. J. (1985). Implicit theory of intelligence, creativity, and wisdom. *Journal of Personality and Social Psychology*, 49(3), 607–627.

Sternberg, R. J. (2004). What is wisdom and how can we develop it? *Annals of the American Academy of Political and Social Science*, 591(1), 164–174.

Strijbos, S. (1995). How can systems thinking help us in bridging the gap between science and wisdom? *Systems Practice*, 8(4), 361–376.

Telfer, E. (1990). The unity of the moral virtues in Aristotle's Nicomachean Ethics. *Proceedings of the Aristotelian Society*, 90, 35–48.

Tredget, D. A. (2010). Practical wisdom and the rule of Benedict. *Journal of Management Development*, 29(7/8), 716–723.

Urmson, J. O. (1998). *Aristotle's Ethics*. Oxford, UK: Basil Blackwell.

Walker, L. J. (2005). Toward a virtuous future: The framing of wisdom. *Journal of Financial Planning*, 18(9), 30–34.

Walsh, R. N. (2014). *The world's great wisdom: Timeless teachings from religions and philosophies*. New York: State University of New York Press.

Webster, J. D. (2007). Measuring the character strength of wisdom. *International Journal of Aging and Human Development*, 65(2), 163–183.

Whitehead, A. N. (1967). *The aims of education and other essays*. New York: Free Press.

Yang, S. (2011). East meets west: Cross-cultural perspectives on wisdom and adult education. *New Directions for Adult and Continuing Education*, 131(Fall), 45–54.

Zeleny, M. (2006). Knowledge-information autopoietic cycle: Towards the wisdom system. *International Journal of Management and Decision Making*, 7(1), 3–18.

Zhong, C. (2011). The ethical dangers of deliberative decision making. *Administrative Science Quarterly*, 56(1), 1–25.

Zhu, Y., Rooney, D., & Phillips, N. (2016). Practice-based wisdom theory for integrating institutional logics: A new model for social entrepreneurship learning and education. *Academy of Management Learning & Education*, 15(3), 607–625.

3 Organizational problems

Why decision situations can be more *wicked* than we think

Introduction

In Chapter 2, we defined wisdom in the management context as a manager's capacity to: (a) critically and accurately assess self, others, and the decision situation, and to (b) integrate personal and communal knowledge and values into decisions and actions, in order to (c) achieve the well-being of all involved, over both the short and long term. The definition underscores that both decision making and wisdom are central features of management. We believe this is because wisdom is necessary when dealing with the complexities that are inherent in real-world decision situations.

The challenges and problems of the 21st century, which have become more complex, polycausal, and contradictory, are profoundly affecting business and society. There are no simple responses and solutions available for these challenges and problems. In a word, they are *wicked*.

To cope with them, we need new ways of thinking and acting. We believe the fundamental characteristics of wisdom – derived from the disciplines of philosophy, psychology, and management and integrated in a way that offers practical effectiveness – give managers, leaders, and organizations the best chance to meet these challenges and problems. An understanding of what is important, an ethical orientation, humbleness, self-knowledge, experience, judgement, insight, and a pragmatic and prudent approach to challenges, as well as the 'stuff' of MBA programmes – area knowledge, as well as technical and analytical skills – can form the basis of an integrated approach to dealing with problems both simple and wicked. In this chapter, we learn more about the nature of problems, and in particular what distinguishes simple problems from complex problems and complex problems from wicked problems. The more we understand the nature of problems, the better we are prepared to understand and deal wisely with emergent decision situations.

Since World War II, globalization has resulted in remarkable and fundamental changes in industries and nations around the world. Many companies and whole industries have transitioned from being domestic operations into global businesses. Globalization has increased the economic, technical, political, and social interdependences between nations. Advances in telecommunication technologies have connected more people and organizations around the world. Cultural exchange and international trade have been instrumental in the evolution of nations. Physical borders are becoming less important and nations are becoming economically, if not culturally, integrated. Macro issues such as poverty, health and education, human rights, labour rights, extremism and war, climate change, and other global issues are increasingly being addressed collaboratively at the level of nations.

Globalization has also created a need for business leaders who can go beyond dealing merely with the technical or financial issues of their teams and organizations. Leaders, and forms of leadership, are needed, who are committed not only to their teams and organizations, but also to the well-being of others in the wider community. An example of this new form of leadership is reflected in the relatively new area of business diplomacy, which emphasizes geopolitical risk management, extends outside of organizations to non-business stakeholders, and operates across geographical areas (Kesteleyn, Riordan, & Ruël, 2014).

Throughout the book and as defined in this chapter, we use the term 'wicked', instead of 'complex', to characterize the multi-stakeholder value-laden challenges that managers experience in today's business world. 'Wicked', not in the sense of being evil, but because wicked problems are both problematic and pernicious to address (Marshak, 2009; McGrath & McGonagle, 2016), often incomplete, contradictory, and related to changing requirements that are difficult to diagnose. In relation to business and management, wicked implies being tied to multiple stakeholder interests, gaps in knowledge, and scientific uncertainty and fragmentation (Head & Alford, 2008). Wicked problems encompass highly complex issues with undefined or multiple causes that are often difficult to understand and to articulate (McGrath & McGonagle, 2016). Thus, when we talk about wicked problems in this book, we are considering the problem itself, the wider circumstances around the problem, as well as the understanding, analysis, and processing of the problem, or in the terminology of this book, the decision situation.

Simple, complex, and wicked problems

Conventional problems, from simple to complicated, are addressed by organizations every day. Business models and methodologies often address conventional problems and ways of solving such problems. However, such strategies and business models as well as common practices (rules of thumb) may not be appropriate when approaching wicked problems because these problems require fundamentally different assumptions, thought processes, and methods to reach a solution (McMillan & Overall, 2016).

As wicked problems demonstrate many of the characteristics of complex problems, the differences between complexity and wickedness may pose some confusion. For this reason, we first discuss how complex problems are different from simple ones, and then how wicked problems are different from complex problems.

From simple to complex problems

Derived from Latin, 'complexity' means 'to twine' and refers to the dynamic interactions of organisms with the environment (Morrison, 2002). From this perspective, the world is considered to be an unordered entity, and there is no simple relationship between cause and effect (Snowden & Boone, 2007). A definition provided by the Santa Fe Group clearly explains complexity (Battram, 1998):

> Complexity refers to the condition of the universe which is integrated and yet too rich and varied for us to understand in simple common mechanistic or linear ways. We can understand many parts of the universe in these ways but the larger and more intricately related phenomena can only be understood by principles and

patterns – not in detail. Complexity deals with the nature of emergence, innovation, learning and adaption.

(p. v)

Complexity is often defined in opposition to simplicity (Tredinnick, 2009). Simplicity refers to the condition where the number of states and dimensions of a phenomenon is limited and identifiable. Simple phenomena can for the most part be clearly described. In the decision-making context, a simple problem has a definite number of causes, alternatives, or aspects. Simple problems have easily identifiable structures. The problems can be characterized as (Hocking, Brown, & Harris, 2016, p. 27):

- identifiable and formulaic,
- having clear distinction between problem and solution,
- having a clearly identifiable end point (known as the answer),
- being able to test the solution as either correct or false,
- having a finite list of permissible operations,
- having identifiable discrepancy between what is and what ought to be,
- being able to treat each problem as a definable and isolated whole,
- requiring solutions that are limited, repeatable, and generalizable and
- enabling the problem solver to be blameless.

The problems can be broken down into smaller and simpler sub-components. The causes are limited and can be identified by examining the problem situation. Simple problems can be solved with the knowledge and procedures available to the decision maker. In such cases, for the decision maker it is clear who the stakeholders are, the causes behind the issue, and who has the required knowledge and capability to address the challenge. The solutions can be developed and implemented with relatively less time and energy. The decision maker can follow predesigned procedures and steps to articulate the problem, develop alternatives, and implement the best alternative. The same procedures or solutions applied to previously addressed problems can be applied to address the current problem.

Complex problems, in contrast, have innumerable possible states, interactions among agents are not structured, and the behaviour of individual elements and the system as a whole is not easily predictable (Battram, 1998). Successful solutions to complex problems frequently require multiple forms of expertise. For example, dealing with a customer's complaint about the quality of the company's services or products can be a complex decision situation. Companies often have clear procedures to deal with situations such as customer complaints. The situation can be addressed by the customer service manager. The problem, however, may just be the tip of the iceberg and in fact represent a more complex issue. For example, the decision situation (the customer complaint) may be reflecting a more systemic problem that could be located in the production line, delivery, or payment procedures. In such a situation, an effective solution to what turns out to be a complex decision situation may require multiple areas of specialized expertise.

Ralph Stacey has written extensively on complexity and organizations. He (2012; Stacey & Mowles, 2016) has proposed a matrix model of complexity for management decision-making settings, suggesting that managers may choose different forms of decision making based on two dimensions: *the degree of certainty* and *the level of agreement* (Figure 3.1).

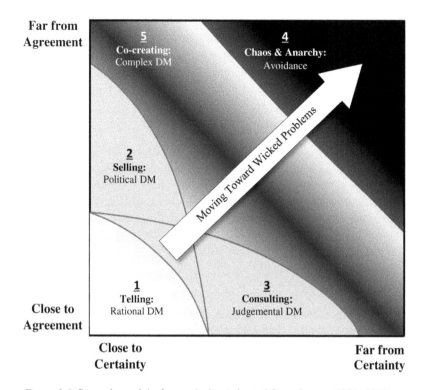

Figure 3.1 Stacey's model of complexity (adapted from Stacey, 2002, 2010)

The degree of certainty refers to the extent to which the situation is unique or new to the decision maker. When the certainty is high, the decision maker can extrapolate from previous experiences to predict the consequences of the decisions. The degree of agreement refers to the extent to which the group, team, or organization agree upon a decision problem or decision.

One of five forms of decision making may be used depending on the two dimensions: rational decision making, political decision making, judgemental decision making, complex decision making, and the avoidance strategy (Stacey, 2002). When the situation is close to certainty and agreement, the decision maker makes rational decisions by gathering data to predict the future. When uncertainty is low, but the level of disagreement is high, or vice versa, the decision maker chooses either political decision making or judgement decision making, respectively. Judgemental decisions are the ones that are made based on shared visions, rather than on specific plans. Political decisions are more based on negotiation and/or coalition, as neither shared visions nor plans work in the situation where disagreement is high, but uncertainty is low.

Situations that are characterized as relatively high in uncertainty and disagreement represent complex decision-making situations. In a complex situation, traditional management approaches are not effective, and the decision maker, therefore, needs to be more creative, innovative, and intuitive in decision making (Stacey, 2002). Stacey (2002) suggests that organizations should avoid situations where there is a little disagreement and uncertainty is extremely high, as the situations lead to anarchy, where visioning, planning, and negotiation do not work. As the avoidance strategy can be disastrous in the long run, decision makers should actively work to reduce disagreement and create certainty to whatever extent possible. As illustrated the arrow in Figure 3.1 wicked problems represent a high level of uncertainty in the decision situation, and among stakeholders and substantial disagreement among stakeholders. We discuss wicked problems in the following section.

From complex to wicked problems

Although Rittel (1972) is often thought to have coined the term 'wicked problems', in 1967 Churchman defined wicked problems in a guest editorial of a special issue of *Management Science* as: "a class of social problems, which are ill-formulated; where the information is confusing; where there are many clients and decision makers with conflicting values; and where the ramifications in the whole system are thoroughly confusing" (as cited in McMillan & Overall, 2016, p. 36). The idea of wicked problems, however, gained significant recognition when Rittel and Webber (1973) published their joint paper on a general theory of planning. Thereafter, the concept was applied across various disciplines from social sciences to government policy (Hocking et al., 2016).

In essence, a wicked problem is a highly complex problem, embodying all the characteristics of complexity but in greater number and with greater intensity. Characteristics of wicked problems include a plurality of elements and phenomena, nonlinear interconnectedness, uncertain causes and unpredictable outcomes, an emergent and adaptive nature, and multidimensional and complicated cause-effect relationships (Keene, 2000; Morrison, 2002; Snowden & Boone, 2007; Stacey, 1996). Wicked problems, however, are more challenging to deal with in that they are often highly value-laden due to the involvement of multiple stakeholders and society as a whole. Many strategic management decisions can potentially affect the well-being of a wide range of stakeholders from the managers themselves, to employees, and to external stakeholders and society. The growing demands by social organizations and governments on organizations to provide products and services (and ways of producing them) that are environmentally sustainable is an example of how organization and management roles and responsibilities go beyond merely the financial success of the organization.

Wicked problems are also known as complex issues (McGrath & McGonagle, 2016), entangled problems (Adam, 2016), ill-structured problems (King and Kitchener, 2002), and messes (Horn, 1981, as cited in McMillan & Overall, 2016). Ackoff (1974) identifies three categories of problems:

1. puzzles,
2. problems, and
3. messes.

Puzzles and problems are well-defined. Puzzles have optimal solutions, whereas there is no single solution for problems. Messes are difficult to understand fully; hence it is not easy to determine or to find solutions.

Wicked problems have higher levels of impact and are more difficult to articulate and solve. They are those kind of problems that encompass both the complexity of issues (e.g. multiple stakeholders, multiple and unclear causes, contradictory solutions, etc.), as well as the need for alternative, nonlinear approaches in dealing with such problems.

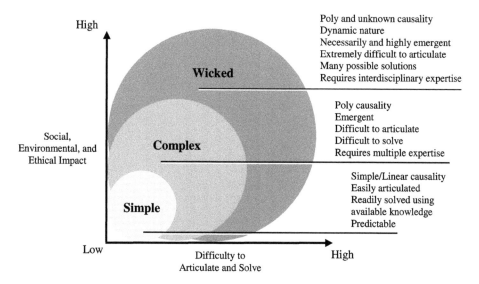

Figure 3.2 From simple to wicked problems

Using the criteria of impact and degree of difficulty of articulation and solution, Figure 3.2 depicts the relationship and key differences between wicked, complex, and simple problems.

Moreover, unlike with complex problems, which may be emergent or non-emergent, wicked problems are necessarily emergent. Emergence refers to the manifestation of new phenomena that are impossible to predict. In such cases, simple common mechanistic or linear ways can fail to help us understand the true nature of a decision situation. Rittel and Webber (1973) identified some key defining characteristics of wicked problems as:

- There is no definitive formulation of a wicked problem.
- Wicked problems have no stopping rule.
- Solutions to wicked problems are not true or false, but better or worse.
- There is no immediate and no ultimate test of a solution to a wicked problem.
- Every solution to a wicked problem is a 'one-shot operation': because there is no opportunity to learn by trial and error, every attempt counts significantly.
- Wicked problems do not have an enumerable (or an exhaustively describable) set of potential solutions, nor is there a well-described set of permissible operations that may be incorporated into the plan.
- Every wicked problem is essentially unique.
- Every wicked problem can be considered to be a symptom of another problem.
- The existence of a discrepancy representing a wicked problem can be explained in numerous ways. The choice of explanation determines the nature of the problem's resolution.

Wicked problems can cover a range of problems from climate change and terrorism to inner-city poverty and cyber-crime (McMillan & Overall, 2016). Drawing on the points made above on simple, complex, and wicked problems, Table 3.1 provides examples of each type of problem in organizational contexts.

Table 3.1 Examples of simple, complex, and wicked problems in organizational context

Characteristics	Simple	Complex	Wicked
	Example: "Budgeting and Providing Equipment for a New Office or Branch"	Example: "Employee Redundancy"	Example: "Deepwater Horizon Oil Spill"
Formulation difficulty	Low *The problem is highly structured and readily definable. The company has clear procedures and rules for procurement.*	Medium to High *The company has clear procedures and rules for employee redundancy. However, the problem could include how to handle employees' unpredictable reactions to the decision.*	High *What is the major problem now and here? Is it how the spill has occurred, who is responsible for the problem, or is it the environmental impact of the oil spill that is important?*
Cause–effect relationship	Known *Buying and installing the required equipment can meet the need for equipment in the new office.*	Difficult to know *What has led the organization and the manager to the point that the company is experiencing excess employees? Does the employee redundancy fix the issue?*	Unknown *Is the issue due to technical failure, human errors, and/or natural causes?* *The issue may be interconnected with other issues within or outside the organization, e.g. lack of appropriate monitoring system, supply chain, etc. Fixing the mechanical failure does not fix the issue. The problem is not completely addressed unless all the mechanical, organizational, and environmental causes and consequences are appropriately fixed.*
Unpredictability and emergence	Low *Procurement is a routine job. Based on the increasing demand for the organization's services in the past, the manager can easily predict what new equipment will be required for the new branch.*	Medium to High *The impact of the decision on the redundant employees' well-being is not clear but based on common experience is likely to be negative. There is no guarantee the organization will not have future employee redundancies.*	High *The problem was emergent. Such an issue is not something that happens on a daily basis.*
Dynamic	Low *The problem is static; the decision situation does not dramatically change during the decision-making process.*	High *The employee's reactions to the manager's decision on the matter may dramatically change the decision situation from an employee redundancy decision to, for example, dealing with all employees protesting against the management. The decision situation, however, is still addressable by the manager based on their authority and legal obligations.*	High *The oil spill may become worse during the repair process, from a simple mechanical issue to an environmentally disastrous problem.*

	Low	Medium to High	High
Multidimensionality and interconnectedness	Buying the equipment is mainly a budgeting concern.	**High** The decision is not a simple organizational decision. The manager may need to consider many other factors than just the excess number of employees. Factors such as the targeted employees' length of service and seniority; remuneration package, and industry norms, as well as the employees' ability to find alternative employment.	**High** The issue has financial, organizational, social, and environmental impacts. The environmental damage that the oil spill has caused is not fixed if the company does not take responsibility in the first place, the spill is not completely and permanently blocked, and many other parties including the government and society do not get involved.
Uncertainty	Uncertainty could be limited to just delivery and setup issues or the possible technical or mechanical failure of the equipment in the future.	**Medium to High** The organization may save money by paying salary to fewer employees. However, the psychological impact of the redundancy on the remaining employees may be negative, and, therefore, significantly affect the individual and organizational overall performance.	**High** Uncertainty around the accuracy and effectiveness of the problem articulation, case identification, and suggested solutions.
Multi-stakeholder	One or few stakeholders are involved. The issue may be limited to one department.	**Medium to High** Multiple stakeholders are involved. Stakeholders may be from inside (e.g. different departments, managers, and employees) and/or outside the organization (e.g. society, vendors, customers, and government).	**High** The issue has financial, organizational, social, and environmental impacts. Stakeholders from both within and outside the organization are involved.
Social involvement and responsibility	The issue does not involve a high level of social responsibility. The responsibility, however, is never zero. The company must consider the ergonomic design of the equipment.	**Low to Relatively High** Although a decision to make employees redundant may be value-laden, the decision maker does not necessarily deviate from their legal obligations.	**Necessarily High** The company is legally, socially, and ethically accountable for the issue and all the possible consequences of the solutions applied.
Ethical burden	In so far as the equipment is not harmful and can facilitate employees' work, the procurement department manager may decide to buy any equipment.	**Medium to High** Although the manager may wish to stop redundancy due to some personal ethical considerations, the employee redundancy may have wider acceptable ethical justifications.	**High** The decision situation does necessarily have ethical aspects, and any actions towards addressing the problem have ethical implications and consequences.

Given the characteristics enumerated in the list above, it is obviously not going to be easy for organizations to solve or even manage wicked problems. Wickedness is the main characteristic of many strategic management situations in today's business environment, in its interdependencies as individuals, groups, organizations, and societies affect and are affected by each other. At the same time, the meaning and concepts of organization and management are getting broader and ever more blurred. To be able to handle wicked issues, managers need to be able to act quickly, responsively, and reliably. Inputs to their decisions could draw on resources and issues at the individual, organizational, national, and international levels (Alammar & Pauleen, 2016).

In such an environment, organizations and management are facing remarkable challenges: for example, the need to adequately organize and manage for issues such as ever-increasing volumes of information, cultural diversity, and globalization of workforces, challenges in becoming more effective both nationally and internationally, and so forth. However, how do wicked problems present themselves in organizational and management contexts? The answer to this question underlines why managers need to be more adaptive than ever to be able to be effective in the contemporary setting. As organizations become more globalized, the skills, competences, and abilities that leaders need undergo a fundamental shift (Alammar & Pauleen, 2016).

"Traditional approaches using bureaucratic systems fail to address wicked problems because their uncertainty characteristics require collaboration that enhances intellectual knowledge diffusion, joint learning and understanding how one issue can be a symptom of a related problem" (McMillan & Overall, 2016, p. 38). Indeed, wicked problems may not even have a final solution (Hocking et al., 2016) as any solution could introduce requirements for changes that are beyond an organization's ability to implement (Rittel & Webber, 1973).

Wisdom and dealing with wicked problems

Although wicked problems encompass characteristics of complex problems, even somewhat unconventional problem-solving approaches such as those proposed by complexity theory may not be effective in dealing with wicked problems. Complexity theory, which is concerned with conceptualizing complexity and its challenges and implications, proposes a different approach. It suggests that complex issues may be better addressed by breaking them into smaller and less complex subsystems or issues, which can then be solved more easily. Wicked problems, however, cannot be deconstructed into simple subunits.

The assumptions underlying complexity theory fail to offer an adequate understanding of wicked problems. Complexity theory is based upon the supposition that reality is what we perceive of the world (Keene, 2000). This is epitomized by subjectivity-objectivity ontologies and thus a Cartesian worldview. The subjective ontology holds the position that no single opinion on a given event is more correct than another as individuals are entitled to their own opinions, while the latter is grounded in the belief that there is only one valid interpretation of any event or issue (Burr & Hofer, 2002). Accordingly, while the objectivist approach may be helpful in dealing with complex problems, this approach cannot be applied to wicked problems as there is no one valid interpretation of any event or issue.

Rittel (1972) labelled complex problems 'wicked problems' since wicked problems cannot be fully resolved without transformative changes to the society that has created and continues to produce the problems. The changes might include fundamental transformation or even radical de- and reconstruction of an individual's, group's, or society's underlying assumptions, values, and paradigms. Because wicked problems arise as a result of person-environment transactions (McGrath & McGonagle, 2016) they tend to be "socially complex and thus need coordination and networking with a variety of stakeholders since they seldom ever sit within the responsibility of one organization" (Beinecke, 2016, p. 17) let alone one person. They are often difficult to diagnose as each problem often appears to be one of a kind (Beinecke, 2016). Being unique, there will be incomplete knowledge or experience on how to deal with them. Moreover, stakeholders may see these one-of-a-kind problems in different ways, resulting in disagreements in understanding just what the problem is. As we have seen before, a manager may not be able to find a single correct way to view a wicked problem (Marshall, 2016).

Indeed, confusion, ambiguity, conflicting values, and disagreements between stakeholders are often signs that distinguish wicked problems from conventional problems in management. McMillan and Overall (2016) identified *potential* wicked problems as those possessing "complexity with conflicts arising from multiple but differing stakeholder views, social and attitudinal variables, varying sequential and simultaneous pressures and timeliness, possible presence of ideological precocity and lack of clarity on end-means relations" (p. 36).

Wicked problems require sophisticated decision-making processes through which the problems are structured or profoundly restructured. During the process, solutions emerge gradually through a process of identifying the internal and external constraints (McMillan & Overall, 2016), as these problems may not just be problems within the organization's boundaries (McGrath & McGonagle, 2016). The academic literature points to some ways to approach wicked problems, particularly with collaborative and collective approaches. For example, according to Zijp, Posthuma, Wintersen, Devilee, and Swartjes (2016), finding management solutions to wicked problems requires a participative, iterative, innovative, and transparent process. Similarly, Hocking et al. (2016) link wicked problems to theories of pattern language, a design-led conversational approach, and collective thinking. They suggest that one approach to wicked problems is through communities that engage in collective learning, thus developing a collective mind, which means having different ways of reflecting on knowledge. "A collective mind rests on the full thinking capacity of each contributing individual: personal, physical, social, ethical, aesthetic, sympathetic and reflective ways of knowing" (Hocking et al., 2016, p. 34).

As discussed above, wicked problems are socially embedded and hence socially complex. As such they are highly susceptible to subjective interpretation and understanding. Moreover, people, including managers and decision makers, are likely to choose to understand and explain a decision situation in a way that best fits their own world view (Rittel & Webber, 1973). Even widely-accepted empirical positivist methods based on the principles of scientific inquiry may fall short in understanding wicked problems.

The fundamentally subjective nature of wicked problems is reflected by almost all the wisdom aspects listed in Table 3.2. The table outlines the main characteristics of wicked problems, as well as the corresponding wisdom aspects identified in Chapter 2. The wisdom aspects will be further refined and explained later in the book (see Chapters 7 and 8). Here we briefly explain how the wisdom aspects can offer effective solutions to wicked problems in complex business settings.

Table 3.2 Wicked problems and wisdom characteristics

Wicked problem characteristics		Wisdom aspects (based on Chapter 2)	Wisdom-based strategies to address the problems
Properties of complex problems	Properties of wicked problems (Rittel & Webber, 1973, pp. 161–166)		
• Plurality of elements • Non-linear interconnectedness • Uncertain causes and unpredictable outcomes • Emergent • Adaptive nature • Multidimensional and complicated cause-effect relationships	There is no definitive formulation of a wicked problem.	• Knowledge • Awareness of the limits of knowledge	Multiple perspectives must be taken into account. The available knowledge may not be sufficient to accurately and comprehensively identify the problem.
	Wicked problems have no stopping rule.	• Awareness of the limits of knowledge • Experience-based	Continuous reflection on the problem situation and the solutions.
	Solutions to wicked problems are not true or false, but good or bad.	• Practice-oriented • Judgement • Non-rationality	Multiple perspectives must be taken into account. Constant reflection on the previous solutions and experiences as well as continuous learning can lead to better solutions.
	There is no immediate and no ultimate test of a solution to a wicked problem.	• Judgement • Awareness of the limits of knowledge	The decision maker needs to be aware that while knowledge and experience are important, they are not sufficient. Each solution may have both intended and unintended consequences. It is therefore critical for the decision maker to consider all the possible consequences of the proposed solutions to the extent possible.
	Every attempt at a solution to a wicked problem is a 'one-shot operation' because there is no opportunity to learn by trial-and-error, every attempt counts significantly.	• Self-transcendence • Ethics • Practice-oriented	The possible consequences of any proposed solution must be carefully analysed. This requires a serious consideration of multiple stakeholders' perspectives.

Wicked problem property	Attributes	Explanation
Wicked problems do not have an enumerable (or an exhaustively describable) set of potential solutions, nor is there a well-described set of permissible operations that may be incorporated into the plan.	• Judgement • Awareness of the limits of knowledge • Emotions	As there is no definite list of possible solutions for a wicked problem, the decision maker's judgement plays a critical role in the decision-making process.
Every wicked problem is essentially unique.	• Awareness of the limits of knowledge • Judgement • Non-rationality	Again, previous knowledge and experience, while important, may not be enough. Each problem needs to be treated as a unique problem, and, therefore, a critical and careful analysis of the problem situation and from different perspectives is vital.
Every wicked problem can be considered to be a cause or effect of another problem.	• Self-transcendence • Awareness of the limits of knowledge • Experience-based • Knowledge	A multi-dimensional analysis of the problem is required. What are the hidden and apparent causes of the problem? What would be the consequences of each solution attempted to address the problem?
The existence of a discrepancy representing a wicked problem can be explained in numerous ways. The choice of explanation determines the nature of the problem's resolution. People may choose the explanation that fits their intentions best.	• Awareness of the limits of knowledge • Non-rationality • Practice-oriented • Emotions • Self-transcendence	As different people may have their own explanation of the problem situation and solutions, consensus on how to define the problem and possible solutions is vital.
The planner has no right to be wrong. Failure is not publicly tolerated.	• Self-transcendence • Ethics • Judgement • Emotions • Awareness of the limits of knowledge	As the public may not accept any failure, reformation of the public's attitude may inevitably be necessary.

We have emphasized that wicked problems are very difficult to articulate, understand, and predict. There might be no obvious reasons for events and phenomena. Knowledge, experience, and previous observations, while helpful in some cases, may fall short in other circumstances. A linear and sequential decision-making process and even gut feelings or intuition may fail when applied to these problems (as discussed in Chapters 4, 5, and 6). Different people may have different opinions and propose various options about the same problem; thus, as required by wisdom, multiple perspectives must be considered when dealing with wicked problems.

Wicked problems do not have stopping rules. That is, the decision maker may not know whether the problem has been solved. There is no rule as to whether the applied solution is the best solution and will completely address the problem. This is because the problem-solving process itself is the process of understanding the problem's nature (Rittel & Webber, 1973). There could always be a better solution, but finding it might be constrained by limited time, budgets, and knowledge. These constraints that can have a 'wicked-like' and ambivalent character, and can have an impact on practices, including those of decision making (Küpers, 2018). A wisdom-based strategy to deal with wicked problems ensures that the decision maker has an accurate awareness of their abilities and limitations. Such awareness requires continuous reflection on the decision maker's knowledge and experiences, on the problem situation, and the available courses of action.

Reflection is an important aspect of wise decision making (this will be discussed further in Chapters 7 and 8), and can help the decision maker to deal with the changing, unordered nature of wicked problems. It is almost impossible to find an absolute and specific answer to a wicked problem. The decision maker needs to be flexible, and constantly reflecting on the solutions as they are applied and as they take effect. The problem situation needs to be continuously examined.

Wicked problems engage social aspects and therefore are in most cases value-laden. Solutions to wicked problems are hardly identifiable and achievable. Even the best possible solutions may fail to completely solve wicked problems. Multiple solutions may exist, all being equally preferable. Each solution to wicked problems may generate waves of consequences over an extended period of time (Rittel & Webber, 1973). Any solution may have a combination of intended and unintended consequences that may produce more problems of even greater severity. Therefore, it is almost impossible to predetermine or understand the effectiveness of solutions, especially within a limited time span. Often only after the solution has been applied do the consequences emerge some time in the future. Moreover, different stakeholders have different interpretations of and reactions to both the problem and the effectiveness of any proposed solution.

Therefore, wisdom requires various stakeholder interests, needs, and perspectives or expectations to be taken into account. The decision maker also needs to consider the limits of their knowledge and abilities to make the best decision. They should operate ethically and be empathetic towards multiple stakeholders. Moreover, the decision maker needs to evaluate all the possible consequences of the available alternatives to the greatest extent possible, before committing to any actions. Accordingly, central to the decision-making process in dealing with wicked problems is reaching consensus on the decision situation. As we have seen, each wicked problem is unique and represents an emergent decision-making situation. This implies that the decision situation` is characterized by circumstances that the organization or the manager has never experienced before and for which their conventional knowledge may be irrelevant, inadequate, or even misleading. Therefore, awareness of the limits of previous knowledge and experiences, among others, is critical. The key role of knowledge and experience in decision making will be discussed further in Chapter 4.

Chapter summary

The challenges that many organizations and managers have to deal with in today's business environment are more than just complex: they are wicked. In this chapter, we have looked at the corresponding contexts of the kinds of decisions that most managers have to make these days. We defined the decision contexts in terms of 'wicked problems'. These are complex problems that are dynamic and emergent in nature. Furthermore, these problems are value-laden as they engage larger social aspects and socio-cultural dimensions of various stakeholders. It is very difficult to articulate the problems, as different stakeholders may have their own needs and interests as well as different interpretations and explanations of the problems and possible solutions.

Furthermore, there are no definitive lists of wicked problems or of acceptable solutions for wicked problems. As they are unique the decision maker's previous knowledge and experience may fail to address these kinds of problems. Looking out through a wisdom lens at wicked problems enables us to perceive and analyse the environment based on appropriate assumptions, including mutual causality, holism, indeterminism, equality, and subjective reality.

Wicked problems challenge a manager's decision-making capacity. Wicked problems may distort a manager's perception of apparent strategic decisions with genuine strategic problems. She may be biased, selective, or focus on the wrong issues when facing and framing difficult situations and problems. This distortion may increase if the wicked problems are addressed by managers with insufficient inexperience and/or inadequate abilities to adequately interpret emergent situations (McMillan & Overall, 2016).

Wicked problems may seem to be 'resistant' to solutions, but there are vital qualities and capabilities that managers can learn and apply to be able to handle or process wicked problems. Helping managers to understand the dynamic and emergent nature of wicked problems and to deal with them is a great challenge and raises many questions. How does an organization or a manager make appropriate decisions and take proper actions when inevitably faced with wicked and complex problems? What does 'appropriate' mean? How can it be qualified ethically in relation to practical wisdom? Before we proceed to the theory of wise management decision making (in Part III), in the next chapters (Part II) we will show why a reliance on previous knowledge and conventional experience may lead to failures when managers confront wicked and complex problems.

References

Ackoff, R. (1974). *Systems, messes, and interactive planning: Redesigning the future.* New York: Wiley Publishing.

Adam, R. J. (2016). *Education for wicked problems and the reconciliation of opposites: A theory of bi-relational development.* Abingdon, UK: Routledge.

Alammar, F., & Pauleen, D. (2016). Business diplomacy management: A conceptual overview and an integrative framework. *International Journal of Diplomacy and Economy*, 3(1), 3–26.

Battram, A. (1998). *Navigating complexity.* London: Robert Hyde House.

Beinecke, R. H. (2016). Leadership for "wicked" school mental health problems. In R. H. Shute & P. T. Slee (Eds.), *Mental health and wellbeing through schools* (pp. 14–27). Abingdon, UK: Routledge.

Burr, J. E., & Hofer, B. K. (2002). Personal epistemology and theory of mind: Deciphering young children's beliefs about knowledge and knowing. *New Ideas in Psychology*, 20(2–3), 199–224.

Head, B., & Alford, J. (2008). Wicked problems: The implications for Public Management. Paper presented at the Panel on Public Management in Practice, International Research Society for Public Management 12th Annual Conference, 26–28 March, Brisbane, Australia.

Hocking, V. T., Brown, V. A., & Harris, J. A. (2016). Tackling wicked problems through collective design. *Intelligent Buildings International*, 8(1), 24–36.

Keene, A. (2000). Complexity theory: The changing role of leadership. *Industrial and Commercial Training*, 32(1), 15–18.

Kesteleyn, J., Riordan, S., & Ruël, H. (2014). Introduction: business diplomacy. *The Hague Journal of Diplomacy*, 9(4), 303–309.

King, P. M., & Kitchener, K. S. (2002). The reflective judgment model: Twenty years of research on epistemic cognition. In B. K. Hofer & P. R. Pintrich (Eds.), *Personal epistemology: The psychology of beliefs about knowledge and knowing* (pp. 37–61). Mahwah, NJ: Lawrence Erlbaum Associates.

Küpers, W. (2018). *Praxis, practices, phronesis and sustainable action in organisation and leadership*. London: Routledge (in press).

Marshak, R. J. (2009). Reflections on wicked problems in organizations. *Journal of Management Inquiry*, 18(1), 58–59.

Marshall, S. (2016). Technological innovation of higher education in New Zealand: A wicked problem? *Studies in Higher Education*, 41(2), 1–14.

McGrath, M., & McGonagle, H. (2016). Exploring "wicked problems" from an occupational perspective: The case of turf cutting in rural Ireland. *Journal of Occupational Science*, 23(3), 1–13.

McMillan, C., & Overall, J. (2016). Wicked problems: Turning strategic management upside down. *Journal of Business Strategy*, 37(1), 34–43.

Morrison, K. (2002). *School leadership and complexity theory*. London: Routledge.

Rittel, H. W. J. (1972). On the planning crisis: Systems analysis of the "first and second generations". *Bedriftsøkonomen*, 8, 390–396.

Rittel, H. W. J., & Webber, M. M. (1973). Dilemmas in a general theory of planning. *Policy Sciences*, 4(2), 155–169.

Snowden, D. J., & Boone, M. E. (2007). A leader's framework. *Harvard Business Review*, 85(11), 68–76.

Stacey, R. D. (1996). *Complexity and creativity in organizations*. San Francisco: Berrett-Koehler Publishers.

Stacey R. D. (2002). *Strategic management and organizational dynamics: The challenge of complexity* (3rd ed.). Harlow, UK: Prentice Hall.

Stacey, R. (2010). *Complexity and organizational reality: The need to rethink management after the collapse of investment capitalism*. Abingdon, UK: Routledge.

Stacey, R. (2012). *The tools and techniques of leadership and management: Meeting the challenge of complexity*. Abingdon, UK: Routledge.

Stacey, R., & Mowles, C. (2016). *Strategic management and organisational dynamics: The challenge of complexity to ways of thinking about organisations* (7th ed.). London: Pearson Education.

Tredinnick, L. (2009). Complexity theory and the web. *Journal of Documentation*, 65(5), 797–813.

Zijp, M. C., Posthuma, L., Wintersen, A., Devilee, J., & Swartjes, F. A. (2016). Definition and use of Solution-focused Sustainability Assessment: A novel approach to generate, explore and decide on sustainable solutions for wicked problems. *Environment International*, 91(May), 319–331.

Part II

Knowledge, information, data/analytics, and decision making

4 Trapped in the past, dealing with the future

The role of knowledge in dealing with decision situations

Introduction

Today's business world operates in a volatile and uncertain environment characterized by a dynamic and increasing rate of change. Advances in technology have increased the pace of action and reaction while growing social awareness causes high levels of uncertainty and ambiguity. Practitioners increasingly face often emergent and frequently unique phenomena. As explained in the previous chapter, problems are often wicked: involving expanding social contexts, multiple factors, and polycausal relationships that are difficult to identify and to process. Organizational and managerial decision making can no longer be made based on simple, linear – if A, then B – processes. As the pace of technological and social changes with its non-causal dynamics intensifies and the future becomes less and less predictable, organizational strategies need to be constantly revised and management must become highly adaptable. To cope with the continual change and transformational dynamics of global environments, competitive markets, and demands of various stakeholders, organizations and leadership must be willing and able to continually change (Cash, 1997).

Knowledge is an important resource and plays a crucial role when dealing with the complex challenges organizations and management face. The ability to effectively manage knowledge at the individual and organizational levels is regarded as a major source of competitive advantage (Grant, 2011; Newman & Conrad, 2000) and ultimately, survival (Davenport & Prusak, 1998; Drucker, 2002). The value of knowledge depends on its intrinsic quality as well as its effective implementation. However, as we argue in this chapter, the use of knowledge that is based on past-oriented informative components (i.e. data, information, and experience) may be insufficient, particularly with regard to problem solving (Churchman, 1971; Davenport & Prusak, 1998; Harris, 2005), or decision making in unforeseen and emergent circumstances (Intezari & Pauleen, 2014).

To be successful, the challenge for organizations and management is to effectively implement the 'right' knowledge (Bierly III, Kessler, & Christensen, 2000). The first step in the successful implementation of knowledge requires a clear understanding of the nature of knowledge and its sources. This requires moving beyond traditional interpretations. Accordingly, in this chapter we discuss and critique conventional information and knowledge management approaches. Investing in and managing knowledge in complex and volatile business contexts and for handling unforeseeable future decision situations must, before anything else, address two fundamental questions:

(1) To what extent should (individual and organizational) information, experience, and previous knowledge be seen as a reliable basis for decision making and action taking when dealing with complex issues in emergent circumstances?

(2) What else can assist us when facing future situations never seen, experienced, or possibly imagined?

To answer these questions, in the first section of this chapter, we look at the nature of knowledge, the sources of knowledge, and the use of knowledge. Then we will discuss the role of knowledge and managing knowledge in complex business environments, the fallibility of knowledge, and the role of wisdom in more effectively applying knowledge in management decision making.

The nature of knowledge

It might sound naive to ask what knowledge is like or what it is supposed to 'do' for organizations. The answer, however, sheds light on the importance and various aspects of the technology and strategies that are designed and used to manage knowledge at individual and organizational levels. The answer may also make it clearer as to why knowledge and knowledge management have become critical aspects of many organizations. Knowing the ultimate goal for developing and using knowledge resources in an organization or in a business field can inform the design and implementation of knowledge management systems.

While knowledge for the sake of knowledge may be virtuous (Trusted, 1997), we believe the key reason for organizations to engage in knowledge management strategies is to ensure that appropriate knowledge is available for the purpose of producing better and wiser management decisions and actions. Such improved decisions promote organizational performance (Walczak, 2005; Martensson, 2000), organizational effectiveness, efficiency, and, in turn, improve competitiveness (Schultze & Leidner, 2002). Knowledge management systems have been developed, designed, and implemented in organizations over the last three decades to help organizations create, share, and apply employee and organizational knowledge to improve performance and maximize profit (Birasnav, 2014; Del Giudice & Della Peruta, 2016; Donate & Guadamillas, 2015; Huseby & Chou, 2003).

In sum, then, the answer to the question, 'what is knowledge supposed to do for organizations?' is that the objective of organizational knowledge is to enable people and organizations to make accurate and wiser decisions, which in turn, promotes organization performance (Martensson, 2000; Van Beveren, 2002). The challenge is making sure the organization's knowledge is relevant and valid. Because of constant change in the business environment, it is critically important to make sure that knowledge used in decision making is up-to-date, relevant, reliable, and ethically qualified. Moreover, knowledge itself is dynamic and constantly developing and changing over time. For these reasons, acquiring and creating knowledge in an organization must be closely aligned with knowledge implementation, the objective of both being improving the organization's ability to effectively handle organizational, market, and environmental changes.

Of course an organization can implement a KMS and use it to support decision making, but the key question is: is the organization's knowledge current, correct, and sufficient for making the most effective decision at a given time? If a manager is making decisions in emergent or complex decision situations based on out-of-date or incorrect knowledge, the 'wrong' kind of experience, or an unrealistic evaluation of the complexity of the decision situation, we can expect the resulting decisions and actions to fail or be only partially successful. This scenario raises critical questions about the applicability of knowledge if the concept of knowledge remains limited to the understanding that a better and wiser decision can be made by solely managing data and information.

Sources of knowledge

As discussed in Chapter 3, solutions to complex and wicked problems require more than just an accumulation of knowledge. Managers frequently deal with problems that are multidimensional, multi-layered, and emergent. The problems are often economically and socially complex, highly value-laden, and hence as described in the previous chapter, *wicked*. Nevertheless, central to successful management decisions is the decision makers' knowledge, expertise, and experience.

There is no universally agreed-upon definition of 'knowledge'. It is a complicated concept and may be defined in different ways depending on the assumptions made about the sources, the nature, and applications of knowledge. As the focus of the book is on decision making in the business context, we focus on the relevant sources and applications of knowledge from a business perspective, rather than engaging in extensive philosophical debates about the nature of knowledge.

In traditional epistemology, knowledge is defined as "justified true belief" (Nonaka, 1994, p. 15), which according to Plato (Fearn, 2005) possesses three rules: (1) it is a true proposition; (2) one believes it; and (3) there is a justification. The definition stands on such broad terms as 'justified', 'true', and 'belief', each of which requires intensive investigation to be defined; moreover, this definition has been logically refuted.[1]

Conceptualizing knowledge as justified true belief implies, as suggested by psychology, that knowledge is a state of mind and also a process. Knowledge is a state of mind as it refers to one's level of awareness of the existence of something (Nugent, 2013). This corresponds to knowledge as 'belief'. The belief must be justified. The 'justification' is the process component of knowledge. Knowledge is a process to understand a specific topic (Nugent, 2013). In this sense, knowledge, as Polanyi (1958, 1966) argues, relies on judgements, and one may or may not always be able to articulate what one knows.

Michael Polanyi, a chemist and philosopher, who has made remarkable contributions to chemistry, economics, social sciences, and philosophy, classifies knowledge under two categories: tacit knowledge and explicit knowledge (Polanyi, 1958, 1966). Tacit knowledge refers to what we know, are aware of, and are able to do, but is almost impossible to articulate and describe analytically. Examples of tacit and embodied knowledge are riding a bicycle, or keeping one's balance when running. Explicit knowledge, in contrast, is knowledge that the knower can articulate in writing, speech, or drawings. Examples of explicit knowledge are the documentation of the process of archiving confidential documents in an organization, or an illustration of the process of receiving and processing online orders in a retailing company's website.

In line with Polanyi's (1962) explicit-tacit knowledge typology is a classification of knowledge as embodied versus knowledge as an entity independent of the person. Embodied knowledge is tied to one's experience and emotions and as such cannot exist outside the person and his experiences (Hassell, 2007). If knowledge is embodied and narrative (Küpers, 2005), then it follows that it cannot be captured and stored as an entity independent of the person who holds the knowledge.

If this is the case, then knowledge cannot be held in computer/information systems. Therefore, information systems can only capture and transmit simple, unstructured, and semi-structured data and information (Hassell, 2007). Conceptualizing knowledge as an embodied entity draws on the philosophical discourses of knowledge sources. There are three main schools of thought that take distinctive stances as to whether knowledge is rooted in one's experiences or is external to the person. These schools include *Empiricism*, *Positivism*, and *Apriorism*.

Empiricism, Positivism, and Apriorism

It would be hubristic to claim that one can clearly identify the real and exact source of knowledge. Being able to find the source(s) of knowledge depends in the first place on how knowledge is defined, which as we have seen above can vary. This is because knowledge is inextricably linked with culture, commitment, and common values (Hassell, 2007), which include those of academic and practice-based disciplines. While some may argue that knowledge is a purely cognitive entity residing in the human mind, others put forward an equally valid argument that knowledge is an embodied phenomenon that cannot exist independent of the person who holds the knowledge.

One rather pragmatic definition provided in the previous section, which reflects our current data and information-driven business environment, explains that knowledge can be understood as information leveraged by individual insight. Although considering knowledge as the output of a simple data- and information-based analysis may not capture the complexity of knowledge, adopting the somewhat linear data, information, knowledge (the knowledge hierarchy, Figure 4.1, discussed below) approach provides a theoretical foundation based on which we can better understand the sources of knowledge. Accordingly, we suggest that data and information serve as important sources of knowledge. When data and information are interpreted and then integrated into one's experience, and when one tailors and mobilizes the data and information, it becomes a knowledge source (Kreiner, 2002; Liew, 2013). In this sense, knowledge is defined as "a capacity that builds on information extracted from data" or "the set of expectations that an observer holds with respect to an event" (Boisot, 1998, pp. xiv, 20). For this reason, other sources of knowledge include one's prior knowledge (Carneiro, 2000; Nielsen, 2006) as well as one's perception, discovery, learning (Harris, 2005), and imagination.

A classical debate about the sources of knowledge draws on the notion of experience. Experience can contribute to one's knowledge. However, one's knowledge may or may not have been necessarily rooted in experience. In the former sense, knowledge can be defined as one's understanding that has been obtained from experience (Roberts & Armitage, 2008).

Kant's perspective on knowledge has become one of the most philosophically influential explanations of the sources of epistemological knowledge. He distinguishes between *a priori* knowledge and *a posteriori* knowledge. A priori knowledge is independent of experience. In contrast, a posteriori knowledge is developed from one's experience (Trusted, 1997). The debate is best reflected by three main schools of thought concerning the source of knowledge: *Empiricism*, *Positivism*, and *Apriorism*.

Empiricism holds that the substantive source of our knowledge of the world is our experience. The primary source of knowledge is one's sensory experience. For scientists, knowledge is acquired mainly by experiments and observation (Kurtus, 2002; Nagel, 2008).

Positivism, which is sometimes referred to as scientific empiricism or logical positivism, is the extended form of and significantly draws on the assumptions of empiricism. Nothing is innate and a proposition is meaningful if its truth is determined by some sense-experience (Kurtus, 2002). Positivism, however, puts more emphasis on the logic of science. Knowledge is derived through mathematical and logical processes. For this reason, verification is essential, and, therefore, specific principles of logic and scientific methods should be used to acquire knowledge. The methodology and precision of mathematics and natural science are used. For positivists, the knowledge that is not supported by validated logical experiments and reliable observatory instruments is not trustworthy and should not be used as a basis for decision making.

Unlike empiricism and positivism, *Apriorism* contends that knowledge can be acquired through non-inductive means. That is, knowledge is innate and independent of experience. The main source of knowledge, according to apriorism, is *a priori knowledge*. People may have ideas that have not been acquired through sense perception or experience.

The Empiricist and Positivist approaches are prevalent in management theory. For example, Davenport and Prusak (1998) argue that knowledge develops through experience. In the same vein, knowledge is defined as a kind of professional experience that is appropriate for the domain (Bourdreau & Couillard, 1999). In management theory, and more specifically, in the field of management decision support systems, knowledge is defined in terms of information processed and applied in a decision situation. This conception of knowledge is represented by a widely accepted model in management theory: the knowledge hierarchy.

The knowledge hierarchy

The knowledge hierarchy has three layers: data, information, and knowledge (Figure 4.1). Data is understood as a "representation of an object" (Miller, Malloy, Masek, & Wild, 2001, p. 364) or a "set of discrete, objective facts about events" (Davenport & Prusak, 1998, p. 2). Information is then defined in terms of data. When the data are put in a meaningful context and processed, information is built (Kock, McQueen, & Baker, 1996; Lillrank, 2003). Data construct the "factual content of information" (Melkas & Harmaakorpi, 2008, p. 108). The third layer is knowledge. According to the knowledge pyramid, knowledge is generally understood as processed and validated information (Firestone, 2003). In human terms, knowledge is differentiated from information and data by suggesting that knowledge is a higher form of information and engages one's interpretation and experience. Unlike information, which mostly deals with descriptions and answers to questions such as 'who', 'what', 'when', 'where', and 'how many', knowledge is more prescriptive and deals with 'how-to' and 'why' questions (Ackoff, 1989).

The knowledge hierarchy draws on the assumption that knowledge can be developed from data and information, and that knowledge can be converted back into information and data. The model continues to form the basis of academic discourses and is also widely implemented in industry (Ardolino et al., 2017; Erikson & Rothberg, 2016, 2017; Kirsch, Hine, & Maybury, 2015). This view allows for knowledge to become a storable entity and located in an information system. This assumption works insofar as we accept that what is stored and managed by the systems as knowledge does not represent

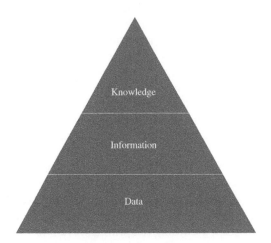

Figure 4.1 The knowledge pyramid

and substitute for the depth and breadth of the knowledge residing in people's minds or bodies (i.e. tacit or embodied knowledge).

Even though the knowledge hierarchy is regarded in the management information systems literature as a reasonable way to position knowledge in relation to data and information (Sumbal, Tsui, & See-to, 2017; Wilson & Campbell, 2016), the model has come in for criticism. For instance, the hierarchy is criticized for failing to consider and explain how each level is transformed into a higher level. That is, the processes through which data is transformed into information and information is transformed into knowledge are unclear (Wognin, Henri, & Marino, 2012).

Another criticism, which is more methodological, is associated with the functionality of the hierarchy in the real world (Frické, 2009). The hierarchy is criticized for drawing on a "pre-emptive acquisition" assumption (Frické, 2009, p. 135). That is, according to the hierarchy, data is collected meaninglessly and mindlessly, in the hope that that one day the data is processed to form information, and that this information will answer questions.

The third criticism that can be directed at the DIK hierarchy concerns the ambiguous conceptualization of knowledge in terms of tacit or explicit knowledge. Articulations of knowledge using statements such as 'processed information', 'information in context', 'validated information', or 'experience in the domain' do not allow for the complex nature of knowledge including implicit or tacit knowledge as understood by Polanyi (1966) or Hassell (2007). This conception leads knowledge as a data- and information-based quality to be bounded to what can be known. This is a highly limiting view of knowledge, when compared for example with the psychological perspective, where growth of knowledge is "conceived in terms of accumulation of skills, habits, vocabulary, information, concepts, and so forth, as each person strives to come closer to the fixed boundary of what can be known" (Meacham, 1990, p. 183).

Taken as a whole, the criticisms of the DIK hierarchy point to significant limitations when it comes to the role of knowledge in decision making. With regard to decision making, the data should be derived by the questions raised in the decision-making process. In this sense, 'data warehouses' for example have no functionality unless the data collection is driven by a decision situation (Pauleen & Wang, 2017). Nevertheless, with the emergence of big data/analytics, business and information systems seem to be betting on the proposition of putting the cart before the horse through the pursuit and collection of vast, ever-increasing amounts of data with the expectation that the data and the analytical tools will answer questions that no one has posed.

Regardless of whether knowledge is accepted as simply a processed form of information (as in the knowledge hierarchy) or argued to be a combination of experience and information exactly tailored to a given context through individuals' perceptions (embodied knowledge), by definition, knowledge is indisputably derived from past-oriented constructive components (i.e. data, information, and experience). This critical fact, we argue, may prevent the effective use of knowledge in future, or emergent, situations (Intezari & Pauleen, 2014, 2017). The Time factor in relation to the nature and sources of knowledge is depicted by Figure 4.2.

Figure 4.2 illustrates the sources of knowledge and how the sources may be time-bounded. One's knowledge may be intuitively derived, or it could be based on conscious analyses and observation of previous experiences as well as data and information. The nature of knowledge (vertical axis) is positioned along a continuum of being either independent of the person or embodied and dependent on the person. The horizontal axis depicts the time-bounded nature of the sources of knowledge.

Intuition, as a way of knowing, refers to the capacity to know something instantaneously and without conscious effort (Nyatanga & Vocht, 2008; Volz & Cramon, 2006). Intuitive knowledge is rooted in one's unconscious analysis of and reflection on previous experiences and observations. Intuition is linked to emotion and feeling (Evans, 2012), and draws on subconscious data and on an internal process of feeling or sensing (Effken, 2001). Intuition allows a decision maker to effectively deal with even complex

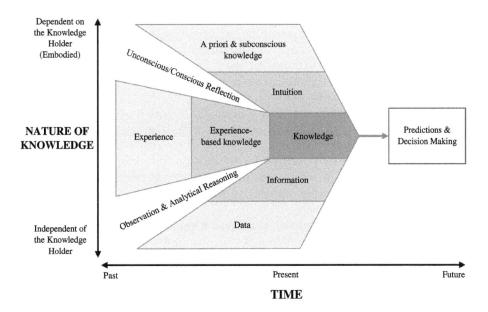

Figure 4.2 The Knowledge–Time Continuum Model of Knowledge Sources

decision situations without any conscious reasoning and objective analysis (Eubanks, Murphy, & Mumford, 2010).

Knowledge can also be developed based on experience. Experience-based knowledge is 'know-how': the knowledge of applying previous experiences, i.e. understanding how experience is related and applied to the current decision situation by reflecting on previous decision-making experiences. Reflection plays a critical role in acquiring experience-based or intuitive knowledge (Intezari & Pauleen, 2013). The contribution of reflection to effective and wise decision making is discussed in detail in Chapters 7 and 8.

It should be understood that many management and decision support systems, in their current form, may fail to offer the knowledge necessary to address wicked problems. Not only is the knowledge stored in information and knowledge systems bereft of human context, but this stored knowledge is also past-oriented, i.e. it is knowledge of the past (as illustrated by Figure 4.2). This implies that existing knowledge is incomplete and so may be insufficient with regard to decision making about the future. If the decision maker fails to accurately assess the decision situation using up-to-date and relevant data and information, the decision is less likely to effectively address the decision problem.

As discussed in the third chapter, through complexity and similar theories and efforts, scholars have tried to give a picture of the unstable and unpredictable nature of the world and future events in order to find a way to cope with complexity and unpredictability by relying on knowledge alone. However, the reliance on knowledge alone may not result in being able to effectively deal with complex problems in unstable environments.

Knowledge fallibility

Knowledge fallibility refers to the extent to which the decision maker's knowledge and experience may fall short in effectively addressing a decision situation. Knowledge fallibility may lead to ineffective and inappropriate decisions and actions. Figure 4.3 illustrates the relationship between the level of (in-)stability of a situation and the chance of knowledge fallibility in the decision situation. 'Stability' and 'instability' in the figure represent two extremes of the same continuum. Along the continuum, multiple combinations of cognitive inconsistency and knowledge fallibility may occur. Cognitive inconsistency refers to the extent to which the decision maker's interpretation of the decision situation at a given time is incompatible with what the reality of the decision situation is. As the strategic decisions and actions that an organization makes and takes rely on the decision makers' interpretation of the environment (DeMeyer, 1991; Schneider & DeMeyer, 1991), different interpretations may lead to different decisions and actions. The instability of the decision situation and environment make it more difficult to have a realistic interpretation of the decision situation, and therefore, may increase cognitive inconsistency.

In an unstable environment, as is the case with decision making around wicked and complex problems, the probability of the decision maker's knowledge fallibility is high. In a decision situation that is characterized as stable, the events are predictable, and problems are non-complex with transparent cause-effect relationships. The previous knowledge and experience are sufficient, and the routine decision-making techniques and procedures are effective to address the problem situations (Figure 4.3).

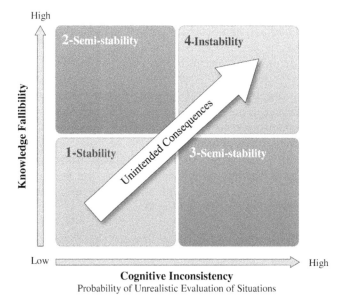

Figure 4.3 Instability and Knowledge Fallibility (adapted from Intezari & Pauleen, 2014, p. 396)

Instability may be the result of sudden and fundamental changes in the decision situation and the environment where the decision is being made. Instability can also be the result of a lack of enough and/or reliable information during the decision-making process, which may lead the decision maker to interpret and analyse the decision situation inaccurately or even incorrectly. In an unstable environment, the problem and the consequences of any possible solution to the problem become less predictable. Emergent problems and unprecedented issues increase the level of instability (Intezari & Pauleen, 2014). When the complexity of the decision situation increases, the probability of an unrealistic evaluation of the situation increases, and the resultant decisions may lead to unintended consequences.

The negative and often unforeseen effects of management decisions that are made solely on data or on data-based knowledge arise from three reasons that Haskins and Nanni have identified as important weaknesses of management information systems (1988, p. 25):

1. "The fact that management information systems present a constrained set of data;
2. The potentially skewed focus of that constrained data set; and
3. The static nature of that constrained dataset".

Some may argue that scenario writing may mitigate the effects of knowledge fallibility and its past-oriented nature when preparing for handling emergent, future, or complex situations. Scenario writing and other similar techniques such as 'future thinking' are management tools used to visualize future events by simulating situations prior to their emergence. Such tools are helpful for gathering information and knowledge, and defining, learning, and practising responses to imagined future situations. However, they might not always effectively prepare managers due to these reasons:

- we make scenarios according to our knowledge, so we cannot imagine what we do not know, especially those situations termed 'unknown unknowns';
- it is impossible to imagine unlimited numbers of possible situations and, in turn, to plan for each one; and
- scenario writing is also based upon experience.

When we claim that a situation is somehow different from that which we have experienced, we are, in fact, comparing it with (our) experienced situation(s). Our experience becomes the basis of comparison. The main point here is that imagining un-experienced situations based on experienced ones is self-limiting; that is to say, our imagination is limited by our experience. In this sense, these kinds of techniques are past-oriented in the same way knowledge is past-oriented. As a result, they may not be particularly helpful for predicting the future, as they do not deal with unknowable future events and circumstances. Kippenberger (1999, p. 6) concurs, stating that:

> The gravest risk [of relying on forecasting techniques alone] is that forecasts tend to project conventional wisdom and current assumptions forward. They fit well with existing mindsets. Yet, time and again, this is inadequate preparation for what the future holds.

So, what might better prepare us for dealing with complex, emergent, and essentially unknowable future decision situations? Because of the unpredictable nature and emergent quality of events in the world, it is not possible to keep fully abreast of the information and knowledge necessary in order to react. Therefore, the focus of organizations and managers should be on finding ways to handle these situations as and when they arise. Kippenberger (1999) states that developing 'insight' is ideal for dealing with unpredictable business environments. Insight refers to one's deep understanding of one's own condition(s) at a given time and in a particular situation, as well as the capacity to explore possible meaningful relationships between apparently unrelated phenomena pertinent to that situation (Intezari & Pauleen, 2013). Fresh thinking, leading to foresight, or even better, insight, is the ideal modus operandi in the current business environment. A better understanding of the relationship between wisdom and knowledge might lead to the kind of fresh thinking needed in management strategies for dealing with emergent and future-oriented decision situations.

Knowledge and wisdom

Although a fourth layer was added to the knowledge hierarchy by the early scholars researching it (cf. Ackoff, 1989), the relationship between the fourth layer – wisdom – and the rest of the pyramid has not been fully explored or properly understood in the management field. In the management literature and in management information systems in particular, a common understanding of wisdom was that wisdom was a higher level of knowledge (Ackoff, 1989; Alter, 1999; Faucher, Everett, & Lawson, 2008; Pantzar, 2000; Tuomi, 2000; Zins, 2007) (Figure 4.4).

One of the main concerns with defining wisdom in terms of knowledge is the conceptualization of knowledge. In the knowledge hierarchy, knowledge is understood as information that is combined with an individual's experience and interpretation (Harris, 2005; Nonaka, 1994). Despite the extensive discourses and discussions in ancient times

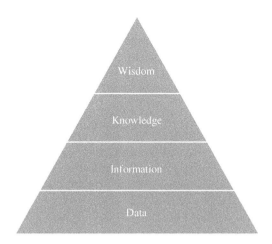

Figure 4.4 Knowledge Hierarchy and Wisdom

and contemporary scientific studies about the nature and the meaning of 'knowledge', there is still no globally-accepted definition of the term, nor how it can be developed. Accordingly, conceptualizing wisdom in terms of knowledge will not result in a clear or appropriate understanding of wisdom.

The importance of the contribution of knowledge in developing wisdom is generally accepted in the knowledge hierarchy and the framework does provide a basic, albeit flawed, understanding of wisdom. Nevertheless, it is widely understood in the philosophical, psychological, and management literature on wisdom that having knowledge alone does not make one wise (Baggini & Fosl, 2007; Intezari & Pauleen, 2017; Meacham, 1990; Nunamaker, Romano, & Briggs, 2002). Rather there are other critical qualities involved in practical wisdom beyond knowledge such as experience, cognition, intelligence, beliefs, values, and judgement that are foundational in the development and enactment of wisdom (Ardelt, 2003; Bierly III et al., 2000; Grint, 2007).

In the following chapters, we explain in detail that approaching decision situations based on, mediated, or enacted by wisdom can be the most responsive, responsible, and effective way of dealing with wicked decision situations. Wisdom as a multidimensional and an overarching quality can integrate various elements that are essential when dealing with difficult decision situations and for achieving the best outcome for the greatest number of stakeholders. As a practice, wisdom can enhance both organizational capacity and the individual manager's capacity to better understand a decision situation and take better, ethical, and more effective actions. Although not a simple practice, wise decision making is achievable and learnable especially by following a set of guidelines as discussed in the following chapters.

Chapter summary

The current business environment can be appropriately characterized as uncertain, unpredictable, complicated, and volatile. We might go so far as to characterize it as 'wicked'. Risk is always present in strategic decision making. Managing uncertain and unpredictable situations and making effective decisions and formulating accurate strategies have been major challenges facing managers and academics for decades. The emergence and practice of knowledge management has been one important response. In this chapter, we have challenged the approach that reliance on previous knowledge alone can lead to effective management decisions in dealing with wicked problems in unstable situations.

The concept of knowledge from the management perspective and common typologies of knowledge were discussed. The knowledge hierarchy as a widely-used model illustrating the nature and relationship of data, information, and knowledge was discussed. Understanding knowledge typologies – such as the knowledge hierarchy, Hassell's concept of embodied knowledge, and Polanyi's tacit-explicit distinction – is central to our understanding of management decision making in today's business context. This is because the design and implementation of management decision support systems and other systems designed to support decision making such as Knowledge Management Systems depend to a high degree on the assumptions underlying these typologies.

The usefulness of knowledge and management decision support systems in decision making is undeniable. Advances in technology and the emergence of business analytics have led many organizations to invest great sums in big data, analytics, and knowledge management systems. However, looking at data and information as the only, or even primary, sources of knowledge may lead to what we call 'knowledge fallibility'. Knowledge fallibility happens when existing knowledge falls short in dealing with unforeseen problems. Computer-based decision making, while common and effective in certain classes of operational decisions, is very likely to lead to situations of knowledge fallibility in the strategic decision-making process, especially if the role of human judgement is omitted.

We conclude the extent to which a decision maker's knowledge and experience, as well as available information and data, can be applied to complex business circumstances, is limited. We believe that experience and knowledge alone are insufficient when confronted with the need to identify and articulate decision situations, particularly those that are complex or wicked. Having or relying on knowledge is not enough. This is a critical, and for some readers a somewhat controversial, proposition. It is, however, central to this book and how we view the management decision-making process and strategies for making it more effective.

Note

1 In one of the cases that Gettier (1963, p. 122) presents,

> Smith and Jones have applied for a certain job. … Smith has strong evidence for the following conjunctive proposition: (d) Jones is the man who will get the job, and Jones has ten coins in his pocket. Smith's evidence for (d) might be that the president of the company assured him that Jones would in the end be selected, and that he, Smith, had counted the coins in Jones's pocket ten minutes ago. Proposition (d) entails: (e) the man who will get the job has ten coins in his pocket.

Another supposition is that "Smith sees the entailment from (d) to (e), and accepts (e) on the grounds of (d), for which he has strong evidence". As seen, "Smith is clearly justified in believing that (e) is true".

Here Gettier changes the situations and shows how the justified true belief may not be knowledge:

Unknown to Smith, he himself, not Jones, will get the job. And, also, unknown to Smith, he himself has ten coins in his pocket. Proposition (e) is then true; though proposition (d), from which Smith inferred (e), is false. Then, all of the following are true: (i) (e) is true, (ii) Smith believes that (e) is true, and (iii) Smith is justified in believing that (e) is true. But it is equally clear that Smith does not KNOW that (e) is true; for (e) is true in virtue of the number of coins in Smith's pocket, while Smith does not know how many coins are in Smith's pocket, and bases his belief in (e) on a count of the coins in Jones's pocket, whom he falsely believes to be the man who will get the job.

References

Ackoff, R. L. (1989). From data to wisdom. *Journal of Applied Systems Analysis*, 16(1), 3–9.

Alter, S. (1999). *Information systems: A management perspective*. Auckland, New Zealand: Addison-Wesley Publishing Co.

Ardelt, M. (2003). Empirical assessment of a three-dimensional wisdom scale. *Research on Aging*, 25(3), 275–324.

Ardolino, M., Rapaccini, M., Saccani, N., Gaiardelli, P., Crespi, G., & Ruggeri, C. (2017). The role of digital technologies for the service transformation of industrial companies. *International Journal of Production Research* (9 May), 1–17.

Baggini, J., & Fosl, P. S. (2007). *The ethics toolkit: A compendium of ethical concepts and methods*. Malden, UK: Blackwell Publishing.

Bierly III, P. E., Kessler, E. H., & Christensen, E. W. (2000). Organizational learning, knowledge and wisdom. *Journal of Organizational Change Management*, 13(6), 595–618.

Birasnav, M. (2014). Knowledge management and organizational performance in the service industry: The role of transformational leadership beyond the effects of transactional leadership. *Journal of Business Research*, 67(8), 1622–1629.

Boisot, M. (1998). *Knowledge asset: Securing a competitive advantage in the information economy*. New York: Oxford University Press.

Bourdreau, A., & Couillard, G. (1999). Systems integration and knowledge management. *Information Systems Management*, 16(4), 24–32.

Carneiro, A. (2000). How does knowledge management influence innovation and competitiveness? *Journal of Knowledge Management*, 4(2), 87–98.

Cash, M. (1997). Stories within a story: Parables from 'the New Zealand experiment'. *The Learning Organization, 4*(4), 159–167.

Churchman, C. W. (1971). *The design of inquiring systems: Basic concepts of systems and organization*. New York: Basic Books.

Davenport, T. H., & Prusak, L. (1998). *Working knowledge: How organizations manage what they know*. Boston: Harvard Business School Press.

Del Giudice, M., & Della Peruta, M. R. (2016). The impact of IT-based knowledge management systems on internal venturing and innovation: A structural equation modeling approach to corporate performance. *Journal of Knowledge Management*, 20(3), 484–498.

DeMeyer, A. (1991). Tech talk: how managers are stimulating global R&D communication, *Sloan Management Review*, 32(3), 49–58.

Donate, M. J., & Guadamillas, F. (2015). An empirical study on the relationships between knowledge management, knowledge-oriented human resource practices and innovation. *Knowledge Management Research & Practice*, 13(2), 134–148.

Drucker, P. F. (2002). "They're not employees, they are people", *Harvard Business Review*, 80(2), 70–77.

Effken, J. A. (2001). Informational basis for expert intuition. *Journal of Advanced Nursing*, 34(2), 246–255.

Erickson, G. S., & Rothberg, H. N. (2016). Intangible dynamics in financial services. *Journal of Service Theory and Practice*, 26(5), 642–656.

Erickson, G. S., & Rothberg, H. N. (2017). Healthcare and hospitality: Intangible dynamics for evaluating industry sectors. *The Service Industries Journal*, 37(9–10), 589–606.

Eubanks, D. L., Murphy, S. T., & Mumford, M. D. (2010). Intuition as an influence on creative problem-solving: The effects of intuition, positive affect, and training. *Creativity Research Journal*, 22(2), 170–184.

Evans, J. S. B. T. (2012). Spot the difference: Distinguishing between two kinds of processing. *Mind & Society*, 11(1), 121–131.

Faucher, J.-B. P. L., Everett, A. M., & Lawson, R. (2008). Reconstituting knowledge management. *Journal of Knowledge Management*, 12(3), 3–16.

Fearn, N. (2005). *Philosophy: The latest answers to the oldest questions*. London: Atlantic Books.

Firestone, J. M. (2003). *Enterprise information portals and knowledge management*. Boston: Butterworth-Heinemann.

Frické, M. (2009). The knowledge pyramid: A critique of the DIKW hierarchy. *Journal of Information Science*, 35(2), 131–142.

Gettier, E. L. (1963). Is justified true belief knowledge? *Analysis*, 23(6), 121–123.

Grant, K. (2011). Knowledge Management, an enduring but confusing fashion. *Electronic Journal of Knowledge Management*, 9(2), 117–131.

Grint, K. (2007). Learning to lead: Can Aristotle help us find the road to wisdom? *Leadership*, 3(2), 231–246.

Harris, P. R. (2005). *Managing the knowledge culture*. Amherst, MA: HRD Press.

Haskins, M. E., & Nanni Jr., A. J. (1988). MIS influences on managers: Hidden side effects. *Management Decision*, 26(3), 25–31.

Hassell, L. (2007). A continental philosophy perspective on knowledge management. *Information Systems Journal*, 17(2), 185–195.

Huseby, T., & Chou, S. T. (2003). Applying a knowledge-focused management philosophy to immature economies. *Industrial Management & Data Systems*, 103(2), 126–132.

Intezari, A., & Pauleen, D. J. (2013). Students of wisdom: An integral meta-competencies theory of practical wisdom. In W. Küpers & D. J. Pauleen (Eds.), *A handbook of practical wisdom: Leadership, organization and integral business practice* (pp. 155–174). Aldershot, UK: Gower.

Intezari, A., & Pauleen, D. J. (2014). Management wisdom in perspective: Are you virtuous enough to succeed in volatile times? *Journal of Business Ethics*, 120(3), 393–404.

Intezari, A., & Pauleen, D. J. (2017). The past-present-future conundrum: Extending time-bound knowledge. *International Journal of Knowledge Management*, 13(1), 1–15.

Kippenberger, T. (1999). Thinking about the future. *The Antidote*, (22), 4–6.

Kirsch, P., Hine, A., & Maybury, T. (2015). A model for the implementation of industry-wide knowledge sharing to improve risk management practice. *Safety Science*, 80(Dec), 66–76.

Kock, N., McQueen, R., & Baker, M. (1996). Learning and process improvement in knowledge organisations: A critical analysis of four contemporary myths. *The Learning Organisation*, 3(1), 31–41.

Kreiner, K. (2002). Tacit knowledge management: The role of artifacts. *Journal of Knowledge Management*, 6(2), 112–123.

Küpers, W. (2005). Embodied implicit and narrative knowing in organizations. *Journal of Knowledge Management*, 9(6), 113–133.

Kurtus, R. (2002). Epistemology: The philosophy of knowledge. 27 January. Retrieved from www.school-for-champions.com/knowledge/epistemology.htm#.WkHiylWWavE

Liew, A. (2013). DIKIW: Data, information, knowledge, intelligence, wisdom and their interrelationships. *Business Management Dynamics*, 2(10), 49–62.

Lillrank, P. (2003). The quality of information. *International Journal of Quality & Reliability Management*, 20(6), 691–703.

Martensson, M. (2000). A critical review of knowledge management as a management tool. *Journal of Knowledge Management*, 4(3), 204–216.

Meacham, J. A. (1990). The loss of wisdom. In R. J. Sternberg (Ed.), *Wisdom: Its nature, origins, and development* (pp. 181–211). New York: Cambridge University Press.

Melkas, H., & Harmaakorpi, V. (2008). Data, information and knowledge in regional innovation networks: Quality considerations and brokerage functions. *European Journal of Innovation Management*, 11(1), 103–124.

Miller, B., Malloy, M. A., Masek, E., & Wild, C. (2001). Towards a framework for managing the information environment. *Information Knowledge Systems Management*, 2(4), 359–384.

Nagel, J. (2008). Knowledge ascriptions and the psychological consequences of changing stakes. *Australasian Journal of Philosophy*, 86(2), 279–294.

Newman, B., & Conrad, K. W. (2000). A framework for characterizing knowledge management methods, practices and technologies. In U. Reimer, (Ed.), *Proceedings of the Third International Conference on Practical Aspects of Knowledge Management (PAKM2000) Basel, Switzerland, 30–31 Oct. 2000*. Retrieved from: http://ceur-ws.org/Vol-34/newman_conrad.pdf.

Nielsen, A. P. (2006). Understanding dynamic capabilities through knowledge management. *Journal of Knowledge Management*, 10(4), 59–71.

Nonaka, I. (1994). A dynamic theory of organizational knowledge creation. *Organization Science*, 5(1), 14–37.

Nugent, P. (2013). Knowledge. Retrieved from: https://psychologydictionary.org/knowledge/.

Nunamaker Jr., J. F., Romano Jr., N. C., & Briggs, R. O. (2002). Increasing intellectual bandwidth: Generating value from intellectual capital with information technology. *Group Decision and Negotiation*, 11(2), 69–86.

Nyatanga, B., & Vocht, H. D. (2008). Intuition in clinical decision-making: A psychological penumbra. *International Journal of Palliative Nursing*, 14(10), 492–496.

Pantzar, E. (2000). Knowledge and wisdom in the information society. *Foresight, The Journal of Future Studies, Strategic Thinking and Policy*, 2(2), 230–236.

Pauleen, D. & Wang, W (2017). "Does Big Data Mean Big Knowledge? KM perspectives on big data and analytics". *Journal of Knowledge Management*, 21(1), 1–6.

Polanyi, M. (1958). *Personal knowledge: Towards a post-critical philosophy*. Chicago: University of Chicago Press.

Polanyi, M. (1962). Tacit knowing: Its bearing on some problems of philosophy. *Reviews of Modern Physics*, 34(4), 601–615.

Polanyi, M. (1966). *The tacit dimension*. London: Routledge & Kegan Paul.

Roberts, J., & Armitage, J. (2008). The ignorance economy. *Prometheus*, 26(4), 335–354.

Schneider, S. C., & DeMeyer, A. (1991). Interpreting and responding to strategic issues: The impact of national culture. *Strategic Management Journal*, 12(4), 307–320.

Schultz, U., & Leidner, D. E. (2002). Studying knowledge management in information systems research: Discourses and theoretical assumptions. *MIS Quarterly*, 26(3), 213–242.

Sumbal, M. S., Tsui, E., & See-to, E. W. K. (2017). Interrelationship between big data and knowledge management: An exploratory study in the oil and gas sector. *Journal of Knowledge Management*, 21(1), 180–196.

Tuomi, I. (2000). Data is more than knowledge. *Journal of Management Information Systems*, 16(3), 103–117.

Trusted, J. (1997). *An introduction to the philosophy of knowledge*. London: Macmillan Press.

Van Beveren, J. (2002). A model of knowledge acquisition that refocuses knowledge management. *Journal of Knowledge Management*, 6(1), 18–22.

Volz, K. G., & Cramon, D. Y. (2006). What neuroscience can tell about intuitive processes in the context of perceptual discovery. *Journal of Cognitive Neuroscience*, 18(12), 2077–2087.

Walczak, S. (2005). Organizational knowledge management structure. *The Learning Organization*, 12(4), 330–339.

Wilson, J. P., & Campbell, L. (2016). Developing a knowledge management policy for ISO 9001: 2015. *Journal of Knowledge Management*, 20(4), 829–844.

Wognin, R., Henri, F., & Marino, O. (2012). Data, information, knowledge, wisdom: A revised model for agents-based knowledge management systems. In L. Moller & J. B. Huett (Eds.), *The next generation of distance education: Unconstrained learning* (pp. 181–189). New York: Springer.

Zins, C. (2007). Conceptual approaches for defining data, information, and knowledge. *Journal of the American Society for Information Science and Technology*, 58(4), 479–493.

5 Big data and analytics

Is it a game changer for decision making?

Introduction

In Chapter 4 we saw how the data, information, knowledge (DIK) hierarchy has shaped thinking on the nature and sources of knowledge. Although we, and many other academics and practitioners, have expressed doubt and criticism about the basic assumptions of the model and also the effect it has had on management, and knowledge management in particular, its paradigmatic influence remains strong. With the advent of big data and analytics the influence of data on management practice is likely to grow stronger.

Two trends have driven the rise of big data and analytics. The first is the rise of the Internet (and related networks), mobile devices, and other recent technological advances; the second is the ever-increasing power of computers. Together these two sets of technologies have made available both vast amounts of data and the ability to analyse that data in real or near-real time. According to IBM's Big Data and Analytics Hub, "10 billion mobile phones will be in use by 2020, 294 billion emails sent are every day, and trillions of sensors monitor and track with each other, populating the Internet of Things with real time data" (IBM, 2011). The reach of big data and analytic knowledge is impressive and pervasive (Pauleen, Rooney, & Intezari, 2017).

According to Erickson and Rothberg (2014), applying analytical and intelligent tools in various fields has provided evidence that valuable intangible assets can be identified both inside and outside a company. Big data and analytics' fundamental capacity to bring to light heretofore hidden data patterns brings important possibilities to management decision making. Davenport also sees potential benefits from analysing big data, particularly because big data is often about the external world – both customers and non-customers alike – so it can provide new perspectives on the business environment (Pauleen, 2017a).

Like many technological breakthroughs before, big data and analytics has hit the popular and academic presses like a wave. While other technologies sometimes fade away or are replaced by newer ones, we feel that the growing ubiquity of data and the increasing power of analytics will come to dominate information and even management discourse. This includes the ways they can augment, or even replace, human decision making. When it comes to management decision making, however, we strongly believe that while organizations must make the best possible use of big data and analytics, they must also temper this use with wise and prudent decision-making processes.

In the business context, big data and analytics are often discussed together. Data and analytics are not new to business. Data have been used in traditional functions such as business intelligence since the 1950s (Petter, DeLone, & McLean, 2012). While big data and analytics are sometimes confused with each other, with the terms being used interchangeably (McAfee & Brynjolfsson, 2012), they are in fact two separate things. Big data refers to the huge volumes of data that are continuously produced in different forms and by numerous data sources. Big data is discussed in detail below. Analytics refers to the techniques for exploring and investigating data using statistical and operations analyses to gain insight, usually to improve decision making.

Although big data and analytics are two different things, they are joined in the sense that they each derive their value from the other. Big data without analytics is of no value whatsoever, while analytics without big data is akin to traditional data analysis; it certainly has value, but not of the potential magnitude that big data would confer. In this book we acknowledge this joining of the two technologies by generally linking them together through the term 'big data and analytics'.

In this chapter, we introduce big data and analytics in some depth. We look at how big data and analytics can be used with both positive and negative effect in decision making. We also discuss the relationship between big data and knowledge and their incorporation into tactical and strategic decision making when dealing with complex and wicked problems.

Big data and analytics

As mentioned above, while big data and analytics represent two different technologies, it is difficult to discuss one without the other. Here we describe the two technologies separately, while noting just how interlinked they are. It is worth noting that data and analytics have been around for some time. Since the 1950s, traditional data sets were housed in so-called data warehouses and managed by database management systems (DBMS). This data was analysed with data analytics and used to support decisions and business processes (Chen, Chiang, & Storey, 2012; Davenport, 2013; Intezari & Gressel, 2017). Some argue that the changes in big data analytics are evolutionary (Davenport, 2013); others say they are revolutionary (Bryant, Katz, & Lazowska, 2008).

The evolution from traditional data to big data can be described as happening in three stages (Davenport, 2013). The first stage, Analytics 1.0, is the era of Business Intelligence (BI). At this stage, data was used in business applications such as managing information about customers, optimizing production, as well as improving and supporting decision making. The data used by companies at this stage were mostly structured, stored in relational Database Management Systems, and mainly used for business reporting purposes (Chen et al., 2012). Davenport (2013) calls the second phase Analytics 2.0. The collected data, at this stage, is web-based and the application of data revolves around the use of the Internet and social media to improve business functions. The nature of the data is unstructured. The data is used to optimize the company's online presence and analyse customer online behaviour (Chen et al., 2012). The current era of big data evolution is Analytics 3.0. Compared with the first two stages, Analytics 3.0 offers more data-enriched contributions and to a wider range of industries and companies from start-ups to multinational conglomerates (Davenport, 2013). Data are mobile and sensor-based and adapted to a specific location or context, which offers the ability to provide more targeted services to users (Chen et al., 2012).

Big data and analytics have also been characterized as revolutionary, as they offer new opportunities for providing newly and rapidly available insight based on data. As discussed below, big data is different from standard data. Big data offers a significantly high volume of data, generated in or near-real time, and in a wide range of formats. Accordingly, operating and implementing big data and producing value requires highly-specialized analytical tools, more complicated techniques, and more highly trained analysts. For example, a firm can now better understand, in near-real time, how its customers feel about the firm's products and services by applying sentiment analyses, or natural language processing tools, to customers' comments on social media.

We are less concerned with whether big data and analytics are evolutionary or revolutionary and more concerned with how the scope of these changes can potentially have an impact on management decision making.

What is big data?

The term 'big data' was coined by Doug Laney in 2001 while at the IT research and advisory firm Gartner (Laney, 2001). Big data can be defined as huge amounts of structured or unstructured data generated moment by moment by a wide range of technologies and data sources, including, but not limited to, social media, sensors, mobile devices, Internet of Things, radio frequency identification (RFID), customer transactions, and so forth (Kacfah Emani, Cullot, & Nicolle, 2015). Big data is generally defined and distinguished from traditional data by three characteristics, known as the 3Vs: volume, velocity, and variety (Kudyba, 2014; McAfee & Brynjolfsson 2012; Russom, 2011).

Big data involves enormous volumes of data that far exceed the size of traditional datasets. Such volumes of data cannot be readily stored, managed, nor analysed using traditional database management systems (Watson & Marjanovic, 2013). Storing data in the 'cloud' and advanced analytics are required.

Big data is also different from the traditional data in terms of the speed of data creation and analysis (Velocity). Big data are processed in real time or near-real time (Hazen, Boone, Ezell, & Jones-Farmer, 2014; McAfee & Brynjolfsson, 2012) through "continuous flows and processes" (Davenport et al., 2013, p. 23). Unlike traditional data, which are collected from past events, big data and analytics represent the analysis of live or near-live streaming data providing information about real-time events (Davenport, 2014). The criticism of the slow process of rational decision making (discussed in Chapter 6) may arguably be addressed by this characteristic of velocity. Big data and analytics offer the opportunity for simultaneous data gathering and analysis, which can provide decision makers with more flexibility and the possibility of faster decisions (Chen et al., 2012; O'Leary, 2013). Operational management decisions also can hugely benefit from velocity. Operational decisions are often based on pre-defined rules and very strict procedures, which can be automated. For example, in a manufacturing company, feeding defect-detecting machinery with real-time data can improve the effectiveness and pace of an assembly line. The velocity of data is also crucial for tactical or even strategic decision making, since certain decisions can be influenced by up-to-the-minute data that is simultaneously being gathered and analysed.

In addition to volume and velocity, big data comes from diverse sources and in different formats (Variety) (Davenport, 2013; McAfee & Brynjolfsson, 2012). Data can be structured (such as click stream counts) or unstructured (customers' comments on social media). Data can be collected from sources internal or external to the organization and from formal or informal sources. Data sources may include business reports,

Table 5.1 Distinctive big data characteristics and decision making

Dimension	Description	Decision-making
Volume	Enormous amount of data that cannot be handled by traditional databases and analytical technologies.	Data is an important source of information when making decisions (Chapters 4 and 6). Big data volume, however, may pose challenges to the decision maker; e.g., how much data is enough? Which data to use?
Velocity	Data is continuously produced and processed in or near real-time.	Can enable the decision maker to have real-time information and a more accurate understanding of the decision situation.
Variety	Data are generated in different formats and from diverse sources and technologies.	Different data sources and formats may provide new insight into the decision-situation and reveal different aspects of the decision situation.

communications over social networks, sensor data, GPS signals, and as numerical or graphical, textual, audio, or video files and so on (Davenport, 2013; O'Leary, 2013). In the past, data sources were often internal to the organization and structured such as the data produced by ERP or CRM systems.

Two additional Vs – value and veracity – have also been identified, extending the characteristics of big data to 5Vs (Kacfah Emani et al., 2015). Value and veracity, however, are not distinct characteristics of big data only, as these two Vs can be applied to traditional data as well. For this reason, we did not include the two characteristics in Table 5.1. The value and veracity of data, however, have particular relevance to the use of big data. Veracity means that the data sources need to be appropriate and credible so that the data they produce is reliable and trustworthy (Jagadish et al., 2014; Sathi, 2012). Value refers to the economic benefits that the use of big data offers (Bumblauskas et al., 2017; Colombo & Ferrari, 2015; Mishra et al., 2017). In decision making, the veracity of the data set that is used in the decision-making process is critical; it is what gives the data set value. If the data is corrupted in any way, there is no value in it and indeed it is likely to harm the decision-making process and output.

An example of a potentially corrupted data set, according to Snowden, is one of the key sources of big data: social media (Pauleen, 2017b). According to Snowden, social media is an unconstrained system, where a significant percentage (30–40%) of 'tweets' on any given subject are bot-generated. Bot-generated means the data (tweets) are being generated by computer programs, not humans. If organizations are basing decisions, for example on marketing products, on information derived from computer-generated data, they need to be very clear about the veracity and value of such data. As Snowden explains:

> you can't really trust social media within half an hour of a catastrophe, because people start to play games with it; anything explicit will sooner or later be gamed. If an algorithm can interpret it, then an algorithm can be generated to create it.
>
> (Pauleen, 2017b, p. 13)

The source and the timing of big data can be seen to be critical factors in judging its veracity and value. For managers to make effective use of big data it "requires one to create value against the volume, variety and veracity of data while it is still in motion (velocity), not just after it is at rest" (Kacfah Emani et al., 2015, p. 72).

Big data is so large that traditional infrastructure cannot contain it. In tandem with the increase in data sources and the power of analytics, data warehousing has also grown. Big data is now primarily held and analysed in the 'cloud'. Cloud computing is the leasing of computer resources and technologies over the Internet (Kroenke & Boyle, 2017).

What is analytics?

Since 1990, business intelligence and analytics (BI&A) has evolved from a mere IT resource to "an organizational capability of strategic importance" (Lahrmann, Marx, Winter, & Wortmann, 2011, p. 1). According to the IT research and advisory firm Gartner, business intelligence is an umbrella term that covers analytics, big data, infrastructure, and best practices that enable access to and analysis of data to improve decisions and organizational performance (Gartner, 2018). Similarly, Chen and Storey (2012) define BI&A as "the techniques, technologies, systems, practices, methodologies, and applications that analyse critical business data to help an enterprise better understand its business and market, and make timely business decisions" (p. 1166).

Analytics is the term specifically used to describe data analysis applications (Watson, 2014) and includes the use of tools to analyse all data, not necessarily big data. Simply collecting and storing big data creates no value. When analytics is performed, the data can be turned into information that can then be used: for example, to improve decision making within a business (Watson, 2014).

The growth in data has been accompanied by the increasing power and sophistication of analytic technologies. Chen and Storey (2012) trace the evolution of big data and analytics as BI&A 1.0 (databases), BI&A 2.0 (Internet-based data), through to BI&A 3.0 (data from mobile phones, tablets, wearables, etc.). The "big impact" from these huge amounts of data is the "new science, discovery and insights ... obtained from the highly detailed, contextualized and rich contents of relevance to any business or organization" (p. 1168). According to Chen and Storey (2012), the reach and impact of BI&A lends itself to greatly influencing areas as diverse as e-commerce, market intelligence, e-government, science and technology, health and well-being, and security and public safety.

Advanced analytics, in contrast to traditional analytics, can be considered a collection of sophisticated tools and multiple analytic methods that primarily serve the discovery and exploration of large, detailed, and varied datasets (Russom, 2011). Analytics can provide estimative results as well as actionable descriptive, predictive, and prescriptive results (Kaisler, Armour, Espinosa, & Money, 2013). Tools and techniques that are considered part of advanced analytics are, for example, complex NoSQL queries, data mining, and statistical analysis, as well as data visualization (Russom, 2011).

While equipped for big data sets, these techniques can also be employed for the exploration of traditional datasets, as Bose (2009, p. 156) defines advanced analytics as "a general term which simply means applying various advanced analytic techniques to data to answer questions or solve problems". Managers mainly employ them for predictive and prescriptive purposes to predict and optimize outcomes (Barton, 2012;

Gartner, 2014), but the techniques can also benefit descriptive analytics. These three types of analytics – descriptive, predictive, and prescriptive – are characterized by their purpose and the tools they utilize, as described below.

Descriptive analytics is used to describe events and phenomena to determine past and present opportunities or potential problems (Delen & Demirkan, 2013). Examples of descriptive analytics include using business reporting tools (e.g. Balance Scorecards, Customer Survey Reports, and Web Traffic Reports). Organizations use the information gained from the reports to identify and tackle various shortcomings and improve their future performance (Davenport, 2013; Delen & Demirkan, 2013). The velocity aspect of big data can provide real-time information about what is actually going on at a given time, and, therefore, offers detailed insight into an organization's situation and customer base (LaValle, Lesser, Shockley, Hopkins, & Kruschwitz, 2011; Watson & Marjanovic, 2013). Descriptive analytics can be very advantageous in the problem-finding phase of decision making. Using real-time data can provide a more accurate understanding of the decision situation.

Predictive analytics utilizes "data and mathematical techniques to discover explanatory and predictive patterns [...] representing the inherent relationships between data inputs and outputs" (Delen & Demirkan, 2013, p. 361). Managers can use the analytics to gain insight about future situations. Predictive analytics can be linked to the future-thinking aspect of wise decision making (as discussed in Chapters 7 and 8) and can possibly lead to better anticipation of decision consequences. Predictive analytics enables the decision maker to make more appropriate decisions, by drawing on a more forward-looking analysis of the current and future conditions (Davenport, 2013). Predictive analytics utilizes qualitative and quantitative techniques to analyse various scenarios to explain how purposeful or unplanned alterations to a given condition can lead to different observations and experiences (Waller & Fawcett, 2013).

At some point in the management decision-making process, especially once the problem has been defined, and various possible alternatives have been created and analysed, the decision maker needs to decide what alternative to choose and how to put it into action. *Prescriptive analytics* can offer significant benefits at this stage, by providing information about which alternatives are optimal, which can help to determine the best course of action (Davenport, 2013; Delen & Demirkan, 2013). Prescriptive analytics can be very useful in both the problem-finding and problem-solving phases. Embedding prescriptive analytics may reduce deviation from the optimal solution. Prescriptive analytics draws on the assumptions of the rational school of decision making and leads to more rational models. Rational models assume that the optimal outcome is logically expected to be achieved if the decision maker strictly follows specific rules and procedures (Bazerman & Moore, 2009). We shall further discuss the rational approach to decision making in Chapter 6. Table 5.2 summarizes the three kinds of analytics and their relationship to decision making.

For decision making, the benefits of using big data and analytics depend on the extent to which the information gained from the analysis is valid and able to be incorporated into the decision-making process.

How can big data and analytics be used in decision making?

According to Davenport (Pauleen, 2017a), the most sophisticated organizations today are using big data combined with 'small' (traditional) data and traditional decision

Table 5.2 Analytics types

Analytics type	Description	Decision making
Descriptive analytics	Analytics that is used to describe events and phenomena in order to determine well-defined past and present opportunities or potential problems.	Descriptive analytics can be useful in the problem-finding phase of decision making. Using real-time data can provide a more accurate understanding of the decision situation.
Predictive analytics	Analytics that is used to discover predictive patterns by exploring the inherent relationships among phenomena in the past and present.	Advantageous when various alternatives need to be developed and analysed; Is closely linked to the future-thinking aspect of wise decision making and can lead to better understanding of a decision's consequences.
Prescriptive analytics	Analytics used to provide information about what alternatives exist and how they can be implemented to achieve expected outcomes.	Draws on the assumptions of rational decision making. Very useful in both the problem-finding and problem-solving phases; Can reduce deviation from the optimal solution in decision situations that require high levels of rationality.

support systems and newer "data products".[1] This, he says, is dramatically increasing the scope and scale of analytical activity for these organizations, resulting in more data-based decisions.

Earlier we described Analytics 1.0, 2.0, and 3.0. Davenport describes the next level up, "analytics 4.0", as highly automated and networked environments in which most or all decisions are made without human intervention. Financial trading and electricity flows fall into this category. Unfortunately, he says, we do not understand these environments very well and they often break down. We need much better insights about how they work before they arrive on a large scale (Pauleen, 2017a).

To be clear, big data and analytics are "not a single out-of-the-box product" (Loshin, 2013, p. 21). Making effective use of big data demands a complicated combination of tools, techniques, skills, and knowledge, and as we will argue later, wisdom (Weerasinghe, Pauleen, Scahill, & Taskin, 2018). Companies that were born in the Internet era – such as Google, Facebook, and Amazon – were built around big data (Davenport & Dyché, 2013); thus, these companies and their managers generally possess the capabilities and mind-set to manage and make use of it.

Companies that existed before the Internet era are also looking into opportunities to develop their businesses by effectively using big data and analytics (Bholat, 2015). To integrate these technologies, traditional businesses may need to make many changes, not only with their technological infrastructure, but also with their human resources. Data scientists may be needed and they will be working together with business analysts (Davenport & Dyché, 2013) and of course, business managers. It will be challenging to integrate these people and technologies into a seamless whole that will be able to exchange relevant information and knowledge in an effective decision-making process.

Later in this chapter we identify the key features that big data and knowledge systems should have to facilitate the seamless integration of big data and knowledge into the decision-making process.

In a recent interview (Pauleen, 2017a), Tom Davenport, noted academic and management consultant, commented on important trends in big data and analytics. He pointed out that big data and analytics environments already involve many automated decisions in mechanical and low-end service processes. While big data and analytics is now penetrating knowledge work such as human decision making, he finds companies are still not aware of this potential. Specifically, he thinks cognitive computing or artificial intelligence, which stands at the intersection of big data, analytics, and knowledge management, will be able to make sense of massive amounts of data that will not only inform human decision making but soon be able to make decisions (Pauleen, 2017a). According to Davenport, this will have tremendous implications for how organizations are run. However, he offers the caveat that "most organizations don't even know what their most important decisions are, and they couldn't tell you whether their decisions are getting better or not, probably because decision-making is all tied up with power, ego, and so forth" (Pauleen, 2017a, p. 8).

Essentially what Davenport is saying is that although organizations have access to cutting-edge technologies with great potential to locate emerging decision situations and in many cases to effectively deal with them, the limitations in doing so are human, and in particular, human traits that are the antithesis of wisdom. According to Davenport the goal of big data and quantitative analysis is to extract insights (usually prescriptive or predictive) from the analysis of the data and use them to inform decisions. Business intelligence has the same goal, but it is usually done through the use of descriptive analytics or reporting. All three should be used to inform decisions and actions, although, Davenport says, there is often a poor connection between the sourcing of data or knowledge, the analysis thereof, and the decisions being made (Pauleen, 2017a).

Snowden relates his concern that managers make the assumption that computer algorithms interpret facts the same way that human beings interpret them, which he says is dubious (Pauleen, 2017b). Human beings have evolved for abductive thinking, whereas big data actually takes a deductive or inductive approach to interpretation. Snowden also worries that analytics is becoming a substitute for human judgement. He believes that while big data and analytics are useful techniques, they have been overhyped, and they have not actually been 'qualified' or proven reliable. In complex or wicked decision situations, where problems do not have an enumerable or a well-described set of potential solutions, analytics may provide only partial help at best. In such situations, human judgement, experience, knowledge, and expertise will be essential.

As we shall see in the following chapters, one of the key aspects of good decision making is being able to judge what is good and useful data or information for the decision situation at hand and then using it appropriately in the decision-making process. What Davenport and Snowden are saying is that so far, they are not seeing managers and organizations effectively using big data and analytics in decision situations.

There are other reasons to be concerned about whether big data and analytics by themselves can substitute for human experience, knowledge, and judgement. The critical research and practitioner literature brings issues around the efficacy of predictive analytics into sharper focus (Pauleen et al., 2017). It argues that historical data are being used as building blocks to create predictive analytic knowledge and that one result of this is that "Judgment and incentive [...] are rendered explicitly in quantitative terms" to "manufacture the simulation of security" (Danisch, 2011, pp. 246–247). This reliance on analytics-derived knowledge may be robbing people of the opportunity to exercise and develop common sense or practical wisdom (cf. Danisch, 2011; Schwartz & Sharpe, 2010) and resilience in the face of ambiguity and uncertainty.

This danger was made shockingly obvious in the recent global financial crises where it was shown that unwise behaviours around information generation and use were contributing factors (Pauleen et al., 2017). The Financial Crises Inquiry Commission (2011) had this to say about predictive analytics: "Financial institutions and credit rating agencies embraced mathematical models as reliable predictors of risks, replacing judgment in too many instances. Too often, risk management became risk justification" (xix).

Caution is urged when it comes to the use of big data and analytics as these will involve new ways of deciding and managing (Davenport, 2006). Pauleen et al. (2017) suggest that organizations and managers will want to be aware that such use may have the effects of helping to diminish wisdom, resilience, and common sense.

In the rush to embrace big data and analytics, the role of knowledge should not be overlooked.[2] Pauleen and Wang (2017) argue that knowledge plays a fundamental role in the management and use of big data and analytics. Their argument turns the DIK hierarchy discussed in Chapter 4 literally on its head as the premise of their argument is that knowledge is central to any discussion around big data and analytics for two rather simple and obvious reasons.

First, it is human knowledge that developed the capabilities of big data and analytics; that is, without knowledge, big data and analytics do not exist. Human knowledge and experience are necessary to decide where to collect data and the analytics for analysing it (Pauleen & Wang, 2017). The second is that it is human knowledge that will decide how the information generated from big data and analytics will be used (Pauleen & Wang, 2017). Whether the data generated are used in operational, tactical, or strategic areas, knowledge will guide its use. It is impossible, therefore, to negate the influence of human knowledge and experience when discussing the influences on and the impact of big data and analytics.

According to Pauleen and Wang (2017), although big data may (theoretically) be collected and analysed without any particular objective in mind, in the vast majority of cases, the collection and analysis of big data will be initiated for three main reasons: supporting operations, exploring new business opportunities, and providing up-to-date information for tactical and strategic decision making.

For operations, big data and analytics can be used to develop automated responses to pre-defined existing problems. In such cases, data may be collected via enterprise-wide and inter-organizational information systems. Managers can use data analytics applications to get needed information in areas as diverse, for example, as warehouse stocking, geographical information for agricultural management, or traffic trends for city planning.

Another motivation to use big data and analytics can be to explore new business opportunities. In this case, there is no clear organizational problem to be solved, but the technologies can be used to look for new patterns that can lead to new opportunities or support strategic initiatives. Amazon Web Services and Google Cloud Platform provide such services to help companies identify new opportunities (aws.amazon.com; cloud.google.com).

The third main reason, and the one we are most concerned about in this book, is the use of big data and analytics to support tactical and strategic decision making to deal with wicked problems and achieve organizational goals. Below we discuss this important application of big data and analytics.

From big data to knowledge in tactical and strategic decision making

Decision situations at the tactical and strategic levels are often ambiguous and complex. Mathematical modelling can be used to determine relationships between variables and develop descriptive, predictive, or prescriptive models of the strategic decision situations. Nevertheless, because of the considerable ambiguity, uncertainty, and risk associated with these decisions (McKenzie, van Winkelen, & Grewal, 2011), effective use of big data and analytics requires high levels of human judgement, experience, expertise, and knowledge to judge the value of the data and understand the implications of the analysis for the decision situation.

Organizations need to link their strategic decision making with their knowledge assets (Nonaka, 1988, 1994). Therefore, to extract useful decision-making knowledge from big data, organizational knowledge systems need to be linked to their big data and analytics capabilities (Intezari & Gressel, 2017). Linking knowledge management with big data and analytics can facilitate the integration of human knowledge and insight into the interpretation and implementation of big data and analytics in strategic decision situations. Intezari and Gressel (2017) suggest that such big data-supported knowledge systems should be social, cross-integral, integrative, simple, and understandable as well as dynamic and agile.

The *social* aspect is critical as the exchange of knowledge through social connections can enhance the formulation and implementation of organizational strategies (Ahearne, Lam, & Kraus, 2014). Successful incorporation of big data into strategic decisions requires the effective collaboration between those who are involved in the decision-making process. These may include the strategy analysts, data analysts, and management decision makers. Cooperation and communication between these key specialists reduce the chance of misalignment between big data analyses and the organization's strategic goals.

Closely linked to the social aspect of the big data knowledge systems is the multi-language processing feature. The systems need to be *cross-lingual*, supporting natural language processing, to effectively capture, process, and disseminate the knowledge required for interpreting big data analysis and incorporate the analytics into strategic decision making. This aspect can make big data knowledge systems more *integrative* in collecting, consolidating, and connecting fragmented and scattered as well as structured and unstructured data and knowledge. To this end, the systems should be *simple and understandable*. That is, the systems need to be designed in such a way that the decision maker and all other participants involved in the system can understand and have confidence in using them.

Big data knowledge systems should also be *dynamic* and *agile* (Intezari & Gressel, 2017), as the speed of tactical and strategic decision making is directly related to organizational performance (Baum & Wally, 2003; Eisenhardt, 1989). Davenport (2013) emphasizes that the primary objective of using big data is to make decisions in real time. For this reason, the big data knowledge systems should enable strategy analysts and managers to handle the velocity of big data and transform the data into useful knowledge.

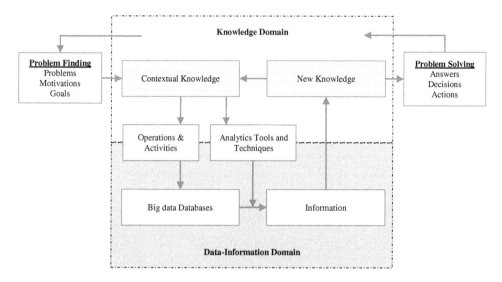

Figure 5.1 Big data, analytics, and knowledge management (adapted from Pauleen & Wang, 2017)

Pauleen and Wang (2017) developed a big data/analytics knowledge management model that illustrates how what they call 'contextual' organizational knowledge is used to manage the use of big data and analytics (Figure 5.1). Contextual knowledge includes the tacit knowledge of employees, implicit knowledge contained in organizational processes and activities, outputs such as products and services, and stakeholders throughout the supply chain including intended markets (Aspers, 2006). This contextual knowledge can function at operational, tactical, and/or strategic levels.

At operational levels managers and practitioners need to use knowledge to set up infrastructure and organizational systems parameters to establish the environments for data collection. This is commonly seen, for example, in enterprise systems environments where the configuration of business rules and parameters has to be done before transactions can occur.

At more tactical or strategic levels, knowledge can bring focus to more complex environments such as global supply chains in which big data such as multinational consumers' data and multi-source marketing data (e.g. the integration of population census, product types, and regional industrial profiles) might be stored in various database management systems and IT platforms. The use of big data at these levels will require knowledge to integrate additional infrastructure and IT staff support.

Higher levels of knowledge in the form of human inputs are exemplified when analysts analyse big data with either a specific purpose in mind or when exploring new opportunities. In such cases, an analyst would apply contextual knowledge (in the form of human knowledge and experience) to extract relevant information from big data. In addition, contextual knowledge is applied when choosing the analytic tools used in new knowledge identifying processes. For example, key search words via text mining may be presented by data attributes of frequency, region, and gender. It will be the analysts' decision regarding which key words will be analysed.

In this third situation, the combination of data analysis and human input will generate new knowledge. This new knowledge provides insight into how to address

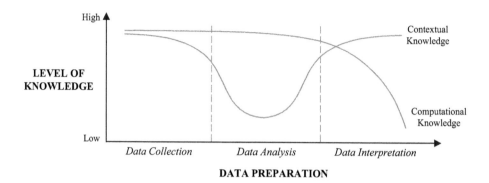

High

LEVEL OF
KNOWLEDGE

Contextual
Knowledge

Computational
Knowledge

Low

Data Collection   Data Analysis   Data Interpretation

DATA PREPARATION

Figure 5.2 Data preparation for decision-making

previously-defined problems or to initiate subsequent organizational actions. A good example of creating knowledge based on big data and analytics to initiate new actions is Amazon's recommender system, which uses customer data and dedicated analytics to suggest products to customers.

Finally, the output of the model results in decisions, answers, and actions. In each case, according to Pauleen and Wang (2017), whether at the operations, tactical, or strategic level, (human) knowledge will be required to make the best use of whatever the big data and the analytics have offered.

In addition to contextual knowledge, computational knowledge also plays an important role in the use of big data and analytics in the 'data preparation process' (Figure 5.2). The quality of a data-based decision depends on the decision maker's knowledge to transform the data into knowledge and to apply the results of the analytics to the decision situation. The depth, breadth, and accuracy of the data analysis also determine the quality of the decision. Both contextual and computational knowledge play a role in the preparation of data for decision making at three levels: the data collection level, the data analysis level, and the data interpretation level.

The data collection phase encompasses three activities: data identification, data collection, and data evaluation. Before the manager is able to make a data-based decision, the required data need to be identified and collected from credible sources and stored in reliable data storage. The data sources must be credible to ensure data correctness and accuracy (Sathi, 2012). The data collection phase also includes cleansing data and making them ready for future use. Then the relevance and accuracy of the data must be evaluated in relation to the decision situation.

Once the required data is retrieved from the data set, the data needs to be analysed. In this phase, data is analysed using analytics techniques, tools, and statistical algorithms. To have a reliable output from the data preparation process, it is necessary to ensure that correct techniques and tools are used for analysing the data. Data collection and analysis phases require a high level of computational knowledge, which refers to the analytics expert's knowledge of and skills in using computers and statistical software packages.

Unlike the data analysis phase, which requires a high level of technical knowledge about analytics techniques and tools, the data collection and data interpretation phases engage extensive knowledge about the context of the decision. Contextual knowledge is the decision maker's knowledge about the decision situation, including the problem, motivations, and desired goals. Contextual knowledge is often held by the manager and decision maker, whereas computational knowledge is held by the data analyst. As seen in Figure 5.2, the data collection phase requires high levels of both computational and contextual knowledge. The decision maker and data analyst should collaborate to determine what data is required in a given decision situation, what data sources should be used, and how to collect the data.

The output of the data analysis can be formatted as numbers, charts, or statements, and, as discussed earlier in the chapter, can be descriptive, predictive, or prescriptive in effect. In phase three, data interpretation, the outputs of data analysis are interpreted by the decision maker to identify the possible solutions and to determine how the results can be applied to the decision situation. As discussed above, human knowledge and experience are necessary to decide where to collect data and which analytics to apply as well as how the information generated from big data and analytics will be used (Pauleen & Wang, 2017).

Before we move on to Chapter 6 and discuss different approaches to management decision making, we think it is important to know that data-based decisions, especially the decisions that are driven by big data and analytics, are significantly technology-bounded. Due to the volume and velocity of big data, it is almost impossible to perform the data collection and data analysis without implementing appropriate technologies such as Internet-linked computers, advanced database management systems, and complicated statistical software packages.

Moreover, data-based decisions may pose significant communication challenges to the decision maker. In the decision situations where the data analyst (who is mainly involved in the data collection and data analysis phases) and the decision maker (who interprets and uses the results of the analysis) are not the same person, effective communication becomes critically important in data analytics and decision making. The data analyst's lack of contextual knowledge as well as the decision maker's lack of computational knowledge may cause problems when it comes to providing information in decision situations. For example, if the decision maker's data needs are miscommunicated to the big data and analytics expert, inaccurate or insufficient data may be collected and inaccurate analysis may be applied to the data by the analytics expert. Similarly, if the decision maker does not have a certain level of computational knowledge, she is likely to misunderstand the complexity involved in data collection and analysis, and also misinterpret the results of the data analysis.

As pointed out above, Internet-based companies that have emerged in the age of big data and analytics have tended to address these issues by employing staff with multiple knowledge sets. More traditional companies, however, are finding these issues challenging to resolve. We suggest that both the management decision makers and analysts should have a certain level of both computational and contextual knowledge.

Chapter summary

In this chapter, we looked at big data and analytics. Big data and analytics represent two different technologies. Nevertheless, it is difficult to discuss one without the other. Big data is different from traditional data and characterized in terms of volume, velocity, and variety. Analytics refers to the use of sophisticated tools and methods that primarily serve the discovery and exploration of large, detailed, and varied datasets. Analytics is performed to turn data into information that can then be used to improve performance within a business. There are three types of analytics: descriptive, predictive, and prescriptive.

We also looked at the use of big data and analytics in organizations. The potential of these technologies in automating business functions and increasing business opportunities is significant. The risk, however, as we have pointed out, is that these technologies may subsume the essential characteristics of human decision making including judgement, experience, expertise, and knowledge. It is human knowledge that will decide where to collect data, what analytics to apply for analysis, and how the information generated from big data and analytics will be used.

We also discussed the role of knowledge as a critical mediator between big data and analytics and human decision making. Knowledge as a mediator manifests both in technical and human circumstances. In technical circumstances, knowledge and knowledge management systems can act to ascertain and augment the value of big data and analytics use in organizations. In terms of human input, it is the shared knowledge of data scientists, business analysts, and management decision makers and the way they understand and use data and analytics that will lead to effective decision making. Decision-making processes and the specific role of knowledge in decision making are discussed in detail in the next chapter.

Notes

1 Data products are sets of (analysed) data that can be purchased from third-party providers.
2 A recent special issue in the *Journal of Knowledge Management* – 2017 *21*(1) – focused on the relationships between knowledge, knowledge management, and big data and analytics. The articles covered the technologies of big data and analytics as well as their uses in management and decision making.

References

Ahearne, M., Lam, S. K., & Kraus, F. (2014). Performance impact of middle managers' adaptive strategy implementation: The role of social capital. *Strategic Management Journal*, 35 (1), 68–87.

Aspers, P. (2006). Contextual knowledge. *Current Sociology*, 54(5), 745–763.

Barton, D. (2012). Making advanced analytics work for you. *Harvard Business Review, 9010*, 78–83.

Baum, J. R., & Wally, S. (2003). Strategic decision speed and firm performance. *Strategic Management Journal*, 24(11), 1107–1129.

Bazerman, M. H., & Moore, D. A. (2009). *Judgment in managerial decision making* (7th ed.). Hoboken, NJ: John Wiley & Sons.

Bholat, D. (2015). Big data and central banks. *Bank of England Quarterly Bulletin*, 55(1), 86–93.

Bose, R. (2009). Advanced analytics: Opportunities and challenges. *Industrial Management & Data Systems*, 109(2), 155–172.

Bryant, R., Katz, R. H., & Lazowska, E. D. (2008). Big-data computing: Creating revolutionary breakthroughs in commerce, science and society. Computing Research Initiatives for the 21st Century, Computing Research Association, Version 8. Retrieved from www.cra.org/ccc/docs/init/Big_Data.pdf.

Bumblauskas, D., Nold, H., Bumblauskas, P., & Igou, A. (2017). Big data analytics: Transforming data to action. *Business Process Management Journal*, 23(3), 703–720.

Chen, H., Chiang, R. H. L., & Storey, V. C. (2012). Business intelligence and analytics: From big data to big impact. *MIS Quarterly*, 36(4), 1165–1188.

Colombo, P., & Ferrari, E. (2015). Privacy aware access control for big data: A research roadmap. *Big Data Research*, 2(4), 145–154.

Danisch, R. (2011). Risk assessment as rhetorical practice: The ironic mathematics behind terrorism, banking, and public policy. *Public Understanding of Science*, 22(2), 236–251.

Davenport, T. H. (2006). Competing on analytics. *Harvard Business Review*, 84(1), 98–107.

Davenport, T. H. (2013). Analytics 3.0. *Harvard Business Review*, 91(12), 64–72.

Davenport, T. H. (2014). *Big data at work: Dispelling the myth, uncovering the opportunities.* Boston: Harvard Business Review Press.

Davenport, T. H., & Dyché, J. (2013). Big data in big companies. International Institute for Analytics. Retrieved from http://docs.media.bitpipe.com/io_10x/io_102267/item_725049/Big-Data-in-Big-Companies.pdf.

Davenport, T. H., Barth, P., & Bean, R. (2013). How "big data" is different. *MIT Sloan Management Review*, 54(1), 22–24.

Delen, D., & Demirkan, H. (2013). Data, information and analytics as services. *Decision Support Systems*, 55(1), 359–363.

Eisenhardt, K. M. (1989). Making fast strategic decisions in high-velocity environments. *The Academy of Management Journal*, 32(3), 543–576.

Erickson, S., & Rothberg, H. (2014). Big data and knowledge management: Establishing a conceptual foundation. *The Electric Journal of Knowledge Management*, 12(2), 83–154.

Financial Crisis Inquiry Commission (2011). *The Financial Crisis Inquiry Report: Final Report of the National Commission on the Causes of the Financial and Economic Crisis in the United States*. Washington, DC: Financial Crisis Inquiry Commission.

Gartner. (2014). Gartner says advanced analytics is a top business priority [Press release]. Retrieved from www.gartner.com/newsroom/id/2881218.

Gartner. (2018). Business intelligence (BI). Retrieved from www.gartner.com/it-glossary/business-intelligence-bi/.

Hazen, B. T., Boone, C. A., Ezell, J. D., & Jones-Farmer, L. A. (2014). Data quality for data science, predictive analytics, and big data in supply chain management: An introduction to the problem and suggestions for research and applications. *International Journal of Production Economics*, 154(1), 72–80.

IBM (2011). The 2011 IBM Tech Trends Report: The clouds are rolling in... is your business ready? Retrieved from www.ibm.com/developerworks/community/blogs/ff67b471-79df-4bef-9593-4802def4013d/entry/2011_ibm_tech_trends_report_the_clouds_are_rolling_in_is_your_business_ready5?lang=en.

Intezari, A., & Gressel, S. (2017). Information and reformation in KM systems: Big data and strategic decision-making. *Journal of Knowledge Management*, 21(1), 71–91.

Jagadish, H. V., Gehrke, J., Labrinidis, A., Papakonstantinou, Y., Patel, J. M., Ramakrishnan, R., & Shahabi, C. (2014). Big data and its technical challenges. *Communications of the ACM*, 57(7), 86–94.

Kacfah Emani, C., Cullot, N., & Nicolle, C. (2015). Understandable big data: A survey. *Computer Science Review*, 17 (Aug.), 70–81.

Kaisler, S., Armour, F., Espinosa, J. A., & Money, W. (2013). Big data: Issues and challenges moving forward. Paper presented at the 46th Hawaii International Conference on System Sciences, Wailea, Maui, HI, 7–10 January.

Kroenke, D., & Boyle, R. (2017). *Using MIS* (9 Ed.). Harlow, England: Pearson Education.

Kudyba, S. (2014). *Big data, mining, and analytics: Components of strategic decision making*. Boca Raton, FL: CRC Press.

Lahrmann, G., Marx, F., Winter, R., & Wortmann, F. (2011). Business models and the internet of things. *Proceedings of the 44th Hawaii International Conference on System Sciences (HICSS)*, pp. 1–10. Berlin: Springer.

Laney, D. (2001). 3D data management: Controlling data volume, velocity, and variety. Application Delivery Strategies, META Group. 6 February. Retrieved from https://blogs.gartner.com/doug-laney/files/2012/01/ad949-3D-Data-Management-Controlling-Data-Volume-Velocity-and-Variety.pdf.

LaValle, S., Lesser, E., Shockley, R., Hopkins, M., & Kruschwitz, N. (2011). Big data, analytics and the path from insights to value. *MIT Sloan Management Review*, 52(2), 21–32.

Loshin, D. (2013). *Big data analytics: From strategic planning to enterprise integration with tools, techniques, NoSQL, and Graph*. Amsterdam: Morgan Kaufmann.

McAfee, A., & Brynjolfsson, E. (2012). Big data: The management revolution. *Harvard Business Review*, 90(10), 60–66.

McKenzie, J., van Winkelen, C., & Grewal, S. (2011). Developing organisational decision-making capability: A knowledge manager's guide. *Journal of Knowledge Management*, 15(3), 403–421.

Mishra, D., Luo, Z., Jiang, S., Papadopoulos, T., & Dubey, R. (2017). A bibliographic study on big data: concepts, trends and challenges. *Business Process Management Journal*, 23(3), 555–573.

Nonaka, I. (1988). Creating organizational order out of chaos: Self-renewal in Japanese firms. *California Management Review*, 30(3), 57–73.

Nonaka, I. (1994). 211 A dynamic theory of organizational knowledge creation. *Organization Science*, 5(1), 14–37.

O'Leary, D. E. (2013). Artificial intelligence and big data. *IEEE Intelligent Systems*, 28(2), 96–99.

Pauleen, D. J. (2017a). Davenport and Prusak on KM and big data/analytics: Interview with David J. Pauleen. *Journal of Knowledge Management*, 21(1), 7–11.

Pauleen, D. J. (2017b). Dave Snowden on KM and big data/analytics: Interview with David J. Pauleen. *Journal of Knowledge Management*, 21(1), 12–17.

Pauleen, D. J., & Wang, W. Y. C. (2017). Does big data mean big knowledge? KM perspectives on big data and analytics. *Journal of Knowledge Management*, 21(1), 1–6.

Pauleen, D. J., Rooney, D., & Intezari, A. (2017). Big data, little wisdom: trouble brewing? Ethical implications for the information systems discipline. *Social Epistemology*, 31(4), 9–33.

Petter, S., DeLone, W., & McLean, E. R. (2012). The past, present, and future of IS success. *Journal of the Association for Information Systems*, 13(5), 341–362.

Russom, P. (2011). *Big data analytics*. TDWI Best Practices Report, Fourth Quarter. Renton, WA: Transforming Data with Intelligence.

Sathi, A. (2012). *Big data analytics: Disruptive technologies for changing the game*. Boise, ID: MC Press.

Schwartz, B., & Sharpe, K. (2010). *Practical wisdom: The right way to do the right thing*. New York: Riverhead Books.

Watson, H. J. (2014). Tutorial: Big data analytics: Concepts, technologies, and applications. *Communications of the Association for Information Systems*, 34(1), 1247–1268.

Watson, H. J., & Marjanovic, O. (2013). Big data: The fourth data management generation. *Business Intelligence Journal*, 18(3), 4–8.

Weerasinghe, K., Pauleen, D. J., Scahill, S., & Taskin, N. (2018, in press). A theoretical framework of big data in healthcare. *Australasian Journal of Information Systems*, 22.

6 Decision making, the core of what managers do

Introduction

Porter (1985) emphasizes that at the core of the success or failure of a firm is the competitive ability to make decisions. Decision making is integrated into every sort of management activity, to the extent that Herbert Simon (1960) considers 'decision making' and the whole process of management to be synonymous. Being central to what managers do (Hickson, Butler, Cary, Mallory, & Wilson, 1989; Michel, 2007; Stewart, 2006) decision making can certainly be considered a critical management skill. Making decisions in the dynamic and uncertain environment of the current business world and making decisions that involve wicked problems require managers to possess and utilize a variety of skills and to have access to current and trustworthy information and knowledge sources.

In the previous chapters, we discussed the nature and value of knowledge and its relation to information and time as well as the potential influence of big data and analytics in understanding and approaching decision situations. We also discussed how the nature of a problem can affect the decision process. As discussed in Chapter 3, prudent and considered decision-making processes are required to effectively address wicked problems. We believe reliance on data and information alone is unlikely to provide an accurate understanding of a wicked problem or to offer effective solutions. Decision making itself is part of the process of understanding the problem. In this chapter, we will introduce the key aspects of decision making, particularly management decision making, and discuss different approaches to decision making. This chapter sets the stage for this book's core argument presented in the following chapters: that wisdom must play a critical mediating role in approaching decision situations and in the decision-making process itself.

Decision making

A 'decision' is defined as an "answer to some problem or a choice between two or more alternatives" (Rowe & Boulgarides, 1983, p. 4). Mintzberg, Raisinghani, and Théorêt (1976) define 'decision' as "a specific commitment to action (usually a commitment of resources)" (p. 246). Harrison (1999) defines 'decision' as being:

> a moment, in an on-going process of evaluating alternatives for meeting an objective, at which expectations about a particular course of action impel the decision maker to select that course of action most likely to result in attaining the objectives.
>
> (p. 5)

Decision making is defined as a mental activity in order to choose among alternatives (Galotti, 2002), or as a mental process of "option generation and comparison" (Schraagen, Klein, & Hoffman, 2008, p. 4). Beach and Connolly (2005) characterize decision making as a sequential process that engages three phases of diagnosis, action selection, and implementation. Of interest to the thesis of this book, Saaty (1994) raises the notions of learning, judgement, and emotions in the decision-making process.

In essence, the core aspects of any decision-making process concern comparison and choice. The most pertinent questions for a decision maker may well concern:

- how much information and knowledge to bring to bear when making a decision;
- what decision-making process to use to make effective and efficient decisions; and
- how to gauge the results or consequences of the decision.

In Chapter 4 we discussed how knowledge has both explicit and tacit components: information-based knowledge and embodied knowledge. Embodied knowledge can include experience as well as cognitive and physical abilities. Information-based knowledge in decision making can include all types of information and data, including, as we have seen in Chapter 5, big data and computer-generated analytics. Having data, information, and knowledge is an essential prerequisite in the decision-making process. Just how much knowledge and information to use in a decision is a key part of the decision-making process, as is knowledge of the decision-making process itself. Indeed, there are many different decision making processes a decision maker might choose to use when making a decision. The most effective decisions will be based on the right amount of information and knowledge and the correct choice and use of a decision-making process. Both of these, as well as the ability to gauge the effects and consequences of decisions, we suggest, may most effectively be determined by wisdom.

Why decisions are made

In organizations, decisions can be made to solve problems, enhance performance, and advance strategy. Decision situations can be categorized in terms of the visibility of the issue or problem. Some decision situations are visible or easily identifiable by the decision maker. Others might potentially or actively exist yet be hidden to the decision maker. These decision situations can be either internal or external to the organization: (1) internally, decision situations might involve strategies, procedures and policies, culture and climate, employees' satisfaction, commitment, and motivation, as well as the physical environment; and (2) external decision situations might involve changes in customers' expectations and changes associated with socio-political, environmental, and/or economic challenges. When the decision situation is identifiable, i.e. the problem is completely or to some degree visible to the decision maker, the problem-solving aspect of decision making becomes central to the decision-making process. In these situations, the need to find a solution and take appropriate action to address the problem is apparent to the decision maker. The desired outcome, and the alternatives that meet this outcome, must be defined and the best alternative put into action.

Business problems, however, do not necessarily always reveal themselves to the decision maker. They might be hidden as part of the status quo and there may even be resistance to changing the status quo. However, in complex and rapidly changing business environments, and also to meet changing stakeholder expectations, making strategic, and even operational, decisions has become routine for managers. Strategic analysts and managers must actively search for decision-making occasions and constantly monitor the consequences of strategic decisions, continuously working to meet present and future expectations and conditions. This requires managers to have the capacity for both finding and solving problems.

Herbert Simon (1960), a prolific scholar in the decision-making field, explains that decision making is a process that comprises three major phases: finding occasions for decision making, finding possible courses of action, and choosing from the courses of action. Effective solutions draw on an accurate and clear explanation of what the problem and the causes behind it are. In the process of problem finding, the decision maker has to work back from an unknown point to identify the mismatch between the current situation and a feasible and achievable ideal. In this process, the existing or potentially existing problem is articulated and the cause(s) or drivers of the issue are identified. The desired situation or outcome is then portrayed.

As we see, managers must anticipate decision situations and actively search for problems to solve. Traditionally, this was done by constantly measuring current performance against standards. The standards were developed through scientific examination of previous experiences or other benchmarks from other organizations. While mostly focused on the internal aspects of the organization to identify any signs of the need for decision making, the external environment, such as competitors' behaviour, was also monitored.

In the past a manager's capability to anticipate decision situations and identify multiple solution alternatives were significantly limited in depth and scope, compared to what managers can now do utilizing advanced business intelligence systems, big data, and analytics. Managers can now quickly collect data and information from numerous sources inside and outside their organizations, apply sophisticated statistical analyses, and better anticipate decision situations. The emergence of big data and powerful analytics is the hallmark of today's business intelligence technology that gives strong previously unavailable decision-making power to managers.

Big data and analytics, as well as all related decision support technologies, however, do not replace human judgement. People still play the fundamental role of determining how these technologies are to be used in the decision-making process (Pauleen & Wang, 2017). Managers take different approaches to decision making and will individually decide the roles of data, information, knowledge, and personal judgement when making decisions.

Different decision situations will engage different decision-making processes, which then engage a variety of functions. The functions are interrelated in a recursive process of problem finding and problem solving. In the following section we discuss how management decisions are made.

How decisions are made

Management decision making is a multi-stage, multi-criteria process encompassing various phases or functions (Hall & Hofer, 1993; Harrison, 1999; Langley, Mintzberg, Pitcher, Posada, & Saint-Macary, 1995) through which different alternatives are developed, compared, and chosen in order to achieve an optimal outcome in a given situation (Keast & Michael, 2009). Mintzberg et al. (1976) define the 'decision process' as "a set of actions and dynamic factors that begins with the identification of a stimulus for action and ends with the specific commitment to action" (p. 246). There is little consensus among practitioners and scholars about what functions represent a decision-making process as it is actually carried out in the real world, or in what order the functions should be carried out to make the most effective decisions. The decision-making process can be a logical linear process or a non-linear process.

Decision making can be generally characterized as the "purposeful coordination of interrelated activities" in three stages: (1) the pre-decision stage, during which the problem is defined and information is gathered about when the decision is to be made, about the context and scope of the decision, and about who must make the decision; (2) the decision stage, during which alternatives are compared and the best alternative is selected towards identifying a course of action; and (3) the post-decision stage, during which the decision and its implementation are explicitly justified (Zeleny, 2006, p. 4). Similarly, other scholars have categorized decision-making phases into assessment, planning, implementation, and evaluation, which incorporate nine functions in which: (1) the problem is articulated; (2) information is gathered; (3) the problem is verified; (4) the best possible resolution and outcome is articulated; (5) options are listed and tested; (6) the decision is made and implemented; (7) appropriate criteria are defined; (8) results are evaluated, and finally; (9) followed up (Maddalena & Canada, 2007).

One of the classic frameworks of decision-making phases is a five-phase framework introduced by John Dewey in 1910 (Dewey, 1933, p. 107): (1) suggestion; (2) intellectualization of the problem; (3) hypotheses; (4) reasoning; and (5) testing the hypotheses. Another classic explanation of decision making belongs to Simon (1960, 1965). Simon (1960) argues that a large part of an executive's time is spent on searching the economic, technical, social, and political environment to identify decision-demanding situations. This process accounts for the first phase of the decision-making process, the intelligence activity. In the second phase, the design activity, which takes most of the executive's time in the decision-making process, the executive works individually or with his associates to develop and analyse possible courses of action to handle the decision situation. Once the alternatives are developed, the decision maker enters the third phase, the choice activity, and selects a particular course of action from the available alternatives.

Others may identify different numbers of steps in the decision-making process. For example, in another classic classification (Drucker, 1967), the decision-making process is described in terms of six phases: classifying the problem, defining the problem, specifying the answer, deciding what is right, taking action, and providing feedback. Drucker (1967) argues that unless a decision is put into action, it is at best a good intention, not a decision. Accordingly, he includes 'taking action' in the decision-making process, and describe it as the most time-consuming step in the process. Drucker (1967) also emphasizes that an important phase in the decision-making process is 'deciding on what is right'. There are always boundaries around a decision-making process, and the decision maker always has to compromise. As Drucker (1967) put it "the effective executive has to start out with what is 'right' rather than what is acceptable" (p. 55). If the decision maker cannot distinguish the right compromise from the wrong compromise, then he may make the wrong decision.

There is little consensus among practitioners and scholars about what phases comprise a decision-making process. For example, Gibcus, Vermeulen, and Radulova (2008), Bazerman (2006), Harrison (1999), and Saaty (1994) all state that six steps should be taken in the process of decision making though they differ somewhat in emphasis (see

Table 6.1). Noteworthy or interesting additional steps in the decision making process proposed by scholars include: managing barriers (Nutt, 2002), creating imaginative alternatives, clarifying uncertainties, thinking about risk tolerance (Hammond, Keeney, & Raiffa, 1999), and eliciting judgements (Saaty, 1994). Table 6.1 provides examples of the approaches to the decision-making process to demonstrate the diversity of perspectives regarding the functions of the decision-making process.

Despite the diversity of perspectives on the decision phases and functions, Simon's (1960, 1965) intelligence-design-choice model is present in almost all the decision-making process classifications. For example, in a comprehensive description of decision-making processes Mintzberg et al. (1976) delineate the three decision-making phases as the central phases of a strategic decision-making process. Mintzberg and his colleagues conducted a field study of 25 strategic decision processes (decisions such as developing a new container terminal in a port, developing an urban renewal pro-gramme, developing a new runway for an airport, instituting a new treatment in a hos-pital, and developing a new TV programme), and concluded that strategic decision making while being unstructured draws on a basic structure. They identify three phases that are central to strategic decision making: identification, development, and selection. Please note that the three central routines resemble Simon's (1960) trichotomy, although the definitions that Mintzberg et al. (1976) use are slightly different. Mintzberg et al. (1976) define the three phases in terms of seven routines: recognition, diagnosis, search, design, screening, evaluation-choice, and authorization. The routines are described in Table 6.2. Mintzberg et al. (1976) emphasize that strategic decision-making processes are exploratory and cyclical. That is, during the decision-making process the decision maker may have to cycle back to earlier phases.

Mintzberg et al. (1976) go on and explain that the three decision-making phases are supported by three sets of routines: decision control routines, decision communication routines, and political routines. Decision control is meta decision making about the decision-making process itself (meta decision-making is discussed in Chapter 8). During the decision control routines, the decision maker plans his approach to the decision-making process and allocates the required resources for the decision making. The second set of routines, decision communication routines, involves exploring, inves-tigating, and disseminating information about the decision situation and the decision-making progress. The final sets of supporting routines, political routines, are key to strategic decision making. Political activities reflect "the influence of individuals who seek to satisfy their personal and institutional needs by the decisions made in an organ-ization" (Mintzberg et al., 1976. p. 262).

The two phases of development and selection phases deal with the problem-solving part of a decision-making process. For this reason, the development and selection phases can be categorized into one phase: problem solving. Generally speaking, a stra-tegic decision-making process consists of two overriding phases: problem finding and problem solving (Figure 6.1). Problem finding is the process in which the decision maker either actively looks for decision situations, or a decision situation emerges as a result of changes inside or outside the decision maker's environment. In this phase, the decision maker tries to define the problem and determine the scope of decision making. Once a problem is identified and articulated, the problem-solving phase begins. Both of these phases engage numerous functions.

The problem-finding phase generally includes the following functions: (1) evaluating the outcome of a previous decision or recognizing and assessing the current situation;

Table 6.1 Different perspectives on the decision-making process

Theorists	Functions involved in decision-making process		
	1	*2*	*3*
Simon (1960, 1965)	Intelligence: Finding decision-making occasions	Design: Finding possible course of action	Choice: Choosing among courses of action
Mintzberg et al. (1976)	Identification	Development	Selection
Beach and Connolly (2005)	Diagnosing the decision problem	Selecting an action	Implementing the selected action
Maddalena and Canada (2007)	Assessing	Planning	Implementing
Dewey (1933)	Suggestion	Intellectualizing the problem	Developing hypotheses
Rosanas (2013)	Identifying and defining the problem	Establishing the criteria that any solution must meet	Searching for and generating action alternatives
Nutt (2002)	Collecting information	Indicating desired results	Establishing a systematic search for ideas
Galotti (2002)	Setting goals	Gathering information	Decision structuring
Drucker (1967)	Classifying the problem	Defining the problem	Specifying the answer to the problem
Bazerman (2006)	Defining the problem	Identifying criteria	Weighting the criteria
Saaty (1994)	Identifying a problem's key elements	Eliciting judgements	Representing the formed judgements
Gibcus et al. (2008)	Recognition	Formulation	Search
Harrison (1999)	Setting managerial goals	Searching for alternatives	Comparing and evaluating alternatives
Hammond et al. (1999)	Working on the right problem	Specifying objectives	Creating imaginative alternatives

and (2) identifying and articulating the problem. Functions in the problem-solving phase commonly include: (3) setting goals; (4) establishing criteria; (5) generating alternatives; (6) evaluating and selecting the most appropriate alternative; (7) implementing the choice; and (8) evaluating and following up (Table 6.3).

Table 6.3 presents the two phases and functions of decision making. In the discussion below we provide details of the phases and functions, highlighting the roles of information and data, as well as human knowledge, judgement, values, and insight.

In the problem-finding phase, the problem central to the decision situation is either actively sought out and identified or it emerges from environmental circumstances. After a problem is recognized, it must be understood as completely as possible. To understand the problem and the wider decision situation, it is essential to have appropriate knowledge and information (Maddalena & Canada, 2007). Various kinds of knowledge,

4	5	6	7	8
Evaluating				
Reasoning	Testing the hypotheses			
Analysing and comparing action alternatives	Choosing an action alternative as the solution to the problem			
Evaluating ideas	Managing barriers			
Making a final choice	Evaluating			
Deciding what is 'right'	Putting the decision into action	Feedback		
Generating alternatives	Assessing alternatives	Calculating and choosing the highest valued option		
Prioritizing the elements of the hierarchy	Determining an overall outcome	Analysing sensitivity to changes in judgement		
Evaluation	Choice	Implementation		
The act of choice	Implementing decisions	Follow-up and control		
Understanding the consequences	Grappling with trade-offs	Clarifying uncertainties	Thinking about risk tolerance	Considering linked decisions

information, and technical data concerning the problem, the actors involved, objectives, policies, factors influencing the outcomes, time frames, and scenarios are gathered (Saaty, 1994). It is of prime importance for decision makers not only to acquire adequate information, but also to acquire real understanding of the problem, context, and consequences of the decision. Bazerman and Moore (2009) suggest that identifying and defining the problem require accurate judgement; thus they identify three errors that managers often make in this step. The errors are: (1) "defining the problem in terms of a proposed solution"; (2) "missing a bigger problem"; and (3) "diagnosing the problem in terms of its symptoms" (p. 2).

In the problem-solving phase, there are several functions that are commonly applied.

Table 6.2 Strategic decision-making phases and routines (based on Mintzberg et al., 1976)

Strategic decision-making phases	Routines	Description
The Identification Phase	Decision recognition	Problems or opportunities are recognized.
	Diagnosis routine	The evoking stimulus is comprehended and cause-effect relationships are determined.
The Development Phase	Search Routine	This routine is provoked to find ready-made solutions.
	Design Routine	This routine is used to develop custom-made solutions.
The Selection Phase	Screen Routine	This is used to filter out unfeasible ready-made alternatives.
	Evaluation-Choice Routine	The feasible alternatives are investigated and a course of action is selected.
	Authorization Routine	Authorization is sought if the decision maker does not have the authority to implement the decision.

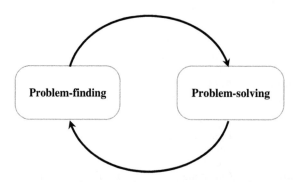

Figure 6.1 Problem-finding and problem-solving as a recursive process

Setting goals

Harrison (1999) identifies 'setting managerial goals' as the first function of the problem-solving phase. A specific goal in the form of a desired result is set, taking into consideration the decision maker's plans for the future, values, principles, and priorities (Galotti, 2002). The goals that are set may be need based (indicating that a problem must be fixed) or opportunistic (in order to make improvements) (Nutt, 2002). In either case, goal setting needs to reflect the organizational mission: i.e. addressing the current decision situation must support the organization's missions and values. For this reason, having a true understanding of and sufficient knowledge and expertise about the decision situation as well as the organizational context of the decision situation is critical for the decision maker. Goals are then used to establish a list of criteria to evaluate the possible solutions.

Table 6.3 Decision-making phases and functions including the use of DIK, insight and judgement

Phases	Decision-making functions		DIK, Insight, and Judgement
Problem finding	Evaluating the current situation decisions, or the outcome of the previous one(s) Follow up	The actual outcomes of the decisions are assessed to see whether or not the desired goals that were set at the time the decision was made were achieved. Possible improvements are identified for future decisions. * Note: in many theories of decision making, this function is identified as the final stage of the decision-making process, following the decision implementation. It is also referred to as the feedback or follow-up stage.	Data and information are central to this function. Data and information are gathered from the previous decision situations.
	Identifying and articulating the problem	The problem is recognized, identified, and defined.	This function engages insight. A correct articulation of the problem requires a better understanding of all the visible and hidden aspects of the decision situation.
Problem solving	Setting goals	A desired status in which the 'solved' problem is defined.	Based on the understanding of the problem, and based on the decision maker's insight and knowledge the desired outcomes are defined.
	Establishing criteria	The information needed for criteria development is gathered. A set of criteria is defined to evaluate and discriminate among alternatives.	Data, information, and knowledge are important in this function. The established criteria should reflect the decision maker's and organization's values. Values ensure that the alternatives that are developed in the following function do not deviate from the decision maker's and organization's fundamental mission, as well as legal and ethical commitments.
	Generating alternatives	Necessary information for developing alternatives is gathered. Possible and available options toward the achievement of the established goal are found and/or developed.	Although gathering reliable data and information is important in this function, generating appropriate alternatives requires a high level of knowledge and expertise. The decision maker needs to have a true understanding of the problem and its dimensions as well as the technical and professional knowledge related to the decision situation. The decision maker may seek advice and conduct consultation with others.

(Continued)

Table 6.3 (Continued)

Phases	Decision-making functions	DIK, Insight, and Judgement
Evaluating and selecting the most appropriate alternative	*The alternatives are judged against the criteria and one is selected.*	*As the function relies on a comparison among multiple alternatives, judgement is central to this function. The judgement is based on the decision maker's knowledge, experience, feelings, and insight.*
Implementing the choice	*The selected alternative is put into action. The decision maker takes the required actions to ensure that the decision is fully implemented during a desired time frame.*	*Knowledge, judgement, and insight are important as to when and how the decision must be implemented, or even withdrawn. The decision maker needs also to ensure that the decision is implemented by using means that are aligned with the organization's values and legal/ethical commitments.*

Establishing criteria

This function involves defining a set of criteria which are then applied to evaluating alternative actions. The function of comparing and contrasting different alternatives is not possible without appropriate criteria. Criteria are the conditions that the decision must meet: "a decision criterion is a fact or circumstance that would make [decision makers] choose a particular alternative, all else being equal" (Rosanas, 2013, p. 31). This function is conducted based on data, information, and knowledge. To establish appropriate criteria, the decision maker must have relevant and reliable knowledge of and information on the decision situation. The decision maker's knowledge of the decision situation needs to be complemented by an understanding of other elements that may be either internal or external to the organization. The criteria should reflect the decision maker's and organization's missions, values systems, and the desired outcomes. This function also requires the consideration of external elements such as professional and standard practices in the business community, and the organization's social responsibilities, as well as legal and ethical commitments. Considering the internal and external factors ensures that the alternatives that deviate from what is central to the decision maker's and organization's mission, and the legal and ethical commitments, will not be considered during the following functions (Intezari, 2016).

Generating alternatives

This function corresponds to the functions of searching for and gathering information (Galotti, 2002; Gibcus et al., 2008) and to the function of generating alternatives examined by Bazerman (2006). Through this function, the information needed for identifying possible courses of action is gathered (Bazerman, 2006; Galotti, 2002). This information may already exist in forms of tacit knowledge or experiential information in the decision maker's mind, or may be gathered through consultation with others or extended research in available databases. The decision maker may rely on his own prior experience or on others' (Rosanas, 2013).

Evaluating and selecting the most appropriate alternative

The decision maker gathers the information needed to see which alternative meets the criteria (Galotti, 2002), evaluate alternatives, and choose the final option. Different alternatives are compared and rated based on criteria. The pros and cons of each alternative are weighed. Then, one or a group of preferred alternatives are selected that, according to the criteria, are expected to meet the desired goals. The decision maker may seek further information and consultation if needed. At this stage, business intelligence and decision support systems may be very useful in gathering and analysing data and information. The decision maker may also seek new perspectives by getting advice from others from either inside or outside the organization. The function of evaluating and selecting alternatives engages a critical comparison among multiple alternatives, and, therefore, largely relies on the decision maker's judgement. Judgement finds expression in the situations that are not very straightforward (Hare, 1971), and reflects the decision maker's knowledge, experience, feelings, and insight. It is important to envision the possible consequences of each alternative. If the current alternatives do not meet the decision criteria developed in the previous function, the decision maker may also need to go back to re-evaluate the decision goals and generate or consider other alternatives.

Implementing the choice

Once the best alternative is selected, it is time to take action. Generally, the best alternative will be implemented. However, the decision maker may decide not to implement any of the alternatives due to changes in the decision situation. For example, the decision problem has been resolved, or a more significant or urgent decision situation has emerged that must be addressed. Usually though, the decision maker will go ahead and put the preferred alternative into action. Implementing a choice may be seen as separate from the decision-making process (Bazerman, 2006; Saaty, 1994), or it may be referred to as the ultimate point of the process (Harrison, 1999).

Rosanas (2013) argues that the final choice is put into action by 'real people', not 'abstract agents', and that people with different priorities and preferences may (want to) take a different course of action depending on their particular knowledge and abilities. In this respect, Drucker (1967) writes: "unless a decision has 'degenerated into work', it is not a decision; it is at best a good intention" (p. 92). The decision maker needs to take into account how and who is going to implement the decision. As Drucker (1967) suggests, the implementation commitment should not outweigh the capacities of those who are going to carry it out. Furthermore, it must be ensured that the decision is not implemented in ways that deviate from the organization's values, legal/ethical commitments, and stakeholders' legitimate expectations.

Following up

Drucker (1967) underlines that people are fallible and decisions are made by people. Therefore, the following-up function is critically important in the decision-making process. The implemented decision needs to be actively observed and critically assessed by the decision maker to understand whether or not the desired goals have been achieved. This function indicates what improvements are required to make better decisions in the future. Active observation and critical assessment, however, are often neglected or missing in many management decision-making processes. This could be due to external limitations, such as time and budget limitations, or because of the decision maker's intention, which might involve political or ethical concerns. The decision maker may refuse to apply the function just to avoid receiving negative feedback, or endangering his reputation by getting labelled as incompetent if the decision failed. From the wisdom perspective, we emphasize that the problem-solving phase must be followed by active observation and critical assessment of the consequences of the decision. This function is associated with reflection and learning: critical components of wisdom. Accordingly, information reporting and monitoring must be put in place to continuously test the actual results against the decision maker's expected outcomes.

Although the decision-making functions are presented above as a sequential or linear process, many decision-making processes will be non-sequential or non-linear (McKenna & Martin-Smith, 2005). Broadly speaking, these two major approaches to decision making are described as rational and non-rational. The two approaches encompass different understandings of the source of knowledge and its role in decision making. It is worth making the effort to understand the distinction between these two approaches as we feel both are important in effective decision making. It is also worth trying to understand why the rational approach dominates business decision making and management education. We do both in the sections below.

Rational vs. naturalist approaches to decision making

As previously discussed in Chapters 4 and 5, in the knowledge management discipline, the sources of knowledge are primarily identified as data and information, experience, and a priori and subconscious knowledge. Two main schools of thought on decision making and how they utilize knowledge and information are evident: the rationalist and the naturalist. The two schools have different approaches to decision making, approaches that in part reflect their views on the sources of information, knowledge, experience, intuition, and insight. We discuss the different approaches and their perspectives on knowledge.

The rationalist school of decision making takes a logical approach to decision making and aims to identify the steps that a decision maker should take to achieve optimal outcomes (Betsch & Held, 2012). In contrast, the naturalist approach wants to understand how decisions are actually made in situ (Messick & Bazerman, 2001). The rationalist models of decision making are normative and prescriptive. That is, the optimal outcome is logically expected to be achieved if the decision maker strictly follows specific rules and procedures and precisely assesses the values and risk preferences during the decision-making process (Bazerman & Moore, 2009). The naturalist models, however, are descriptive in nature. The theories seek to provide a description of the decision makers' cognitive and behavioural processes as they engage in making different kinds of decisions in their natural environments (Beach & Connolly, 2005). Decision-making investigations in the naturalistic school concentrate on the decision maker and complex decision-making situations where the decision maker is faced with limited resources and time (Rosen, Salas, Lynos, & Fiore, 2008).

According to the rational models of decision making, a decision is a logical and linear step-by-step process (Miller, Hickson, & Wilsdon, 2002), through which a decision is made based on clearly defined, rational processes which include defining, diagnosing, designing, and deciding (Mintzberg & Westley, 2001). From this perspective, decision making may be defined as "an orderly process, beginning with the discovery

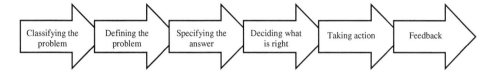

Figure 6.2 Drucker's effective decision-making process

by the decision maker of a discrepancy between the perceived state of affairs and the desired state. This desired state is usually between an ideal and a realistically attainable state" (Bass, 1983, p. 4).

Rationalists assume that the decision maker can: (1) perfectly recognize, identify, and diagnose the problem; (2) identify and stringently establish all criteria; (3) accurately set all the criteria by rating them based on their preferences; (4) perfectly know all the possible alternatives; (5) precisely assess all the alternatives against each criterion; and (6) accurately calculate and select the alternative that has the highest value (Bazerman & Moore, 2009). Data and information are, therefore, important elements in rationalist decision making. Expected outcomes and all probabilities are evaluated and measured against objective (rather than subjective) criteria. Relevant, reliable, and sufficient data and information can significantly enhance the accuracy of the objective evaluation.

Figure 6.2 by Drucker is an example of the rational decision-making process. Drucker (1967) believes that decision making relies on systematic processes with clearly defined elements.

Unlike the rationalists, naturalists do not believe that the functions of decision making in actual practice follow a set order of tasks. A manager may make a decision without necessarily going through a process of ordered phases. The functions of decision making can overlap, some functions can be skipped, and a different order may be followed. Moreover, the importance of each function in the whole process of decision making may vary, depending on the problem situation or other factors. So, according to the naturalists, providing an understanding of decisions as simple sequential functions does not grasp the complex nature of decision making.

The naturalist models are based on the assumption that people may deviate consciously or unconsciously from the principles of rational decision making in the real-world setting due to various reasons. These may include 'bounded rationality', which is discussed in more depth below (Simon, 1955, 1959), politics and power (Pettigrew, 2002; Schein, 1985), bounded willpower, and bounded self-interest (Thaler, 2000), ethics and moral considerations (Holian, 2002; Kohlberg, 1984), knowledge fallibility, and the imperfect and fallible technology and techniques that are used to gather and analyse data and information (Intezari & Pauleen, 2014; as discussed in Chapter 5).

Rational decision-making theory is also criticized for underestimating or even ignoring the influence of the decision maker's experience, environmental factors, the complexity of the task (Cannon-Bowers & Salas, 1998), emotions (Hess & Bacigalupo, 2011; Sevdalis, Petrides, & Harvey, 2007), individual differences, and divergent perceptions (Carnevale, Inbar, & Lerner, 2011; Shiloh, Koren, & Zakay, 2001). Other critiques include being choice-centric (with little support for other phases in the process of decision making) (Smith, 2008), as well as failing to predict human behaviour (Wendt, 1975) and to account for conflicts of interest (Simon, 1959) (Table 6.4). All these critiques and constraints of rational decision making are summarized in Table 6.4.

One of the classic and fundamental criticisms of rational decision making is the concept of bounded rationality, which is largely associated with many of the criticisms and constraints outlined in Table 6.4. The theory of bounded rationality argues that limited human cognitive capacities and the complexity of modern organizations mean the decision maker is unable to make perfectly rational decisions (Simon, 1945, 1960), and also that the influence of constraining factors beyond rationality is significant in decision making (Rosanas, 2013). Such constraints include: the vague and unclear nature of the issues under decision; misrepresented, incomplete, or unavailable information about the alternatives; disagreement on the criteria against which alternatives must be evaluated; and limited time and energy – which are all likely to lead to decision outcomes that are 'satisfying' and sufficient, rather than optimal (Miller et al., 2002).

Human rationality is bounded due to three major reasons (Rosanas, 2013):

- the decision maker's lack of understanding of the decision situation and preferences;
- the decision maker's lack of understanding of possible alternatives and inability to pick the best alternative; and/or
- the decision maker's inability to compare criteria.

Shiloh et al. (2001) investigated how individual variations in the decision situation affect decision making. They report that decision complexity (the number of alternatives, the number of the attributes and outcomes of each alternative, and personal variables such as deficiencies in skills, information, and readiness) can increase decision-making difficulties. They go on to argue that in addition to decision complexity and personal characteristics, the decision maker's perception of the complexity of the decision structure and difficulty (subjective decision complexity) affects his decisions. Individuals differ in their abilities to recognize and assess a problem situation, and may approach and tackle decision situations in entirely different ways.

Furthermore, constraints such as limited knowledge and information, restricted time and budget, as well as social and political considerations, among others, can affect the decision-making process. For example, to avoid further negative impacts of a decision situation on the organization, a manager, without completely examining all the aspects of the decision situation, may decide to partly and temporarily fix the problem by applying the first and easiest solution that appears to be applicable at a given time. Under time constraints, a manager may just trust his intuition and make a successful decision without even being able to clearly explain how they reached the decision.

As we can see, much of what the naturalists and bounded rationality theorists are saying resonates with how wicked problems were described in Chapter 3, i.e. wicked problems include: the problem itself, the wider circumstances around the problem, as well as the understanding, analysis, and processing of the problem. In upcoming chapters we will look at the role wisdom can play in decision making and this will include among other things the use of rational and non-rational approaches to the decision situation. In the following section, we will look at how others have approached this area in the decision-making literature.

Table 6.4 Critiques and constraints of rational decision making

Critiques	Scholars	Description
Bounded rationality	Simon (1955)	The decision maker is not capable of looking at all possible choices and their outcomes.
Less-than-perfect nature of data and information gathering and analysing techniques and technology	Chapter 4; Intezari & Pauleen (2014); Simon (1955)	Associated with the previous critique, a decision maker's bounded rationality may be due to the (poor) quality of the data and information. The means that are used to collect the data and information required for decision making may fail to provide ideal or even adequate data, information, and analysis.
Ignorance of the decision maker's experience, environmental factors, ignorance of the complexity of the task	Cannon-Bowers & Salas (1998)	Decision making is an experience-based process. That is, people make decisions in the field setting, based on their experience. Decision makers are different in terms of the amounts of experience that they bring to the decision-making situation. Decision situations may be simple, complex, or wicked.
Politics and power	Pettigrew (2002); Schein (1985)	Factors beyond the decision maker's control such as political considerations or pressure from authorities in more powerful positions may limit the decision maker's ability to make a purely rational decision.
Inability to predict human behaviour	Wendt (1975)	Rational decision-making models are too strict for predicting human behaviour. The complexity of human behaviour is underestimated.
Fails to consider conflicts of interest	Simon (1959)	Profit maximization is seen as an adequate description of the goals of an organization. Conflicts of interest may be ignored.
Bounded willpower, and bounded self-interest	Mullainathan & Thaler (2001); Thaler (2000)	Willpower: The decision maker may make decisions that are not in his or her long-term interests. Bounded self-interest: people may be willing to sacrifice their own interests to help others.
Individual differences, various subjective perceptions	Carnevale et al. (2011); Galotti et al. (2006); Shiloh et al. (2001)	Different people approach decision situations in different ways (Galotti et al., 2006). One single rational decision-making model may or may not be applicable in different decision situations, or for different people. This is mainly because the nature and structure of a problem and decision is characterized largely based on the decision maker's subjective perceptions (Shiloh et al., 2001). Therefore, different decision makers, or the same decision maker in different decision situations may make different decisions.
Omitting or undervaluing the role of emotions and feelings	Hess & Bacigalupo (2011); Sevdalis et al. (2007)	The rational decision-making models fail to take into account and provide a full explanation of how the decision maker's feelings and emotions influence or are incorporated into the decision.

(Continued)

Table 6.4 (Continued)

Critiques	Scholars	Description
Choice-centric	Smith (2008)	Decision making is a multi-phased process. The rational theory of decision making over emphasizes the function of choosing alternatives. The theory offers little support for other phases in the process of decision making.
Risk behaviour	Kahneman & Tversky (1979)	People may deviate from rational decision making, since they take different risk actions depending on the decision situation. For instance, people tend to take more risks in the decision situation that is described as a choice between two losses. However, people may be risk-averse when the same decision situation requires a choice between two gains.
Over-emphasis on future risks and rewards	Arkes & Blumer (1985); Staw (1976)	For example, when allocating resources, decision makers often tend to be affected by their past investments, rather than by attending solely to future risks and rewards.
Ethics and morality	Arnold, Dorminey, Neidermeyer, & Neidermeyer (2013); Holian (2002); Kohlberg (1984); Lindblom (1959); Maddalena & Canada (2007); Rest (1984, 1986)	This critique fails to explain how a rationalist decision maker handles norms or morality when evaluating alternatives in their decisions.
Knowledge fallibility	Chapter 4; Intezari & Pauleen (2014; 2017); Tannenbaum (1964)	The future is uncertain and knowledge of relevant existing facts may be inadequate. The decision maker can never have complete knowledge of all facts and factors underlying their choices. Moreover, gathering more data and information does not necessarily reduce uncertainty. In fact, uncertainty may be a result of an overload of information and/or the lack of effective organization and analysis of the data and information.

The dual process decision making

We made the case in Chapter 3 that business decision making today is tremendously complex due to rapid environmental changes, global complexity, vastly increased social interaction, and issues of sustainability and corporate social responsibility (McKenna & Martin-Smith, 2005). Although a classification of rational or non-rational processes can provide a clear and broad understanding of the core components of the decision situation, articulating management decision making as purely rational or non-rational does not represent how management decisions are actually made in the real world. In fact, it is almost impossible to make a purely rational or non-rational decision. Most decisions represent various combinations of the two approaches. This is because many of the decision situations that managers encounter are too complex to be readily fixed by following a set of pre-determined decision procedures or by completely trusting one's intuition and gut feeling.

Dual process theories of reasoning (Elqayam & Over, 2012; Kahneman & Frederick, 2002; Thompson & Morsanyi, 2012) suggest that decision making is based on two distinct processes of intuitive and analytic thinking (Evans, 2009, 2012; Kahneman, 2003). Intuitive thinking (also known as System 1) is typically characterized as automatic, holistic, implicit, emotional, and often unconscious or preconscious, and can lead to fast, instantaneous (and less rational) decisions (Kahneman, 2003; Stanovich & West, 2000). On the other hand, analytic (or System 2) thinking is controlled, deliberate, demanding, explicit, and often linked with conscious awareness and reasoning, and leads to rational decisions (Stanovich & Toplak, 2012; Stanovich & West, 2000). While these systems can act separately, they are often found to work in tandem (Bazerman & Moore, 2013). The two systems complement each other. System 2 can be applied to monitor the quality of the decision output from System 1. If the intuitive decision resulting from System 1 is tentative, unclear, or biased, then System 2 can be used to override or correct the automatic decision (Evans, 2003; Gilhooly & Murphy, 2005; Kahneman, 2003; Wray & Wray, 2017). On the other hand, System 1 processes can support System 2 by providing a cognitive shortcut by stopping "the combinatorial explosion of possibilities that would occur if an intelligent system [or hyper-rational person] tried to calculate the utility of all possible future outcomes" (Stanovich & West, 2000, p. 710). The monitoring of System 1 by System 2 leads to a more controlled process, which is often related to the concept of rationality in decision making (Evans, 2003). While System 1 is often applied in decision situations that concern the present moment, System 2 is more often applied in decision situations that relate to the future (Thaler, 2000).

The System 2 process, compared to System 1, is slower, more effortful, conscious, logical, and explicit (Bazerman, 2006). This is due to the emphasis that rational decision making puts on considering all the aspects involved and their interrelationships with the problem (Gibcus et al., 2008; Klein & Weiss, 2007). Intuitive or holistic decisions, in contrast, are typically made implicitly, emotionally, automatically, quickly, and effortlessly (Bazerman, 2006), and have such advantages as flexibility and creativity (Khatri & Ng, 2000; Morera & Budescu, 2001). Most of the decisions in life, according to Bazerman (2006), are of this kind. According to Klein and Weiss (2007), non-rational decision making is creative and suitable for non-conventional situations, while rational decision making benefits from accuracy in data processing and is appropriate for conventional circumstances.

In line with the above discussion of dual process decision making, Mintzberg and Westley (2010) argue that decision making is not necessarily always a 'thinking first' process, a linear process which begins with 'defining the problem' and then evaluating and choosing from alternatives. They propose a model of decision making that suggests that the 'thinking first' style, which corresponds to rational decision making, must be complemented by two other decision-making styles: 'seeing first' and 'doing first'. They argue that decisions may be driven by what is seen, as opposed to what is thought. They emphasize the role of seeing, or insight, in making decisions by saying "no one should

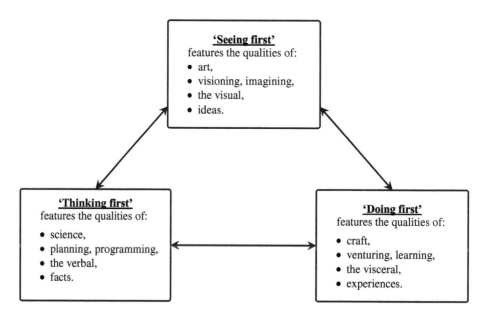

Figure 6.3 Characteristics of the three approaches to making decisions (based on Mintzberg & Westley, 2001, p. 91)

accept any theory of decision making that ignores insight" (Mintzberg & Westley, 2010, p. 76). With regard to 'doing first' decision making, they argue that the decision maker may not be able to see or even think of a problem. In these cases, doing first may drive thinking: "successful people know that when they are stuck, they must experiment. Thinking may drive doing, but doing just as surely drives thinking. We don't just think in order to act, we act in order to think" (Mintzberg & Westley, 2010, p. 76). Figure 6.3 outlines the characteristics of the three approaches to making decisions.

Mintzberg and Westley (2010) suggest that when a decision situation is clear, the data are reliable, the context is structured, thought can be pinned down, and discipline can be applied, then the 'thinking first' decision-making approach works best. This approach resonates with the type one decision making (i.e. rational decision-making) discussed by Stacey (2002) in relation to complexity theory. Stacey (2002) suggests that in decision situations where certainty and the agreement among those involved in decision making are high, the decision maker can use the data gathered in the past to predict the future (Stacey's model has been discussed in Chapter 3). In situations where developing a solution requires consideration of various factors, commitment to the solution, and communication across boundaries, are critical; the best decision-making approach is 'seeing first'. 'Doing first' works best in novel and confusing situations, when complicated specifications are barriers, and "a few simple relationship rules can help people move forward" (p. 81).

In decision situations where the decision maker does not adhere to the principles of rational decision making (i.e. making non-rational decisions, Figure 6.4), knowledge and information can lead to better decisions in so far as the decision maker's interpretation of his previous experiences allow (see Chapter 4). The nature and structure of a problem and decision are characterized largely based on the decision maker's subjective perceptions (Shiloh et al., 2001). Therefore, different decision makers, or the same decision maker in different decision situations, may make different decisions. The decision maker's experiences and expertise have significant impact on the person's interpretation of the available data and information. An experienced manager may be in a better situation to understand how relevant or reliable the available data, information, and knowledge are to the decision situation. A fundamental perspective of the naturalist stance on decision making is that decision making is an experience-based process. That is, people make decisions in the field setting, based on their experience (Zsambok, 1997) and the decision situation they face. Decision makers are different in terms of the depth of experience that they bring to the decision making situation.

Unlike the rational approach that assumes that gathering more data and information can reduce uncertainty, the natural approach underlines that too much information not only does not reduce uncertainty but can increase confusion and uncertainty. In other words, as far as data and information are concerned, decision uncertainty may result from the lack of effective organization of data and information, not just the absence of data and information. Moreover, in dealing with wicked or ill-defined problems, where the decision goals cannot be specifically defined in advance, the rational models of decision making may fall short because the models are based on the assumption that an effective decision-making process begins with a clear definition of the goal.

Figure 6.4 expands on Figure 4.2 (The Knowledge–Time Continuum Model, from Chapter 4) by incorporating the kinds of decision making discussed in this chapter. Non-rational and intuitive decisions are made based upon the decision maker's a priori and subconscious knowledge. As explained above, these decisions are usually made faster than the other two decision-making types. The process of making decisions based on data and information is slower as it requires collecting sufficient data, evaluating the validity of the dataset, and applying advanced analytical skills and knowledge to gain insight into the decision situation. Experience-based decisions are made based on the decision maker's reflection on his experiences with the same or similar decision situations in the past. The decision maker then tries to find out how the solutions applied to address the past decision situation can be applied to the current one. If the decision maker cannot find any exact match for the current decision situation, then he may combine his experience-based decision making with either or both non-rational and data-based decision making, much as dual process theories propose.

The complexity of management decision situations can require sophisticated decision-making processes that can bring rationality and non-rationality together in an integrated and dynamic fashion. The level of the integration of the rational and non-rational cannot be predetermined. While some decision situations require a more rational and data-based analytical examination of the problem and solutions, others may require the manager's urgent and prompt reaction and intuitive decision. A manager familiar with both rational and non-rational decision making is in a better position to make effective decisions. Rational decision making advocates believe that the decision-making process can be predetermined. In contrast, the naturalists hold that every decision maker is a unique person in a unique decision situation, and, therefore, the way that they make a decision varies from person to person and from situation to situation. For this reason, the rational theories of decision making are more prescriptive compared with the descriptive theories that are proposed by naturalists (Bazerman & Moore, 2009; Rosen et al., 2008).

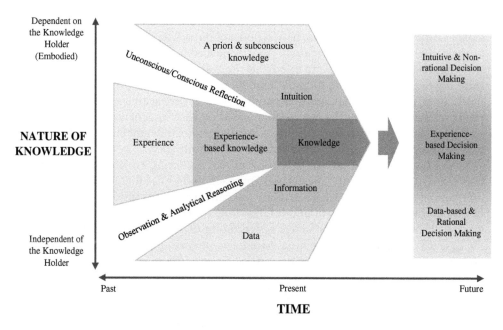

Figure 6.4 Decision types and knowledge sources

Despite the numerous critiques, rational decision making has endured and persisted in organizational decision making.

Why is rational decision making still influential in organizations?

Most decision-making theories in the management literature are based on the primacy of rationality and seek to develop normative models and methods that aim at optimizing decisions. This is not surprising given the rational, logical bent of Western philosophy and later academic disciplines such as the sciences, psychology and others, which as we saw in Chapters 1 and 2 have formed the basis of a great deal of management thinking. Yet as we have seen, much decision making is made 'naturally' based on the uniqueness of the decision situation, interpretation, and the skill and knowledge set brought by the decision maker. So why does the primacy of rational decision making persist if not in situ, then in classrooms and boardrooms?

A theory by Cabantous and Gond (2011) might explain this paradox. They proposed that a social construction of rationality undergirds rational decision making in organizations. They conceptualize rational decision making as performative praxis and argue that rational decision making is a set of activities whereby actors (including organizational members, technology developers, consultants, and academics) collectively support the production of rational decisions, thus granting social reality to rational choice theory. This social construction of rationality has become a 'convention' in organizational settings, i.e. a social norm that guides decisions and actions. In conventionalizing rationality in organizations, business schools and other management education have embedded students and future managers in rational choice theory.

This cognitive embeddedness in rational choice theory is sustained by an 'engineering rationality', which refers to managers' attempts to make rational decisions by relying heavily on decision-making tools, e.g. software and decision support systems, in order to overcome their bounded rationality. The conventionalization and engineering of rational thought are complemented by rationality 'commodification'. Rational decision making has become a convention embedded in tools and practices (engineering) and has become a commodity which is sold to managers and organizations by academics, consultants, and managers. These three mechanisms support the spread of rational choice theory in organizations (Cabantous & Gond, 2011). This relationship is illustrated in Figure 6.5.

'Actors' refers to the whole range of people who are directly or indirectly involved in decision making, whether they are within the organization e.g. managers and employees, or from outside the organization e.g. independent consultants. Regarding rational decision making as praxis, Cabantous and Gond (2011) argue that it is "a purposeful effort of managers in search of rationality", and has a performative effect as it leads rational

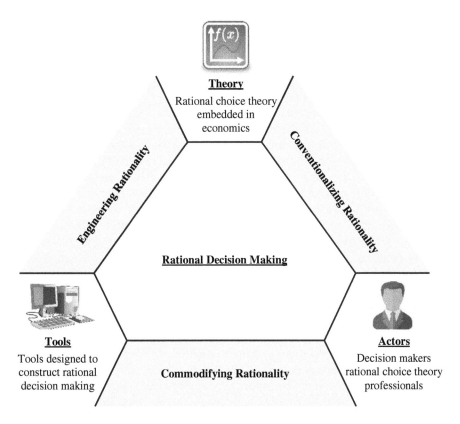

Figure 6.5 Rational decision-making as performative praxis (adapted from Cabantous & Gond, 2011, p. 578)*

* adapted with permission, Cabantous & Gond, Rational decision making as performative praxis: Explaining rationality's éternel retour, *Organization Science*, volume 22, number 3, 2011. Copyright 2018, the institute for operations research and the management sciences, 5521 research park drive, suite 200, Catonsville, Maryland 21228 USA.

choice theory to manifest in reality. Rational choice theory, as a performative theory, influences the social reality in such a way that its predictions and premises become true. Rational decision making as praxis focuses on the actual doing of the 'actors', and underlines the importance of 'tools' and techniques that the actors use in their decision-making activities.

It must be also mentioned that the role of stakeholders in keeping the primacy of rationality in the organizations should not be underestimated. Stakeholders influence managers' decision making to ensure that the managers follow transparent and rational processes to reach a justifiable decision (Dean & Sharfman, 1993; Fredrickson & Iaquinto, 1989). For example, Mintzberg and Waters (1982) study the strategies of a retail chain (over 60 years of the company's history) and show how pressure from the financial community led the managers to be more systematic and rational in their strategic decision making. This underlines the criticality of the wisdom qualities of considering alternative points of view and reconciling different stakeholders' interests (we shall discuss wisdom qualities in the following chapter).

As we have discussed in the previous chapter, big data/analytics are potential game changers in management decision making. They represent a significant enabler of rational decision making in organizations. The increasingly growing volume of data (big data), as well as advances in technology in acquiring and analysing a massive volume of data in a very limited time, may very well significantly improve many management decisions. Real-time analytics and deep contextual analysis of data can help managers identify trends, anticipate changes in the market, mitigate risks, provide customized services, and improve customer experience.

As mentioned in this chapter, the complexity of many decisions that managers encounter requires more complex decision-making processes than just rational and data-based decisions. Effective decisions engage the decision maker's expertise, judgement, interpretation, legal obligations, ethical considerations, social responsibilities, and many other stakeholders' subjective and objective expectations. For this reason, a manager who is familiar with different types of decision making – i.e. rational and non-rational – and can apply each of the two approaches individually or integrally, is more capable of handling complex decision situations. In the previous chapters and this chapter, we have examined knowledge, decision making, and the role of different sources of knowledge in dealing with complex problems. In the following chapters we introduce a model of integral decision making (wise decision making) that shows how both rationality and non-rationality can be brought together into one integrated decision-making process.

Chapter summary

In this chapter we learned about management decision making and the functions involved in the decision-making process. The functions vary from different perspectives. The major decision functions that commonly exist in most decision processes include identifying the problem, setting goals, establishing criteria, generating alternatives, evaluating and selecting the most appropriate alternative, implementing the choice, and following up. The functions are categorized under two major decision phases: problem finding (which includes the functions of identifying the problem and following up) and problem solving (encompassing the other five decision functions).

We then looked at two approaches to decision making; rationalist and naturalist (non-rational). The two approaches are different in their explanation of the decision-making process and the knowledge sources in decision making. Rationalists describe decision making as a clearly defined set of rules and phases. The models that rationalists suggest are prescriptive in nature. That is, the models dictate that to maximize expected outcomes of a decision, the decision maker should strictly follow each and every function that a rational decision-making model outlines. Naturalists are more concerned with how a decision is actually made. They believe that due to many constraints in the real world such as time and budget constraints as well as legal and ethical obligations, a manager as a decision maker does not necessarily follow a set of predefined steps to make a decision. The manager may just rely on his intuition and make an effective decision that is difficult to logically explain. The naturalist models of decision making, therefore, are descriptive rather than prescriptive.

We reviewed the major criticisms of the two approaches, and argued that the decision situations that managers are confronted by are often too complicated to completely address using either of the rational or non-rational approaches individually. In many cases the problems are hidden, partially identifiable, emergent, or a result of previous decisions. To address the decision situations, managers have to go through a cyclical process of problem finding and problem solving. They have to apply multiple decision functions and consider numerous factors such as a diverse range of stakeholders' expectations. By reviewing the critiques that have been made of rational decision-making theory and practice, we hope that perhaps we can go beyond single-minded approaches and develop more holistic, integrated decision-making theory and practice that builds on the best of rational and non-rational theory and practice. We build on this in the following chapters.

References

Arkes, H. R., & Blumer, C. (1985). The psychology of sunk cost. *Organizational Behavior and Human Decision Processes*, 35(1), 125–140.

Arnold Sr, D. F., Dorminey, J. W., Neidermeyer, A. A., & Neidermeyer, P. E. (2013). Internal and external auditor ethical decision-making. *Managerial Auditing Journal*, 28(4), 300–322.

Bass, B. M. (1983). *Organizational decision making*. Homewood, IL: Richard D. Irwin Inc.

Bazerman, M. H. (2006). *Judgment in managerial decision making* (6th ed.). Hoboken, NJ: John Wiley & Sons.

Bazerman, M. H., & Moore, D. A. (2009). *Judgment in managerial decision making* (7th ed.). Hoboken, NJ: John Wiley & Sons.

Beach, L. R., & Connolly, T. (2005). *The psychology of decision making: People in organizations* (2nd ed.). Thousand Oaks, CA: Sage Publications.

Betsch, T., & Held, C. (2012). Rational decision making: Balancing RUN and JUMP modes of analysis. *Mind & Society*, 11(1), 69–80.

Cabantous, L., & Gond, J.-P. (2011). Rational decision making as performative praxis: Explaining rationality's éternel retour. *Organization Science*, 22(3), 573–586.

Cannon-Bowers, J. A., & Salas, E. (Eds.). (1998). *Making decisions under stress: Implications for individual & team training*. Washington, DC: American Psychological Association.

Carnevale, J. J., Inbar, Y., & Lerner, J. S. (2011). Individual differences in need for cognition and decision-making competence among leaders. *Personality and Individual Differences*, 51(3), 274–278.

Cohen, M. S. (1993). Three paradigms for viewing decision biases. In G. Klein, J. Orasanu, R. Calderwood, & C. E. Zsambok (Eds.), *Decision making in action* (pp. 36–50). Norwood, NJ: Ablex.

Dean, J., & Sharfman, M. (1993). Procedural rationality in the strategic decision-making process. *Journal of Management Studies*, 30(4), 587–610.

Dewey, J. (1933). *How we think* (Revised rd.). Boston, MA: D.C. Heath.

Drucker, P. F. (1967). The effective decision. *Harvard Business Review*, 45(1), 92–98.

Elqayam, S., & Over, D. (2012). Probabilities, beliefs, and dual processing: The paradigm shift in the psychology of reasoning. *Mind & Society*, 11(1), 27–40.

Evans, J. S. B. (2003). In two minds: Dual-process accounts of reasoning. *Trends in Cognitive Sciences*, 7(10), 454–459.

Evans, J. St. B. T. (2009). How many dual-process theories do we need? One, two, or many? In J. St. B. T. Evans & K. Frankish (Eds.), *In two minds: Dual processes and beyond* (pp. 33–54). Oxford, UK: Oxford University Press.

Evans, J. St. B. T. (2012). Spot the difference: Distinguishing between two kinds of processing. *Mind & Society*, 11(1), 121–131.

Fredrickson, J. W., & Iaquinto, L. A. (1989). Inertia and creeping rationality in strategic decision processes. *Academy of Management Journal*, 31(5), 16–42.

Galotti, K. M. (2002). *Making decisions that matter: How people face important life choices.* London: Lawrence Erlbaum Associates.

Gibcus, P., Vermeulen, P. A. M., & Radulova, E. (2008). The decision-making entrepreneur: A literature review. In P. A. M. Vermeulen & P. L. Curşeu (Eds.), *Entrepreneurial strategic decision-making: A cognitive perspective* (pp. 11–40). Cheltenham, UK: Edward Elgar Publishing Limited.

Gilhooly, K., & Murphy, P. (2005). Differentiating insight from non-insight problems. *Thinking & Reasoning*, 11(3), 279–302.

Hall, J., & Hofer, C. (1993). Venture capitalists decision criteria in new venture evaluation. *Journal of Business Venturing*, 8(1), 25–42.

Hammond, J. S., Keeney, R. L., & Raiffa, H. (1999). *Smart choices: A practical guide to making better life decisions.* New York: Broadway.

Hare, W. (1971). The teaching of judgment. *British Journal of Educational Studies*, 19(3), 243–249.

Harrison, F. E. (1999). *The managerial decision-making process* (5th ed.). Boston: Houghton Mifflin Company.

Hess, J. D., & Bacigalupo, A. C. (2011). Enhancing decisions and decision-making processes through the application of emotional intelligence skills. *Management Decision*, 49(5), 710–721.

Hickson, D. J., Butler, R. J., Cary, D., Mallory, G. R., & Wilson, D. C. (1989). Decision and organization – Processes of strategic decision making and their explanation. *Public Administration*, 67(4), 373–390.

Holian, R. (2002). Management decision making and ethics: Practices, skills and preferences. *Management Decision*, 40(9), 862–870.

Intezari, A. (2016). Practical wisdom through sustainability: A meta-approach. In A. Habisch & R. Schmidpeter (Eds.), *Cultural roots of sustainable management: Practical wisdom and corporate social responsibility* (pp. 23–37). Basel, Switzerland: Springer.

Intezari, A., & Pauleen, D. J. (2014). Management wisdom in perspective: Are you virtuous enough to succeed in volatile times? *Journal of Business Ethics*, 120(3), 393–404.

Intezari, A., & Pauleen, D. J. (2017). The past-present-future conundrum: Extending time-bound knowledge. *International Journal of Knowledge Management*, 13(1), 1–15.

Kahneman, D. (2003). A perspective on judgment and choice: Mapping bounded rationality. *American Psychologist*, 58(9), 697–720.

Kahneman, D., & Frederick, S. (2002). Representativeness revisited: Attribute substitution in intuitive judgment. In T. Gilovich, D. Griffin, & D. Kahneman (Eds.), *Heuristics and biases: The psychology of intuitive judgment* (pp. 49–81). New York: Cambridge University Press.

Kahneman, D., & Tversky, A. (1979). Prospect theory: An analysis of decision under risk. *Econometrica*, 47(2), 263–291.

Keast, S., & Michael, T. (2009). *Rational decision-making for managers.* Chichester, UK: John Wiley and Sons.

Khatri, N., & Ng, H. A. (2000). The role of intuition in strategic decision making. *Human Relations*, 53(1), 57–86.

Klein, J., & Weiss, I. (2007). Towards an integration of intuitive and systematic decision making in education. *Journal of Educational Administration*, 45(3), 265–277.

Kohlberg, L. (1984). *The philosophy of moral development*. New York: Harper & Row.

Langley, A., Mintzberg, H., Pitcher, E., Posada, E., & Saint-Macary, J. (1995). Opening up decision-making: The view from the black stool. *Organization Science*, 6(3), 260–279.

Lindblom, C. E. (1959). The handling of norms in policy analysis. In M. Abramovitz (Ed.), *The allocation of economic resources: Essays in honor of Bernard Francis Haley* (pp. 160–179). Stanford, CA: Stanford University Press.

Maddalena, V., & Canada, H. (2007). A practical approach to ethical decision-making. *Leadership in Health Services*, 20(2), 71–75.

McKenna, R. J., & Martin-Smith, B. (2005). Decision making as a simplification process: New conceptual perspectives. *Management Decision*, 43(6), 821–836.

Messick, D. M., & Bazerman, M. H. (2001). Ethical leadership and the psychology of decision making. In J. Dienhart, D. Moberg, & R. Duska (Eds.), *The next phase of business ethics: Integrating psychology and ethics* (pp. 213–238). Oxford, UK: JAI Elsevier.

Michel, L. (2007). Understanding decision making in organizations to focus its practices where it matters. *Measuring Business Excellence*, 11(1), 33–45.

Miller, S. J., Hickson, D. J., & Wilsdon, D. C. (2002). Decision-making in organizations. In G. Salaman (Ed.), *Decision making for business: A reader* (pp. 74–92). London: Sage Publications.

Mintzberg, H., & Waters, J. A. (1982). Tracking strategy in the entrepreneurial firm. *Academy of Management Journal*, 25(3), 465–499.

Mintzberg, H., & Westley, F. (2001). Decision making: It's not what you think. *MIT Sloan Management Review*, 42(3), 89–94.

Mintzberg, H., Raisinghani, D., & Théorêt, A. (1976). The structure of "unstructured" decision processes. *Administrative Science Quarterly*, 21(2), 246–275.

Morera, O. F., & Budescu, D. V. (2001). Random error in analytic hierarchies: A comparison of holistic and decompositional decision strategies. *Journal of Behavioral Decision Making*, 14(3), 223–242.

Mullainathan, S., & Thaler, R. H. (2001). Behavioral economics. In N. J. Baltes and P. B. Smelser (Ed.), *International encyclopedia of the social and behavioral sciences* (pp. 1094–1110). Oxford, UK: Pergamon Press.

Nutt, P. C. (2002). *Why decisions fail: Avoiding the blunders and traps that lead to debacles*. San Francisco: Berrett-Koehler Publishers.

Pauleen, D. J., & Wang, W. Y. C. (2017). Does big data mean big knowledge? KM perspectives on big data and analytics. *Journal of Knowledge Management*, 21(1), 1–6.

Pettigrew, A. M. (2002). Decision-making as a political process. In G. Salaman (Ed.), *Decision making for business: A reader* (pp. 97–107). London: Sage Publications.

Porter, M. E. (1985). *Competitive advantage: Creating and sustaining superior performance*. New York: Free Press.

Rest, J. R. (1984). The major components of morality. In W. Kurtines & J. Gewirtz (Eds.), *Morality, moral behaviour, and moral development* (pp. 24–40). New York: John Wiley & Sons.

Rest, J. R. (1986). *Moral development: Advances in research and theory*. New York: Praeger.

Rosanas, J. M. (2013). *Decision-making in an organizational context: Beyond economic criteria*. Basingstoke, UK: Palgrave Macmillan.

Rosen, M. A., Salas, E., Lynos, R., & Fiore, S. M. (2008). Expertise and naturalistic decision making in organizations: Mechanisms of effective decision making. In G. P. Hodgkinson & W. H. Starbuck (Eds.), *The Oxford handbook of organizational decision making* (pp. 211–230). Oxford, UK: Oxford University Press.

Rowe, A. J., & Boulgarides, J. D. (1983). Decision styles: A perspective. *Leadership & Organization Development Journal*, 4(4), 3–9.

Saaty, T. L. (1994). How to make a decision: The analytic hierarchy process. *Informs*, 24(6), 19–43.

Schein, E. H. (1985). *Organizational culture and leadership*. San Francisco: Jossey-Bass.

Schraagen, J. M., Klein, G., & Hoffman, R. R. (2008). The macrocognition framework of naturalistic decision making. In J. M. Schraagen, L. G. Militello, T. Ormerod, & R. Lipshitz (Eds.), *Naturalistic decision making and macrocognition* (pp. 3–25). Aldershot, UK: Ashgate Publishing Limited.

Sevdalis, N., Petrides, K. V., & Harvey, N. (2007). Trait emotional intelligence and decision related emotions. *Personality and Individual Differences*, 42(7), 1347–1358.

Shiloh, S., Koren, S., & Zakay, D. (2001). Individual differences in compensatory decision-making style and need for closure as correlates of subjective decision complexity and difficulty. *Personality and Individual Differences*, 30(4), 699–710.

Simon, H. A. (1945). *Administrative behaviour* (2nd ed.). New York: Free Press.

Simon, H. A. (1955). A behavioral model of rational choice. *The Quarterly Journal of Economics*, 69(1), 99–118.

Simon, H. A. (1959). Theories of decision-making in economics and behavioral science. *The American Economic Review*, 49(3), 253–283.

Simon, H. A. (1960). *The new science of management decision*. New York: Harper & Row.

Simon, H. A. (1965). *The shape of automation*. New York: Harper and Row.

Smith, G. F. (2008). Teaching decision making. In G. P. Hodgkinson & W. H. Starbuck (Eds.), *The Oxford handbook of organizational decision making* (pp. 455–474). Oxford, UK: Oxford University Press.

Stacey R. D. (2002) *Strategic management and organizational dynamics: The challenge of complexity* (3rd ed.). Harlow, UK: Prentice Hall.

Stanovich, K. E., & Toplak, M. E. (2012). Defining features versus incidental correlates of Type 1 and Type 2 processing. *Mind & Society*, 11(1), 3–13.

Stanovich, K. E., & West, R. F. (2000). Individual differences in reasoning: Implications for the rationality debate? *Behavioral and Brain Sciences*, 23(5), 645–726.

Staw, B. M. (1976). Knee-deep in the big muddy: A study of escalating commitment to a chosen course of action. *Organizational Behavior and Human Performance*, 16(1), 27–44.

Stewart, T. (2006). Did you ever have to make up your mind? *Harvard Business Review*, 84(1), 12–12.

Tannenbaum, R. (1964). Managerial decision making, in D. E. Porter and P. B. Applewhite & M. J. Misshauk (Eds.), *Organizational behavior and management* (pp. 419–442) (2nd ed.). Scranton, PA: Intext.

Thaler, R. H. (2000). From homo economicus to homo sapiens. *Journal of Economic Perspectives*, 14(1), 133–141.

Thompson, V., & Morsanyi, K. (2012). Analytic thinking: Do you feel like it? *Mind & Society*, 11(1), 93–105.

Wendt, D. (1975). Some criticism of stochastic models generally used in decision making experiments. *Theory and Decision*, 6(2), 197–212.

Zeleny, M. (2006). Knowledge-information autopoietic cycle: Towards the wisdom system. *International Journal of Management and Decision Making*, 7(1), 3–18.

Zsambok, C. E. (1997). Naturalistic decision making: Where are we now? In C. E. Zsambok & G. Klein (Eds.), *Naturalistic decision making* (pp. 3–16). Mahwah, NJ: Erlbaum.

Part III
Wisdom in management practice

7   Wisdom aspects in the management context

Introduction

In Chapter 4 we discussed the nature and sources of knowledge and in Chapter 5 we examined the role of big data and analytics in decision making. We have learnt that knowledge can be developed based on different sources. Knowledge may be seen as a quality that is attainable through experience and observation (empiricism, objectivism), or is innate and independent of experience and, therefore, can be acquired through non-inductive means (apriorism). We then moved on and in Chapter 6 discussed the processes around decision making and how the different knowledge sources may inform and even lead to different types of decisions. Accordingly, decisions can be data-based and analytical, experience-based, or intuitive.

In this chapter we extend the discussion and argue that what is central to the sources of knowledge, knowing, and (wise) decision making is, above all, the decision maker. Knowledge and processes of knowing reside in the person, regardless of whether the person accumulates the knowledge through analytical observations, experience, or intuition. Judgement plays a fundamental role in transforming data into useful information, and then information into useful knowledge, as well as incorporating one's reflective or unconscious analysis of experiences or a priori knowledge into decision making. We also argued that many management decision situations are too complex to be addressed or dealt with by a simple linear mechanism of decision making. Rather, effective decisions engage and integrate both rationality and non-rationality.

This argument gives rise to a critically important question about how management decision-making techniques, and more importantly the decision support technologies used in today's management context, can ensure that no possible source of knowledge – be it data, experience, or a priori knowledge – is omitted or marginalized by over-emphasis on either the rational or non-rational aspect of decision making. Decision support systems and knowledge management systems, for example, are designed and implemented based on the assumption that knowledge is a form of data and information (as illustrated by the knowledge hierarchy, discussed in Chapter 4). This assumption undermines the role of other knowledge sources, such as experience and a priori and intuitive knowing. As a result, decision-making mechanisms and systems that are designed and developed to support management decisions often fail to facilitate the integration of different knowledge sources into decision making.

In this chapter, we introduce other factors that directly affect the effectiveness of a management decision. We will refine and extend aspects of wisdom discussed in Chapter 2. This extension is based on the findings of an empirical study conducted by the authors (Intezari, 2014; Intezari & Pauleen, 2018), which focused on senior managers making decisions in a management context.

We will review the wisdom aspects that have been identified in the relevant academic and practitioner literature and outline how these aspects correspond with the decision-making approaches described in the previous chapters. This will give the reader an opportunity to compare the literature-based wisdom aspects with the empirically identified ones. This also provides an initial picture of how the general approach to the wisdom aspects relates to decision making. We hope that this will help the reader better understand our model of wise management decision making that will be discussed in the following chapter.

Wisdom aspects: the literature-based approach

In Chapters 1 and 2 we reviewed the philosophy, psychology, and management literature on wisdom and identified ten wisdom aspects. Different wisdom aspects have been identified by scholars across various disciplines as associated with wisdom. Table 6.1 outlines how these wisdom aspects correspond with the decision-making elements and approaches that we have discussed in the previous chapter.

Wisdom corresponds to decision making in various ways. Wisdom is concerned with fundamental matters of life, which in the management context may manifest in practices that lead the organization towards 'success' without compromising the well-being of those associated with the organization, including local and global communities. Wisdom brings to the manager's attention the value that 'true success' is not achieved unless the interests of everyone directly or indirectly affected by the decision are considered and appropriately addressed.

Decision making is closely linked with judgement (Holian, 2006) and ethics (Arnold, Dorminey, Neidermeyer, & Neidermeyer, 2013; Maddalena & Canada, 2007). Wisdom as a moral virtue leads decisions and actions to be necessarily ethical and based on sound judgement. Virtue, according to Aristotle, is concerned with the answer to the question, "How should I act in this particular situation I am situated in?" (Tikkanen, Lamberg, Parvinen, & Kallunki, 2005, p. 5). 'Leading to action', in fact, is the key as to why wisdom is a virtue. Csikszentmihalyi and Rathunde (1990) clarify this: "wisdom is a virtue because by relating in a disinterested way the broadest spectrum of knowledge, it provides the most compelling guide to action" (p. 48). The answer to this question implies that the possible 'action', first, requires a comprehensive understanding of the given context and possible results. That is to say, as soon as one starts thinking what action might be suitable, given the situation, to reach a satisfactory goal, she enters into a cognitive process. For this reason, wisdom can be understood as a cognitive process integrating mind and virtue (Csikszentmihalyi & Rathunde, 1990). An example of a decision-making model that emphasizes the role of morality and judgement is Rest's (1984, 1986) four-component ethical decision-making model, where moral judgement is one of the key components. The other three are moral awareness and perception, moral intent, and moral behaviour.

Rationality and non-rationality are mutually dependent in wise decisions and actions. Effective decisions are made based on reliable knowledge and the awareness that while one's knowledge may be useful in one decision situation, it may fall short in another. The acceptance of the fallibility of knowledge is an essential aspect of wisdom (Meacham, 1990). Decision making is the practice of addressing a decision

Table 7.1 Key aspects of wisdom and their corresponding decision making elements based on the literature

Wisdom aspects	Description	Corresponding elements in decision making
Concerned with fundamental matters of life	Wisdom is related to fundamental and pragmatic aspects of life.	Wisdom is inextricably linked to decision making. Everyone is involved in decision making. In management decision making, the fundamental matters could include the success of the organization without compromising the well-being of anyone who is involved with the organization.
Knowledge	Knowledge is important in making wise decisions and taking wise actions. However, wisdom is more than a mere accumulation of knowledge. Wisdom is also associated with one's ability to use knowledge.	Both rational and non-rational ways of knowing are used in decision making: this includes intuitive, experience-based, and data-based (analytical) knowledge.
Experience	Experience is a critical subcomponent of wisdom. Experience, however, in and of itself, does not necessarily lead to wisdom.	Included in both rational and non-rational decision making. Reflection is vital in being able to incorporate lessons learnt from previous experiences into a decision situation. This can lead to experience-based knowledge, and experience-based decision making. This is also concerned with the development of wisdom (Chapter 9).
Practice-oriented	Wisdom wants to act. Wisdom is a way of being and doing. Wise people are defined as being 'the sort of people who act'. Wisdom is not just about the achievement of good ends, but it is also about how to achieve the ends.	Decision making is the practice of fully addressing a decision situation. Taking action is part of the decision-making process. The action could be the implementation of the selected solution, or halting the implementation (an action, itself).
Ethics	Wisdom and morality are interwoven. Ethics is a critical part of wisdom.	Considering different stakeholders' perspectives including ethics and values, and how these differences may affect decision making.
Self-transcendence	Wisdom is not restricted to the individual level, but it manifests at both individual and social levels. Wisdom is concerned with well-being of self and others.	Self-transcendence is implicit in decisions where the decision maker evaluates the decision situation and the possible solutions by considering the impacts of the decision consequences on self and others, which includes the manager herself, the organization as a whole and all those who are directly and indirectly affected by the decision within and outside the organization.

(Continued)

Table 7.1 (Continued)

Wisdom aspects	Description	Corresponding elements in decision making
Judgement	Wisdom enables people to make good pragmatic judgements about important matters of life.	Judgement is central to decision making and can be expressed in rational and non-rational decision making. Developing alternatives and selecting criteria, and assessing the consequences of the alternatives all draw heavily on the decision maker's judgement.
Non-rationality	Wisdom engages non-rationality, and goes beyond rational and objective understanding of what is already known.	A priori knowledge and intuition are important sources of knowledge in decision making.
Emotions	Wisdom is not a purely cognitive quality. Emotions are acknowledged and moderated in life. Wisdom leads to empathy for others.	Wisdom includes empathetic decision making, i.e. considering the impact of the decision on, and understanding the feelings of, everyone who is directly or indirectly affected by the decision.
Awareness of the limits of knowledge	Wisdom includes the awareness of what is not known. Wise people are aware of the limitations and fallibility of their knowledge.	Relates to both rational and non-rational decision making: both in being aware that more knowledge is not necessarily the answer to all problems and also maintaining a humble attitude regarding the decision maker's own knowledge.

situation by considering and taking appropriate actions based on sound judgement about the decision situation.

The wisdom aspects outlined above and discussed in detail in Chapters 1 and 2 are wisdom aspects that are derived from the philosophy, psychology, and management literature. In the next section, we delve deeper into wisdom aspects in the management context. We will refine and extend the list of the wisdom aspects by incorporating the findings of an empirical study of wisdom conducted by the authors (Intezari, 2014; Intezari & Pauleen, 2018). The authors interviewed more than 30 CEOs and senior managers to investigate how managers can make wise decisions. Descriptive quotes from the study's participants are used in this chapter to illustrate key points and lessons. The linkage between the new list of wisdom aspects and management decision making will be discussed in detail in the following chapter.

Wisdom aspects in the management context

In our study, we identified nine wisdom aspects which are important in management settings. These wisdom aspects are: future thinking, perspective-taking, ethical consideration, cognitive mastery, emotional mastery, self-awareness, other-awareness, internal reflection, and external reflection. Figure 7.1 illustrates the management wisdom aspects.

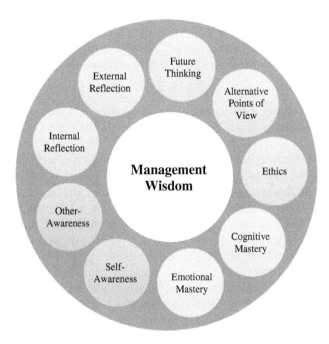

Figure 7.1 Wisdom aspects in the management context

Future thinking

Wisdom is the ability to see beyond the horizon and to take into account long-term and far-reaching consequences, so the future is not forgotten at the moment of decision making (Ackoff, 1999; Hays, 2007). Wisdom requires two future thinking elements:

1. critical analysis of the consequences and ramifications of a decision (action); and
2. short-term and long-term thinking.

As Kemmis and Smith (2008) stress, doing the right thing in uncertain circumstances requires deliberation, i.e. "consideration of what one is really doing in this situation, and what different kinds of consequences will follow for different people if one decides to do one thing, rather than another" (p. 16). In particular, strategic decision situations require a mindful and critical evaluation of the possible consequences of any decisions that might be made. As the impacts of strategic decisions go beyond a short-term time frame, both the short- and long-term consequences of the decisions must be evaluated. The following statement from a senior manager interviewed by the authors underlines that wisdom requires an understanding of the long-term impacts of decisions and actions:

> Potentially an unwise business decision is something that just has a short term view on the world. So an unwise decision to me would be one that just doesn't look very far into the future, and just is dealing with something immediate.

Considering alternative points of view

Although decision makers, regardless of their position in the organization, usually bear ultimate responsibility for their decisions and actions, management decisions should work to consider alternative points of view both from within and outside of the organization. Wisdom requires:

- representing alternative points of view without bias; and
- reconciling individual and communal (different stakeholders') interests.

Kitchener and Brenner (1990) assert that in solving difficult problems, wise people are able to recognize, evaluate, and synthesize alternative interpretations. Biloslavo and McKenna (2013) refer to this quality as 'cognitive complexity' and explain that cognitive complexity refers to the decision maker's ability "to view a given situation from multiple perspectives while screening out irrelevant factors, flexible thinking and possessing a multidimensional view of the world" (p. 118). The multidimensional view of the world is based on an integration of different, and sometimes conflicting, values and interests through the individual and the communal levels. The individual level refers to either an employee vis-à-vis the organization, or an organization vis-à-vis the wider community or society within which the organization is operating. The communal level refers to the wider community as a whole, whether it is the organization vis-à-vis individuals, or society vis-à-vis organizations and individuals. Nonaka and Takeuchi (2011) note that knowledge alone does not result in wise leadership, and therefore businesses, as social phenomena, need to consider people's goals, values, and interests.

To be able to perform wisely in decision situations, considering alternative points of view and individual and communal interests can help a manager overcome the inclination to limit their view to one of personal interest or gain. According to managers interviewed by the authors, wise decisions are made based on a deeper understanding and non-biased view of the subject matter. "Wise managers are prepared to listen not just to themselves, but they will take counsel from really wise counsellors". This was a sentiment from an experienced manager in a law enforcement agency in the public sector. The same emphasis is made by a young female manager of a design company in the private sector:

> I think if you want to be a wise manager, you need to be able to look at problems from a point beyond your position. You should be able to go beyond your personal biased position.

Ethical consideration

Ethics and morality are central to wise management practices (Rooney & McKenna, 2008). Wise management decisions are by definition ethical. Decision makers are not able to decide what is good or bad without a foundation of values (Nonaka & Takeuchi, 2011). Wisdom is not independent of morality (McKenna, 2005; Nonaka & Takeuchi, 2011). An increasingly growing awareness of the impact of organizations on local and global environments, as well as the wicked nature of many socio-economic problems, forces management to prioritize social responsibility. Management decisions and actions that do not comply with ethical codes in the organization, business community, and society are not considered wise. This comment emphasizes the importance of ethics in wise management decisions:

> I don't say that morality and ethics are necessary in wise managerial decisions; I would say they are essential if you want to make a wise decision. [...] I don't believe that businesses can be successful or very successful without being ethical. You have to respect the values that society is respecting.

Being ethical is even more important than being financially successful if management is to achieve long-term and sustainable success. Managers should consider that ethical codes form a mutual compact between themselves and others. A CEO, with 13 years of senior management experience in a large company in the energy industry, clearly underscores the point that ethics (not just financial success) is important for a manager who wants to have long-lasting success:

> I think ethics is incredibly important in wisdom. You end up living by your own morals. And if you don't have your own standards and ethics, so you can't expect others to have any either. So, I wouldn't think that it was a wise decision, if a managerial decision is unethical, even if it was a financially successful one.

A similar point is made by another senior manager, who has 28 years of management experience:

> Ethics to me are part of the framework of decision making so they are one of the foundation stones of making a good decision, in the same way that you can't build a house without a foundation stone. Periodically in business decision making you take that stone out, you try to find a way to make a decision without the stone there. And you know that decision is contrary to your ethics, and if you don't put that stone back in, and make that decision, then that's going to be an unwise decision. And you know it. I know people make decisions all the time without ethics. But I think the best decision is when it is present.

Good decisions are grounded in accepted values in management practices and are also congruent with organizational and social values (Maddalena & Canada, 2007). This aspect of wisdom requires the manager to understand the relationship between ethics and the impact of the organization's operation on society. In the comment below, another manager, with 23 years of management experience in banking, highlights the critical role of ethics. According to the manager's comment, the wise person needs to first be truly aware of the value system of the community and then to be able to consider these moral codes in their decisions. The comment also conveys that ethical considerations include legal aspects:

> A wise decision would be not to do anything that breaches the law. [...] I think they are important, because if you are unethical or immoral, these days you are about to be caught out. [...] I think it is really a part of wisdom: understanding the relationship between morality and society and ethics. And that's all a part of a good business person.

Self-awareness

Self-awareness is a fundamentally important aspect of wisdom in management, where high levels of self-awareness are necessary. Self-awareness refers to the intimate understanding of one's own qualities, characteristics, and abilities. This wisdom aspect deals specifically with the following kinds of awareness:

- awareness of personal strengths and weaknesses, abilities and inabilities;
- knowledge awareness (which includes knowing what one knows, and what one does not know);
- awareness of personal values and interests; and
- awareness of one's own attributes and behavioural characteristics.

Self-awareness refers to understanding strengths and admitting weaknesses. In the following comment, a manager of a technology company mentions self-awareness as being critical to wisdom, in order to understand what motivates oneself, as well as one's abilities, capacities, and weaknesses. The manager also links 'admitting to weaknesses' to self-awareness.

> If you understand yourself, you understand what motivates you, and what is driving the decision that you are making. And that understanding of self is the thing that allows you to understand whether or not the motives are the right ones, and that is the important thing [...]. So, understanding of self is really critical in wisdom: understanding what you do, understanding your abilities, and your capacities, your strengths, and your weaknesses, and being willing to admit to the weaknesses.

Drawing on the Aristotelian approach to wisdom, Korac-Kakabadse, Korac-Kakabadse, and Kouzmin (2001) hold that having a "healthy vision of self", which is constructed based on knowledge and experience, is important for leaders (p. 209). A senior manager points out that self-awareness includes both the awareness of what one knows, and what one does not know. One of the interviewed managers, a senior manager with over 25 years of management experience, believes that a lack of awareness of one's own limitations impedes wise decision making:

> The first thing that actually comes to my mind regarding not being able to make a wise decision is a certain lack of self-awareness of one's own limitations. [...] I think it is a lack of knowledge of their limitations and abilities.

Similarly, another experienced manager (with over 40 years of management experience) highlights the importance of the awareness of one's weaknesses in making wise decisions:

> If you have weaknesses, which we all have, then you prop up your management with those areas of expertise... with greater expertise from someone else. And it is not a bad thing or wrong thing. It is all about piecing together what you can to make your team under your management direction strong.

Being aware of what one does not know is perhaps even more important than being aware of what one knows. Not surprisingly, the awareness of appearing foolish drives management behaviour. Wise leaders fear foolishness, and indeed a fear of foolishness is an important quality for a wise leader, although this fear is often suppressed. Foolishness is a result of a lack of knowledge, or unwillingness to use knowledge, and stands in the way of wisdom (Sternberg, 2004). A wise leader should fear foolishness, and their vulnerability towards foolishness (Solansky, 2014) for that fear may bring wisdom.

Many scholars have asserted that awareness of one's own fallibility, and of what one does not know, is an important aspect of wisdom. For example, Meacham (1983) argues that the essence of wisdom is rooted in recognition of one's limitations and fallibility of knowledge. The wise person "probes inside knowledge" and excels in metacognition, i.e. knowledge about knowledge, which implies that wise people know what they know, know what they do not know, know what they can know (given the limitations of present understandings and of knowledge itself), and know what they cannot know (again, given the limitations imposed on them) (Sternberg, 1990, p. 152).

Wise managers do not consider themselves as being perfect or knowing everything. They are aware of the fact that there may always be the need to get advice from or consult with others. As a 38-year-old manager with 11 years of management experience pointed out:

> A wise manager would have people whom they trust around them, like a really strong team who are not afraid to come and say "Hey, look! There is a little problem brewing here, we need to do something about it". A wise manager would say: "That's awesome. Thanks for bringing that to me. Let's deal with it". And an unwise manager would go: "It will be fine. Don't worry about it", and just ignores it. So, a wise manager would surround themselves with wise people.

Another manager explains why she thinks self-awareness is critical to wisdom. For the manager, self-awareness is not limited to just 'understanding', but rather to being willing to overcome weaknesses by getting help from others. This manager links self-awareness to the success of the organization, asserting that lack of self-awareness will ultimately lead the organization to collapse:

> if you can admit that you are not perfect, that there are gaps in your experience and knowledge, then that means that you can bring someone in to fill those. But if you say "No, I am going to do that all, because I am so good, and I am perfect" then you are going to fall over. And the organization will fall over. And the dreams will fall over, if you are building a dream. So, it is best not to go there. So, that is "understanding of self".

Being aware of weaknesses and inabilities helps the manager realize when she is able or unable to make decisions and take proper actions. This prevents the manager from dealing with decision situations where the manager may not be the right person to make the decision due to lack of knowledge, expertise, or experience. Self-awareness guides the manager in deciding to get help from others and/or build up a better team around them to overcome the weaknesses. The following sentiment from a manager with 11 years of management experience highlights that wisdom in a management setting is concerned with understanding both strengths and weaknesses:

> Knowing what you are really strong at, what you are really weak at, and reflecting "can I improve it? Yes or no?" If yes, then you go ahead and work on it. If no, you don't do it. You focus on what you are good at.

This wisdom aspect of self-awareness is critical in decision making as it also enables the manager to be aware of her own personality and behaviours and understand how they affect her decisions. Being aware of this, a manager can then consciously direct their behaviour towards making appropriate decisions. A young novice manager in the banking industry highlighted this concern:

> Wise managers are very self-aware. I think to a large degree self-awareness gives them the ability to see how their behaviours impact other people, and how they can use their behaviour in a positive way to inform decisions, or to judge before making a decision. And then that helps in the communication of their decisions.

Other-awareness

Wisdom, engaging a "holistic and integrative understanding of the world around us" (Lombardo, 2010, p. 34) serves as a "means to choose one's behaviour based on knowledge and shared values, in order to enhance the well-being of all and awareness that personal actions have social consequences" (Blasi, 2006, p. 407). In addition to self-awareness, other-awareness or awareness of the surrounding environment is a critical aspect of wisdom in the management context. To be able to make proper decisions that effectively address issues at hand, yet for them to be regarded as wise decisions in any given time and situation, managers need to be fully aware of the events going on around them.

This aspect of wisdom refers to a true understanding of various elements in the surrounding environment including:

- awareness of others' strengths and weaknesses, abilities and inabilities;
- awareness of others' knowledge (knowing what others know, and what they do not know);
- awareness of others' values and interests; and
- situational awareness.

In the previous section we saw that wisdom requires a high level of awareness about self, which can help the manager to better understand when a decision situation requires advice and assistance from others. To engage effectively with others, one needs to have a true and accurate understanding of what those around us are capable of and what they value. Other-awareness requires an understanding of the decision situation and the (in-)abilities, strengths, and weaknesses, and knowledge of others involved in the decision situation, as well as the individual and communal values and interests of all stakeholders. This awareness helps managers to better manage others, work with them, and also to know whom to approach to get advice, when needed. This is illustrated in an analogy offered by a manager from the public sector:

The conductor doesn't need to know how to play the trumpet and drums, and the guitar and the violin; but he does need to know how to listen [and] bring those together in harmony to deliver some product better than any of the individuals alone. That is the conductor's skill and that to me is the [wise] manager's skill.

The same sentiment is echoed by another experienced manager from the public sector:

A wise decision is actually recognizing that you don't have the full set of tools and to go and seek support from somebody else to inform your decision that you make.

The interrelationship between an organization and the wider community (business community and society) within which the business operates requires managers to take into account the possible impacts that their businesses may have on the society or that the society may have on their businesses. A manager cannot truly comprehend the interrelationship between management practices and their impacts on various stakeholders if the manager does not have a comprehensive understanding of what is going on around her within and outside the organization. This is indicated by the following comment from an experienced manager with over 30 years of management experience in the private sector:

There are on-going side- and indirect effects that you don't even realize until later on; then you go: "Oh wow! I didn't realize people thought that way". Good decision making around the business means [the] business gets successful. And you are thinking that it is good for your own business and you are only looking at yours. But you don't realize that others are looking from outside of your business. ... Being judged by others does make a huge difference on how people react to them and you realize that you don't operate in a bubble.

Awareness of the variety of perspectives that may exist about the decision situation can help the manager to avoid taking a self-centred or biased position in the decision situation. Other-awareness is linked to another wisdom aspect: considering multiple perspectives, as discussed above. Being aware of the prevalent values and beliefs of the wider community and society may increase the level of acceptance of the management's decision and subsequent action. If the manager's decisions and actions do not comply with the wider community's values, then the manager is not regarded as a wise manager. The person may not be regarded as wise if these personality traits and behavioural characteristics of others are devalued or ignored (Sternberg, 1990).

A manager with 11 years of management experience in the public sector highlights the linkage between self-awareness and considering the decision situation from multiple points of view:

I think that they have to look at it from a number of different perspectives. And I think you have to have taken into account these perspectives. You have to take into account other people's point of view, even if they are different from your own.

Cognitive mastery

Cognitive mastery is another important aspect of management wisdom. Cognition engages the mental activities that are most closely associated with learning, reasoning and decision making:

> Cognition is the ability to process information through perception (stimuli that we receive through our different senses), knowledge acquired through experience, and our subjective characteristics that allow us to integrate all of this information to evaluate and interpret our world. In other words, cognition is the ability that we have to assimilate and process the information that we receive from different sources (perception, experience, beliefs…) to convert them into knowledge. Cognition includes different cognitive processes, like learning, attention, memory, language, reasoning, decision making, etc., which form part of our intellectual development and experience.
>
> (www.cognifit.com/cognition)

Cognitive processes involve what humans perceive from the world and representing it either conceptually or practically, rationally or non-rationally. From a managerial perspective, cognition can be defined as "the conceptual and operational representations that humans develop while interacting with complex systems" (Tikkanen et al., 1990, p. 792). Wisdom as a cognitive process refers to "attempts at understanding the world in a disinterested way, seeking the ultimate consequences of events as well as ultimate causes while preserving the integration of knowledge" (Csikszentmihalyi & Rathunde; 1990, p. 48).

Mastery is a process through which one expands personal capacity and continually improves one's level of proficiency in order to achieve goals (Senge et al., 1994). "Mastery" is, therefore, a continual learning process, not an end state. Cognitive mastery reflects a manager's desire to know the truth (Bergsma & Ardelt, 2012), and refers to the extent to which the manager can effectively handle the intellectual and cognitive aspects of a decision situation, including:

- possessing appropriate knowledge (having expertise);
- being able and knowing how to acquire the required data, information, and knowledge;
- being able and knowing how to use knowledge in the decision situation (i.e. data-based knowledge, experience-based knowledge, and intuitive knowledge – as discussed in Chapters 4 and 6);
- possessing insight (insightful as opposed to superficial); and
- thinking outside the square (being creative and innovative).

Cognitive mastery is more than just a desire to know the truth: it is also concerned with one's knowledge and experience, and the extent to which one is able to apply that knowledge and experience in a given decision situation. It also involves knowing when one does not have enough knowledge and information and being able to obtain what is required. Wisdom requires a reasonable level of manager expertise, knowledge, and experience. As underscored by one of the interviewed managers, wise management practices rely on knowledge-related skills and capabilities, so conversely a lack of knowledge may lead to unwise decisions and actions:

There is always something that you don't know. There is always something out there, there is always knowing where to go to ask about what you don't know, where to get help, or maybe just deciding that you can't make that particular decision. And sometimes a wise decision is just saying "I can't decide", because you just don't know enough to make that decision.

Managers have organizational responsibilities, central to which is the achievement of the organization's goals and continuing success. Managers have to make sure that their organization is effectively and efficiently achieving its short- and long-term mission and goals. Whether the goals are selling products or providing services, knowledge about the organization's core operations and its surrounding environment (e.g. the marketplace, business partners etc.) is critical in making wise decisions and business success. The managers who are considered wise are described as being knowledgeable about the field in which they work:

> In terms of the community that I interact with, there are probably three or four people who I consider as being wise managers. [...]. Mr X is now a professor director, but he is very much a specialist in company culture, and high growth business development. [...] the wisdom that I ascribe to him, I guess centres on the way that he understands the marketplace.

Due to the emergent and unique nature of the complex and wicked problems that managers encounter, they may not always have all the knowledge required to address a particular decision situation, but the manager should be able to acquire the knowledge and information critical to the decision situation. Wisdom in a management context requires a manager to have the ability to find the information, to get advice from others, and to consult experts. The following comments reflect this quality:

> In order to make a wise decision I need to gather some information, and once I've gathered that information I might go and speak to my manager; I'm putting myself into the team members' position now. [I] may talk to my manager, certainly talk to others that I trust or think are wise.

> Wise managers get advice when they need it. And it is up to them to know when they need that advice.

As has been emphasized in other chapters, wisdom is more than just accumulated knowledge. Being knowledgeable and experienced does not equal being wise. Wise management is about being able to implement knowledge and make things happen (Boyatzis, Stubbs, & Taylor, 2002), as these comments attest:

> Just because you have knowledge and experience doesn't mean you are going to use it wisely.

> Experience and knowledge are very important to make wise decisions. You can learn everything at the start, but putting it in practice and understanding how to put it in practice can be a different thing. Wisdom to me is that understanding: understanding how to put your knowledge into practice.

In Chapters 4, 5, and 6, we learnt about three forms of decision making that were distinct in terms of the type of knowledge based on which the decisions were made. These include data-based decision making, experience-based decision making, and non-rational or intuitive decision making. One dimension of this wisdom aspect is the extent to which the decision maker is capable of considering and applying different sources of knowledge to the decision situation. In wise decision making, intuition is considered a reliable source of knowledge. As discussed in the previous chapter, unlike a logically thought-through decision-making process (i.e. rational, data-based decision making), in an intuitively-made decision, the preference for one alternative over another is not necessarily justifiable by applying a set of logical criteria.

In this sense, cognitive mastery refers to the degree to which the decision maker can consider different sources of knowledge, including those sources termed non-rational (e.g. intuition). An experienced manager with 40 years of management experience in the private sector does not believe that reason and intuition are separable in real decision situations. She underlines that wisdom in the management context engages a mixture of both:

> I actually don't think that you can separate logic and intuition in [a] wise decision-making process. I think the separation is artificial, and I don't think it helps. I guess … logically, a business might be in a situation where they are looking at the balance sheet and the numbers are telling them, that they are doing well or they are about to go under. I think there can be situations where one needs to prevail over another. But I think as human beings, you operate from both. And I don't know that it is always constructive to separate them. I think they can be. But wisdom would involve saying in one situation or another "we need to go with one or the other perhaps", being able to use them together or separately, as may be needed.

Wise managers are cognitively adept. They are insightful (as opposed to superficial) and able to think outside the square (not being restricted to conventional thought frameworks) in dealing with wicked problems and complex decision situations. Wisdom means managers will not only make their decisions based on critical, in-depth analysis of the decision situation, but will also bring into play non-rational methods of understanding, such as deep insight. In psychology, 'insight' refers to the understanding one obtains of the functional relationships between component parts of a specific situation in a particular way (Marková, 2005). In management contexts, insight has been defined as "deep understanding, concerning one's own condition(s) in a particular situation at a given time; as well as the capacity to explore possible meaningful relationships between apparently unrelated events and phenomena pertinent to that situation" (Intezari & Pauleen, 2013, p. 160). Put simply, insight uses deep rational and non-rational approaches to enable one to "comprehend the obscure aspects of situations and events, recognize their interrelationships, and gain a true, deeper and wider understanding of the bigger picture and of the dynamics taking place" (Intezari & Pauleen, 2013, p. 160).

A young manager in the finance and banking industry focuses on the need to look at phenomena in detail:

> Some managers just skim really at the surface of the issues, and have no ability to delve into [the] detail of anything. […] Wise managers have that ability to go into detail of the things that matter, but of course to not do that with everything.

The complexity and emergence of decision situations that managers encounter in today's business environment require managers to be creative and innovative to effectively address these situations. Wise managers are able to think differently. They can think both critically and creatively to generate unorthodox yet effective solutions. The following comment from a highly experienced director of a private company in the paper and forestry industry shows that wisdom is linked to the ability to think outside the square:

> They may come with new ideas, new perspectives, looking at something in different ways that you hadn't thought possible. [...] Wisdom is an ability to be able to think outside the square: to be innovative in thinking.

As we have seen in Chapters 5 and 6 certain types of cognitive ability are absolutely vital in decision situations. For example, in data-based decisions a high degree of knowledge and training is often required to understand complex data sets and the analytical tools that process these data sets. Generally speaking, however, successful and wise managerial decision-making processes extend beyond purely rational and cognitive processes. We discussed non-rational cognitive processes such as intuition and insight above, but it is also important to discuss emotions, an important aspect of wisdom. Emotions complete the cognitive dimension of management practices.

Emotional mastery

Wisdom is not merely a cognitive phenomenon, nor is management practice. Wisdom involves emotional and motivational characteristics (Baltes & Kunzmann, 2003; Marker, 2013; Webster, 2007). We found in our studies of management wisdom that wise management decision making is, among others, associated with the capacity to appropriately incorporate emotions into management decisions and actions. We call this aspect of wisdom in the management context emotional mastery.

A decision maker's emotions inevitably influence their interpretations of the decision situation and all other related aspects including the generation and implementation of decision alternatives. Wise people show "emotional mastery" such that their decisions are not dominated by such passions as anger and fear (Birren & Fisher, 1990, p. 321), but neither are their decisions void of emotion. Emotional mastery is concerned with the emotional involvement of the decision maker in the management decision-making process in a way in which emotions are considered yet do not overly dominate the decision-making process. This wisdom aspect deals with the following aspects in management practice:

- emotional regulation (emotional balance, e.g. avoidance of excessive anger, fear, even happiness, as well as resistance against making rash decisions); and
- confidence (feeling confident, but not overly confident).

Emotional mastery refers to the characteristics or qualities that are related to the wise manager's emotions, and the degree to which the manager is able to regulate emotions and to resist becoming overwhelmed by them (Matthews, 1998). It is also concerned with the consequences of decisions and actions on the emotions of others (Blasi, 2006). In this comment, a manager from the private sector in the communication industry affirms the significance of emotions in the decision-making process:

If you entirely remove emotion from the decision-making process, it is probably too dry. I think there are times where you have to apply more logic. I mean there is a balance. [...] you have to be pragmatic on one hand and also understand where emotion is helpful within the decision-making process.

Wisdom in the management setting supports a reasonable level of confidence in decisions and actions. Confidence is central to making effective decisions. A lack of confidence could be a sign of inadequate trust in, awareness of, or understanding about the decision situation, and/or the assessment of the decision maker's knowledge, expertise, experience, or willingness to address the decision situation effectively. This aspect of emotional mastery is reflected in the following comment from another experienced manager:

One of the CEOs I worked with, where I was the Chair of the Board [...], I would consider him to be a wise manager because he has the confidence in his own experience, and he was able to apply that in a practical way. So, to try to explain that better, he is able to make quite a number of decisions quickly and efficiently, based on his own practical experience. So, to me in a sense that was wisdom.

Wise managers are decisive in decision making and resolute in practice. Wise managers are confident about dealing with the issues at hand and confident in the decisions that they make. An experienced general manager of a company operating in the consultancy field emphasizes the importance of confidence for wise managers:

I think wise managers are by nature typically people that are confident. They can sit back and deal with issues, projects, or whatever they may be.

The importance of confidence is significant. As this manager explains, sufficient confidence can be more important than sufficient information when it comes to decision making:

If you're trying to make decisions on things that you need information about, [and] you can't get that information, clearly that's a constraint. But I think wise decision making is at least as often constrained by not having the courage to be able to make a decision. Quite often people seek more and more information to improve their confidence level. Sometimes sufficient confidence is being able to say that I've actually got enough [information] now.

A key aspect of wisdom that serves as a foundation for most of the aspects we have already discussed is reflection. For example, reflection on events experienced during and after decision situations is what makes it possible for a manager to better understand her cognitive abilities or to learn over time how to regulate and eventually master emotions. A manager's wisdom relies on two types of reflection: internal and external.

Internal reflection

Perhaps the most important source of knowledge and insight in decision making is the manager herself. As managers make numerous important decisions as a part of their management responsibility, learning from previous decisions and actions can serve as an important source of knowledge for managers. A manager who is unable to reflect on previous decisions, critically assess them, and apply lessons learnt from those experiences may not be able to understand the interrelationships that underpin decision situations, particularly complex or wicked situations. Our study of management wisdom shows that reflection plays a critical role in wise management practice.

Reflection is an in-depth consideration of phenomena or events by which the person attempts to understand a situation, her thoughts and feelings about it, as well as of those who are involved, in order to better understand the situation and people involved (Bolton, 2010). Reflection "involves reviewing or reliving an experience to bring it into focus. Seemingly innocuous details might prove to be key; seemingly vital details may be irrelevant" (Bolton, 2010, p. 13). By applying internal reflection, a manager can make decisions based on careful consideration and evaluation of her own attributes, capacities, values, and beliefs, and by reflection on her own previous mistakes, successes, and experiences. Internal reflection is concerned with the following aspects:

- critical assessment of previous decisions (learning from one's own mistakes);
- (re)evaluation of one's own values system, interests, and goals; and
- (re)evaluation of one's own knowledge, abilities, emotions, etc.

Success in management requires a high level of flexibility in terms of learning and developing expertise and competencies. To this end, wisdom engages continuous and active reflection on one's own thoughts, attitudes, and behaviours. Internal reflection is a form of self-awareness that helps a decision maker acquire better understanding of themselves and their personal capacities, (in)abilities, and knowledge by comparing that understanding of self with the realities of the external world. This important point is made by an experienced CEO from a non-governmental voluntary association:

> I think self-awareness, the ability to understand one's own fallibilities and weaknesses, fits into experience. So, experience is a great teacher. Experience teaches us where we have made mistakes, if we can learn from our mistakes, if we can look back at our life, and we can say "I did this, this and this. That worked, but those two didn't", that is part of self-awareness. It is a part of knowing where our limitations are, it is part of knowing where our strengths and weaknesses are, but it is also part of recognizing what we did that worked and what we did that didn't work. Self-awareness is absolutely crucial.

The same point is made by a young senior manager:

> Learning from your mistakes [helps with making wise decisions]. I think it's about looking back to see what's happened. [...] I think the unwise man is the person who makes some mistakes and never looks at what they did. And they make the same mistakes again. And they make them again and again. For me being wise is making mistakes, being aware that you've just made a mistake, looking at what's occurred and learning from it to ensure that you don't make the same one again.

The sentiments above emphasize an important aspect of management practice in the real world. A manager cannot always make wise decisions and act wisely in all situations. The wickedness of many management decision situations, as well as the complexity and the constantly changing nature of the business environment, require managers to continuously reflect on their experiences, expertise, and behaviours to succeed. As was the case with knowledge, the accumulation of experience does not necessarily make a manager an effective decision maker. It is more important for a manager to be able to learn from experience, and apply these lessons to future decision situations. This idea is clearly supported by the general manager of a large private accounting company:

> Those whom I consider as being wise, I think they are wise because they have not just experience, but they also delve down to the real causes and effects of what they have learned from that experience.

In wise management practice, learning from experience is accompanied by the necessity of being flexible enough to challenge one's own values and beliefs:

> Wisdom could involve applying one's own values and beliefs to a complex situation, but it could also mean checking and challenging one's own values and beliefs and coming to a different view – and knowing the difference is part of the wisdom dimension.

Questioning and critically re-evaluating one's own underlying assumptions, values, and beliefs is done in light of what is happening in the wider environment (Intezari & Pauleen, 2018). One manager states that although values and beliefs are involved in wisdom, checking those values and beliefs is also associated with wisdom:

> Wise managers do constant re-evaluation of their own values. They know that everything changes around them: people, market, technology, society's values system, everything. So, wise managers always check their knowledge and beliefs for any changes.

Accordingly, internal reflection needs to always be accompanied by another form of reflection: external reflection.

External reflection

As we have previously stated, organizations do not operate in isolation from the business community and society in which they operate. Organizations have an impact on society and are influenced by society. Management is a social practice in that managers' decisions and actions reflect the values and beliefs of the managers, organization, and society. These values and beliefs construct an organization's culture. Organizational culture is a pattern of common assumptions, values, beliefs, and attitudes that influences organizational behaviour (Schein, 1985, 2004). The culture involves patterns of basic assumptions which define the way in which organizational members' perceptions, thoughts, and feelings relate to the problems of internal integration and external adaptation (Ravasi & Schultz, 2006; Schein, 1985). Organizational culture is not separate from the culture of the society in which the organization operates. For this reason, being aware of and actively reflecting on the values and beliefs that are prevalent – or which may be changing – in the society is central to the success of management practice. As a complement to internal reflection, external reflection is an important aspect of management wisdom. Wisdom requires reflection on:

- critical assessment of others' decisions (learning from others' mistakes);
- (re)evaluation of others' values systems, interests, and goals; and
- (re)evaluation of others' knowledge and abilities.

By reflecting on stakeholders' and society's values and beliefs, a manager can be in a better position to see whether or not management decisions and practices are aligned with what the society promotes. A manager highlights the importance of considering the community and society's values and beliefs in management practice:

> You [need] to be outward-looking and understanding of what is important to the community around you, their values and beliefs, […] and being aware that in five years those things may be different. So you have to continuously ask the question, have to be continually seeking information, trying to understand, and then change the way you are doing things.

Cultures are dynamic so societies' values and beliefs continuously change and transform over time. Accordingly, wise managers continuously reflect on the stakeholders' and society's values systems and interests to ensure that the management decisions and practices are always done based on a true understanding of the contemporary values of the society within which they are operating.

> If you look at history, there are decisions and approaches taken at that time in history that would have been considered very wise. But as our society values change over time, we look back and would say perhaps they weren't ethical by today's values, by today's standards. So, [wisdom] is very much driven or shaped by the current contemporary values of a society within which we operate.

Another aspect of external reflection is learning from others' mistakes. Most of the managers interviewed by the authors considered wise managers able to learn from others. For them, wise managers not only learn from their own mistakes, they also try not to make the same mistakes as others. The owner and CEO of a private company operating in the resource management consulting industry explicitly highlights that learning from experiences is not restricted to one's own mistakes and successes. He asserts:

> Wisdom is not just based on your experience. Wise managers need to have the ability to learn from other people's mistakes and successes. So, not just your own personal experiences, but others' as well. To look to others and see what they've done well and what they've done poorly, and to learn from those mistakes or successes. And to think "how does that apply to me?"

Similarly, another CEO with more than 30 years of management experience mentions that the development of wisdom requires reflection through which the person can learn from others:

> I think wise managers learn from others, from others' mistakes. Because by nature being wise would suggest that you have a degree of humbleness and openness. You

didn't get that wisdom when you are born; you got it from being open and exposing yourself to others. If you don't invest in your wisdom, it'll go away.

Wisdom aspects summary

The nine wisdom aspects discussed here are interrelated. While there might be many other factors that can affect the effectiveness of management practice, and which may not be completely under the manager's control, the wisdom aspects are under the manager's control. The nine wisdom aspects and the associated descriptions are summarized in Table 7.2.

Table 7.2 Wisdom aspects and their descriptive points

Wisdom aspects	Descriptive points
Future Thinking	- Analysing outcomes and ramifications - Short-term and long-te rm thinking
Perspective Taking	- Representing alternative points of view (including impartiality – openness to others' ideas) - Reconciling individual and communal (different stakeholders') interests
Ethical Consideration	- Consideration of moral and ethical codes
Self-Awareness	- Awareness of personal (in-)abilities, strengths and weaknesses - Awareness of what one's own knowledge (which includes knowing what one knows, and what one does not know) - Awareness of one's personality (values, interests and behavioural characteristics)
Other-Awareness	- Awareness of others' (in-)abilities, strengths and weaknesses - Awareness of others' knowledge (knowing what others know, and what they do not know) - Awareness of others' personality (values, interests and behavioural characteristics) - Situational awareness
Cognitive Mastery	- Possessing relevant knowledge (having expertise) - Knowing how and being able to acquire the required data, information, and knowledge - Knowing how and being able to use knowledge in the decision situation - Possessing insight (insightful as opposed to superficial) - Thinking outside the square (being creative and innovative)
Emotional Mastery	- Emotional regulation (emotional balance, e.g. avoidance of excessive anger, fear, even happiness, as well as resistance against making rash decisions) - Confidence (feeling confident, but not overly confident)
Internal Reflection	- (Re)evaluation of one's own core assumptions, values system, and interests - (Re)evaluation of one's own knowledge and abilities - Critical assessment of previous decisions (learning from one's own mistakes)
External Reflection	- (Re)evaluation of others' (including individuals and society) core assumptions, values system, and interests - (Re)Evaluation of others' knowledge and abilities - Critical assessment of others' decisions (learning from others)

Although we have not yet discussed in detail how the wisdom aspects are interrelated, wise management practice suggests all the wisdom aspects will be present and integrated in important management decisions and actions. In the next chapter we further discuss the wisdom aspects and introduce an integral model of wise management decision making.

Chapter summary

In this chapter, we discussed the main aspects of management wisdom. Based on an overview of wisdom aspects that we had discussed in Chapter 2, we briefly explained the relationship between wisdom and decision making. We then identified empirically nine wisdom aspects including future thinking, considering alternative points of view, ethics, cognitive mastery, emotional mastery, self-awareness, other-awareness, internal reflection, and external reflection. These factors affect the effectiveness of decision making. Due to the complex and dynamic nature of each of the wisdom aspects, the aspects overlap and are interrelated.

It is difficult to draw a line which neatly separates the different wisdom aspects. As we shall argue in the following chapter, the wisdom aspects need to be viewed as an integrated whole, a holonic nexus. In the following chapter we discuss in detail the wisdom aspects and their interrelationships. We will also introduce the model central to this book's thesis, an Integral Model of Wise Decision Making. This model reinforces that the nine wisdom aspects are interrelated qualities, which need to be simultaneously present in the decision-making process in order for managers to be more cognizant of decision situations as they emerge and to enhance the effectiveness of the decision-making process and ultimately of the decisions made and the actions implemented.

References

Ackoff, R. L. (1999). On learning and the systems that facilitate it. *Reflection*, 1(1), 14–29.

Arnold Sr., D. F., Dorminey, J. W., Neidermeyer, A. A., & Neidermeyer, P. E. (2013). Internal and external auditor ethical decision-making. *Managerial Auditing Journal*, 28(4), 300–322.

Baltes, P. B., & Kunzmann, U. (2003). Wisdom: The peak of human excellence in the orchestration of mind and virtue. *The Psychologist*, 16(3), 131–133.

Bergsma, A., & Ardelt, M. (2012). Self-reported wisdom and happiness: An empirical investigation. *Journal of Happiness Studies*, 13(3), 481–499.

Biloslavo, R., & McKenna, B. (2013). Testing a 4-dimensional model of wisdom on wise political leaders. In W. Küpers & D. J. Pauleen (Eds.), *A handbook of practical wisdom: Leadership, organization and integral business practice* (pp. 111–132). Aldershot, UK: Gower.

Birren, J. E., & Fisher, L. M. (1990). The elements of wisdom: Overview and integration. In R. J. Sternberg (Ed.), *Wisdom: Its nature, origins, and development* (pp. 317–332). Cambridge, UK: Cambridge University Press.

Blasi, P. (2006). The European university – Towards a wisdom-based society. *Higher Education in Europe*, 31(4), 403–407.

Bolton, G. (2010). *Reflective practice: Writing & professional development* (3rd ed.). London: Sage.

Boyatzis, R. E., Stubbs, E. C., & Taylor, S. N. (2002). Learning cognitive and emotional intelligence competencies through graduate management education. *Academy of Management Learning and Education*, 1(2), 150–162.

Csikszentmihalyi, M., & Rathunde, K. (1990). The psychology of wisdom: An evolutionary inter-pretation. In R. J. Sternberg (Ed.), *Wisdom: Its nature, origins, and development* (pp. 25–51). New York: Cambridge.

Hays, J. M. (2007). Dynamics of organizational wisdom. *The Business Renaissance Quarterly*, 2(4), 77–122.

Holian, R. (2006). Management decision making, ethical issues and 'emotional' intelligence. *Management Decision*, 44(8), 1122–1138.

Intezari, A. (2014). *Wisdom and decision making: Grounding theory in management practice. School of Management*. Massey University, Auckland, New Zealand.

Intezari, A., & Pauleen, D. J. (2013). Students of wisdom: An integral Meta-competencies theory of practical wisdom. In W. Küpers & D. J. Pauleen (Eds.), *A handbook of practical wisdom: Leadership, organization and integral business practice* (pp. 155–174). Aldershot, UK: Gower.

Intezari, A. & Pauleen, D. J. (2018). Conceptualizing wise management decision-making: A grounded theory approach. *Decision Sciences*, 49(2), 335–400.

Kemmis, S., & Smith, T. J. (2008). Personal praxis: Learning through experience. In S. Kemmis & T. J. Smith (Eds.), *Enabling praxis: Challenges for education* (pp. 15–35). Rotterdam: Sense Publishers.

Kitchener, K. S., & Brenner, H. G. (1990). Wisdom and reflective judgment: Knowing in the face of uncertainty. In R. J. Sternberg (Ed.) *Wisdom: Its nature, origins, and development* (pp. 212–229). New York: Cambridge University Press.

Korac-Kakabadse, N., Korac-Kakabadse, A., & Kouzmin, A. (2001). Leadership renewal: Towards the philosophy of wisdom. *International Review of Administrative Sciences*, 67(2), 207–227.

Lombardo, T. (2010). Wisdom facing forward what it means to have heightened. *Futurist*, 44(5), 34–42.

Maddalena, V., & Canada, H. (2007). A practical approach to ethical decision-making. *Leadership in Health Services*, 20(2), 71–75.

Marker, A. W. (2013). The development of practical wisdom: Its critical role in sustainable per-formance. *Performance Improvement*, 52(4), 11–21.

Marková, I. S. (2005). *Insight in psychiatry*. Cambridge, UK: Cambridge University Press.

Matthews, P. (1998). What lies beyond knowledge management: Wisdom creation and versatility. *Journal of Knowledge Management*, 1(3), 207–214.

McKenna, B. (2005). Wisdom, ethics and the postmodern organization. In D. Rooney, G. Hearn, & A. Ninan (Eds.), *Handbook on the knowledge economy* (pp. 37–53). Cheltenham, UK: Edward Elgar.

Meacham, J. A. (1990). The loss of wisdom. In R. J. Sternberg (Ed.), *Wisdom: Its nature, origins, and development* (pp. 181–211). New York: Cambridge University Press.

Nonaka, I., & Takeuchi, H. (2011). The big idea: The wise leader. *Harvard Business Review*, 89(5), 58–67.

Ravasi, D., & Schultz, M. (2006). Responding to organizational identity threats: Exploring the role of organizational culture. *Academy of Management Journal*, 49(3), 433–458.

Rest, J. R. (1984). The major components of morality. In W. Kurtines & J. Gewirtz (Eds.), *Morality, moral behaviour, and moral development* (pp. 24–40). New York: John Wiley & Sons.

Rest, J. R. (1986). *Moral development: Advances in research and theory*. New York: Praeger.

Rooney, D., & McKenna, B. (2008). Wisdom in public administration: Looking for a sociology of wise practice. *Public Administration Review*, 68(4), 709–721.

Schein, E. H. (1985). Defining organizational culture. *Classics of Organization Theory*, 3, 490–502.

Schein, E. H. (2004). Learning when and how to lie: A neglected aspect of organizational and occupational socialization. *Human Relations* , 57(3), 260–273.

Senge, P. M. (1990). *The fifth discipline: The art and practice of the learning organization*. New York: Currency Doubleday.

Solansky, S. T. (2014). To fear foolishness for the sake of wisdom: a message to leaders. *Journal of Business Ethics*, 122(1), 39–51.

Sternberg, R. J. (1990). Wisdom and its relations to intelligence and creativity. In R. J. Sternberg (Ed.), *Wisdom: Its nature, origins, and development* (pp. 142–159). New York: Cambridge University Press.

Sternberg, R. J. (2004). Words to the wise about wisdom? *Human Development*, 47(5), 286–289.

Tikkanen, H., Lamberg, J. A., Parvinen, P., & Kallunki, J. P. (2005). Managerial cognition, action and the business model of the firm. *Management Decision*, 43(6), 789–809.

Webster, J. D. (2007). Measuring the character strength of wisdom. *International Journal of Aging and Human Development*, 65(2), 163–183.

8 Wise management decision making

Introduction

We have covered a great deal of ground in this book. We have learnt about the complexity of decision situations, and the diversity of approaches to making decisions. We have also learned about data, analytics, information, and knowledge, as well as the role of experience and intuition that can support decision making. We have addressed wisdom in general and in the previous chapter we reviewed major aspects of wisdom empirically explored in business contexts.

In this chapter, we learn more about these wisdom aspects. We will introduce a model of wise management decision making. This model provides a framework for making effective decisions in complex decision situations. Drawing on practical guidelines it explains how various wisdom aspects, the major knowledge sources, and multiple decision-making approaches can be brought together in the decision-making process. While the theory has implications at various managerial levels and with different kinds of decisions, it is more concerned with strategic management decisions. These decisions usually deal with mid- and long-term plans or strategies, have potentially profound impacts on multiple stakeholders, and are, therefore, often characterized by high levels of ambiguity and uncertainty. The increasing complexity of decision making in contemporary business is also influenced by various factors such as competition, time and budget and other constraints, the increasing pace of innovation, new technologies, politics and power, as well as regulations and environmental and social responsibilities. For this reason, effective strategic management decisions engage a number of qualities including sound judgement, relevant experience, ethics, awareness, intuition, emotions, empathy, and importantly the responsibility of the decision consequences.

The ability to link the human factors and the factors around the decision situation will aid managers in making more effective and wise decisions while facing complex or wicked problems (Chapter 3). Unlike the DIKW hierarchy (discussed in Chapter 4), the theory of wise management decision making underscores the point that it is too simplistic to assume that wisdom is just a higher level of knowledge. The theory offers an overarching and integrative approach to handle the complexity surrounding management strategic decision making by integrating multiple factors, levels, and dimensions. The nine wisdom aspects discussed in the previous chapter are refined and categorized under four categories (henceforth, called 'wisdom principles').

The wisdom principles include:

- Multi-Perspective Consideration (MPC),
- Self-Other Awareness (SOA),
- Emotional-Cognitive Mastery (ECM), and
- Internal and External Reflection (IER).

These wisdom principles guide the decision maker's approach to decision making holistically, rather than just providing a set or order of specific and fragmented decision functions. As discussed in Chapter 6, decision making may be characterized as a linear process (as offered by the rational approach) (Drucker, 1967), or non-linear (as offered by the naturalist approach). As Mintzberg and Westley (2001), and McKenna and Martin-Smith (2005) emphasize, in real-world settings decisions are not always the outcome of a pre-defined set of sequential activities; rather they are often made through a non-sequential or non-linear process. Wise decision making does not neatly fall into any of the categories. Wise decision making is a multi-faceted process, which acknowledges that a multiplicity of interconnected factors can influence the quality of the decisions. The model that we introduce in this chapter is more a meta decision-making model, which provides a meta approach to the whole process of decision making.

Meta decision-making level

Strategic management decisions require multiple, ongoing, and often simultaneous decisions. As Simon (1960) long ago emphasized, each phase of a decision-making process is itself a decision-making process. For example, to articulate the problem in the problem-finding phase, decisions need to be made about what information to gather and from what sources. Should the manager trust his intuition, or does he need to investigate specific sources of data and information in order to provide explicit explanations of the problem? Similarly, the problem-solving phase may call for a new decision-making process, which may have its own problem-finding and problem-solving phases. For example, the 'alternative development' phase requires decision making on what criteria to use to assess alternatives.

In addition to sub-decisions, strategic decision making usually includes a pre-decision-making stage. The pre-decision-making stage determines the decision maker's approach to the whole decision-making process. When a decision maker encounters a decision situation, even before (or as) he begins to apply decision functions to find and apply a solution, he (simultaneously) plans his approach to the decision making (Mintzberg, Raisinghani, & Théorêt, 1976). In addition to making a decision on budgeting and resourcing the strategic decision-making process, the manager continuously and critically (re-)evaluates his position, as the decision maker, in relation to the decision process and multiple stakeholders. This pre-decision-making stage can be referred to as 'decision planning' (Minzberg et al., 1976, p. 261). We call it the meta decision-making process. Meta decision making is when the decision maker makes decisions about the decision-making process itself (Figure 8.1).

Although meta decision making is critical to the success of strategic decision making, the decision-making process is something of a black box. This is because the process of making decisions about the yet to be determined decision-making process is happening inside the decision maker's mind and it is not documented (Minzberg et al., 1976). Among the early researchers who have noted this pre-decision-making stage are

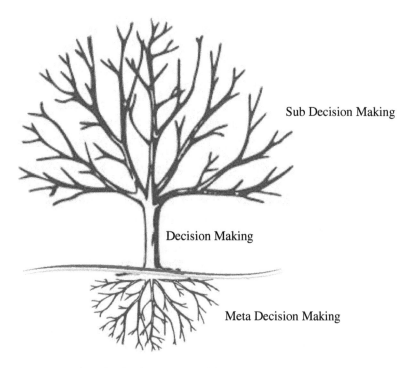

Sub Decision Making

Decision Making

Meta Decision Making

Figure 8.1 Three levels of strategic decision making

Cyert, Simon, and Trow (1956), and Newell and Simon (1972). The multi-level nature of management strategic decisions is well captured in a statement by Simon (1960). He describes decision making as consisting of "wheels within wheels within wheels" (p. 3).

At the meta decision-making stage, upon encountering the decision situation, the manager, based on prior knowledge and experience, makes suppositions about the decision situation, and begins to make decisions on how to handle the decision-making process. The suppositions involve matters such as the significance and scope of the issue, whether or not the decision can be effectively handled using a rational or non-rational approach, and allocating organizational resources. The meta decision-making stage has significant impact on the success or failure of a decision. For example, if a manager identifies a decision situation as being a non-significant one, he may decide not to get involved in the decision-making process and delegate the decision making to lower-level managers. This decision may lead to disastrous consequences, for example, when the manager's supposition about the decision situation was wrong and the manager assigned to handle the decision situation fails to do so. Similarly, in a decision situation where multiple perspectives of stakeholders with high levels of experience and a priori knowledge are required, the manager may end up making a poor decision if he characterized the decision situation as requiring data and analytics and a rational decision-making process.

Whatever inferences the manager makes about the decision-making process as a whole will affect all sub-decisions and their effects. For this reason, we have conceptualized a wise management decision-making model as a meta decision-making model. As such it informs all phases and stages of the decision-making process. Essentially, we argue that wise decision making is, or can become, a form of 'embodied knowledge' that manifests habitually when decision situations emerge.

Wise management decision making

Let us begin with a seemingly simple question: What is a wise management decision? Before we delve into the discussion of the theory of wise decision making, it is important to understand first what we mean by decisions by management that qualify as wise. A wise management decision is the decision that achieves the *right ends* using the *right means* at the *right time*. 'Right ends' here refers to the *legitimate* and *ethical* interests of multiple stakeholders involved in and directly or indirectly affected by the decision and subsequent actions. Stakeholders may include employees, managers, the organization as a whole, customers and business partners, the business community, and the wider community (society and the environment). *Right means* implies that the selected alternative should not involve the use of coercion or unethical means; rather the implementation of the right decision should be done with the *right means*, that is, by abiding by legal and ethical obligations. While donating to a charity might be a *right end for an organization*, doing so through a compulsory deduction of employees' salaries would not be a *right means*. The 'right time' means that the decision is made when it will have the most positive impact. If a decision is made later than when it is supposed to be, the scope and the level of the problem's negative impacts may increase. If a decision is made earlier than it should be, i.e. based on the initial signs of a decision situation, the decision maker may not have enough time to investigate all the aspects of the decision situation. The decision maker may make his decision based on a superficial examination of some apparent aspects of the problem, if the decision maker rushes to make the decision.

Wise management decision making explains a meta decision-making perspective that enhances the chances of making an effective strategic decision, given the wickedness of today's management decision situations (Chapter 3), fallibility of knowledge (Chapter 4), the emergence of analytics (Chapter 5), as well as the complexity of management decision-making processes (Chapter 6). While managers may use various mechanisms and techniques to make strategic decisions, an effective strategic decision requires a meta decision-making perspective on how a diverse range of stakeholders' interests can be appropriately addressed while the stakeholders' well-being is achieved to the greatest extent possible.

According to the wise decision-making model, an effective management decision is made based on four principles, which themselves are based on the wisdom aspects discussed in Chapter 7. The first principle is concerned with the extent to which multiple perspectives are taken into account: we call this principle Multi-Perspective Consideration (MPC). The second principle underlies the integration of cognition and emotions in the decision-making process: we call this principle Cognitive-Emotional Mastery (CEM). Another important principle of wise decision making is Self-Other Awareness (SOA). SOA underpins the importance of self-awareness and awareness of the surrounding environment in management decision making. The fourth principle underlies the other principles, and refers to the extent to which the decision maker applies detailed consideration and critical (re-)evaluation of the decision-related facts and assumptions: we call this principle Internal-External Reflection (IER) (Figure 8.2).

The wisdom principles and their relationships are discussed below.

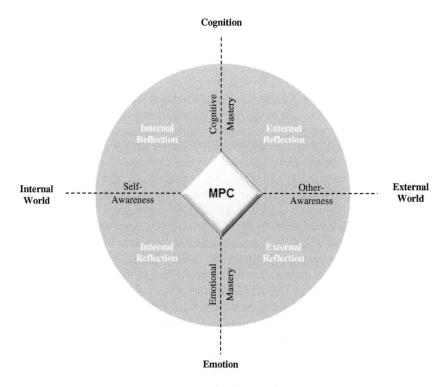

Figure 8.2 Wise management decision-making: the conceptual model

Multi-Perspective Consideration (MPC)

The impacts of strategic decisions are often profound and long-term. For this reason, strategic decisions engage multiple stakeholders. Stakeholders consist of those who are directly and indirectly affected by the decision, including managers (the decision maker or the decision-making team), employees, the organization as an entity, customers, vendors, business partners, and society. Effective management decisions are, therefore, made based on a true understanding of the bigger picture and the subsequent impacts of the decision, alternative points of view, and individual and communal interests and values.

This principle is based on the belief that strategic decisions have social consequences, and, therefore, need to be made based on a true understanding of stakeholders' diverse and sometimes conflicting interests and values. This principle encourages the decision maker to gain a comprehensive understanding of the stakeholders' perspectives, identify the shared values and interests, and make the decision accordingly. Wisdom reflects the recognition of multiple perspectives (Grossman et al., 2012), and requires a holistic and concerted effort to bring a wide range of different aspects of a decision situation into consideration.

Wisdom is intimately linked with ethics (Goede, 2011), and engages the ability to see the bigger picture (Cammock, 2003), beyond the immediate horizon (Hays, 2007). A wise management decision, therefore, not only achieves the organization's legitimate goals, but also enhances the well-being of stakeholders: not just considering and accounting for, for example, financial success, but also the social and environmental effects and implications. MPC refers to the extent to which a decision takes into account the short- and long-term consequences of the available courses of action, alternative points of view, multiple stakeholders' individual and communal interests, as well as legal and ethical commitments. MPC is operationalized in the management decision-making process in the form of three qualities: 'future thinking', 'perspective taking', and 'ethical consideration'.

Future thinking

Making a wise decision requires a critical analysis of the decision's outcomes and ramifications over the short and long term: we call this aspect of the MPC principle 'future thinking'. Both short- and long-term consequences of the decision must be taken into account during the decision-making process. Strategic management is envisioning the future (MacMillan & Tampoe, 2000) and wisdom as "the ability to perceive and evaluate the long-run consequences of behavior" (Ackoff, 1999, p. 14). As we will see in Chapter 9, wise management decision making requires the ability to see beyond what has happened in the past to what will possibly happen in the future. Future thinking is the systematic exploration of and reflection on what will happen in the future, especially as a result of present decisions and actions, as well as how these will be perceived. Although the future may not be precisely predictable, the decision maker can to some extent foresee a continuum of ramifications and changes that will occur stretching into the future. This kind of future-oriented thinking is critical to strategic management decision making in volatile times, as it envisions and illuminates the strategic direction of the organization.

Perspective taking

Understanding the reaction of those who are affected by the decision is important for making right decisions. Wisdom requires a detailed consideration of multiple stakeholders' individual and communal interests, values, and preferences. We call this aspect of MPC 'perspective taking'. Perspective taking refers to:

> understanding the attitudes that others have toward a particular problem or solution. It is empathy applied to problem solving. Perspective taking means being sensitive to other people's perspectives and goals – being able to understand their point of view on different issues.
>
> (Northouse, 2016, p. 49)

A wise solution is developed based on a correct recognition, evaluation, and synthesis of alternative perspectives (Kitchener & Brenner, 1990). Considering multiple perspectives in decision making requires the manager to be impartial and open to divergent points of views and ideas. By listening to different ideas the manager may be able to better understand the decision situation or identify new sources of action to address the decision situation. In this sense, MPC is linked to another wisdom principle, cognitive mastery, which is discussed later in this chapter.

Ethical consideration

Another important aspect of MPC is 'ethical consideration'. The engagement of a wide range of stakeholders in strategic decisions, and the uncertainty underlying strategic decision situations, increase the number and intensity of ethical issues surrounding management decisions and actions. Management practitioners and scholars have been extensively calling for the necessity of and attention to ethics in the field of management (Donaldson, 2007; Smyth, 2008). The influence of ethics in the business world is well reflected by the metaphor of the 'minefield'. Executives work in a 'moral minefield' where apparently harmless decisions can have devastating consequences not only for the decision maker but for all others involved (Messick & Bazerman, 2001). Wise management decision making is an ethical practice in nature, process, and outcome (Intezari & Pauleen, 2014). A wise manager can diagnose circumstances in a way that truth, and creative possibilities, are integrated with ethics (Waddock, 2010).

This focus on the criticality of MPC in wise management decisions concurs with previous studies of wisdom, such as Intezari and Pauleen (2014), Grossman et al. (2012), Erickson (2009), Reznitskaya and Sternberg (2004), and Kitchener and Brenner (1990). Similarly, Nonaka and Takeuchi (2011) stress that wise leadership requires a consideration of people's goals, values, and interests. This wisdom principle also resonates with Sternberg's (1998) Balance Theory, which holds that both individual and communal interests over the short and long terms are inextricably linked to wisdom.

MPC is based on the integration of the decision maker's awareness of self and others, as well as mastery of cognition and emotion (CEM). Taking different perspectives and alternative points of view, unifying diverse interests at the individual and communal levels, and considering one's own values and shared societal values all require a high level of awareness of self and others.

Self-Other Awareness (SOA)

The process of strategic management decision making, characterized in terms of multi-stakeholder engagement and uncertainty, is a process of dealing with divergent interests and potential conflicts. Strategic decision making, therefore, requires a high level of awareness of numerous facets of the decision situation and stakeholders. The awareness ought to be comprehensive and include the decision maker, those around him, the organization, and the surrounding environment. Wisdom includes one's awareness of one's own fallibilities, one's knowledge, and of what one does not know (Meacham, 1990), as well as an integrative and holistic understanding of the surrounding environment (Lombardo, 2010).

SOA refers to extent to which a manager is aware of his 'Internal world' (self-awareness) and the 'External world' (other-awareness). The 'Internal world' corresponds to the manager's internal attributes, which include: (1) strengths, weaknesses, abilities, and inabilities; (2) knowledge (which includes knowing what one knows, and what one does not know); and (3) one's personality (including values, interests, and behavioural characteristics). Self-awareness, therefore, is concerned with the manager's awareness of his internal world.

The 'External world', on the other hand, refers to one's surrounding environment and the decision situation. The management team, employees, external stakeholders' interests, and society's values are, for example, part of the external world. Other-awareness refers to the extent to which the manager is aware of the external world which includes:

- others' strengths and weaknesses, abilities and inabilities;
- others' knowledge (knowing what others know, and what they do not know);
- others' personalities (values, interests, and behavioural characteristics); and
- situational awareness (the key elements of the situation that affect the decision including the constraints imposed by organizational, political, social, or environmental factors).

Robinson (1990) points out that knowing what values, principles, and priorities one holds is a critical part of wisdom. This quality enacts a fundamental role when it comes to decision making. A lack of awareness of what one knows or does not know, as well as one's strengths, weaknesses, and (in-)abilities may turn the manager's attention from a critical meta decision-making level question: 'Am I capable to make the decision?' If he does not ask this question, he may wrongly assume that he is qualified to make a particular decision.

Emphasizing the importance of awareness in decision making, Bazerman and Chugh (2006) refer to 'bounded awareness' (discussed in Chapter 6) and explain that bounded awareness leads the decision maker to unconsciously ignore some information. Bounded awareness may lead executives to make unsound decisions (Bazerman & Chugh, 2006) as it limits the decision maker's MPC. One's awareness of what one knows and does not know, as well as admitting that no-one is omniscient, is a prerequisite for being able to make wise decisions. A lack of awareness of what one does not know or, as Bazerman and Chugh (2006) emphasize, a lack of awareness of the information that might remain out of focus, leads managers to fail to make appropriate decisions at a given time. Wise managers also admit when their ideas or thoughts are implausible or wrong. This awareness enables the manager to attract and be receptive to any ideas that might be useful in addressing the problem at hand. To this end, self-awareness is accompanied by the decision maker's awareness of the external world.

As discussed in Chapter 4, a manager's knowledge and experience may fall short when dealing with wicked decision situations. Accordingly, managers need to be able to acquire required knowledge and information, and also to consider other points of view when dealing with wicked problems. Other-awareness enables the manager to know where to seek advice when needed (Holliday & Chandler, 1986; Korac-Kakabadse, Korac-Kakabadse, & Kouzmin, 2001; Kramer, 1990). A manager who knows what others around him know, or what their strengths, weaknesses, and (in-)abilities are, has the opportunity to reduce his knowledge gap by seeking relevant advice or knowledge. Having a team of people with a range of knowledge and experience can be very useful in making wise decisions by complementing the manager's knowledge and abilities. A strong team that the manager trusts includes people who are not afraid of openly raising concerns and giving honest advice to the manager. Baltes and Staudinger (2000) and Sternberg (1986) argue that wisdom is associated with such competences as the ability to listen to others, evaluate and weigh advice, and to give advice to others.

Other-awareness also engages situational awareness. In complex and dynamic situations, the quality of a decision depends on the decision maker's situational awareness (Endsley, 2004). Situational awareness refers to the decision maker's awareness of what is going on in the environment around him. The environment will include elements and constraints such as:

- organizational (e.g. limited budget and human resources, organizational culture, demands from customers, business partners, or shareholders);
- political (e.g. unexpected changes in legislation, pressures and demands from political parties, and lobbies);
- socio-environmental (e.g. pressures from environmentalists and unions, dominant social values and beliefs); and
- economic (e.g. financial pitfalls, economic changes, and trends in the market).

Situational awareness is concerned with information that is relevant to the task at hand (Endsley, 2004).

Central to situational awareness is the awareness of the values and beliefs that are prevalent in the organization, wider community, and society (Figure 8.2). Effective management decisions are congruent with organizational and social values (Maddalena & Canada, 2007). As Sharp (2007) put it, "It is a serious mistake – a very poor judgment – to think that one can think in terms of what is good for others who are different from oneself, without knowing what they think and believe is good for them" (p. 301).

SOA is interconnected with MPC. Based on SOA, wise managers are able to act effectively in a given context, interact empathically with others, and make sound judgements and decisions by bearing in mind and unifying different points of view. This interconnection also helps the decision maker with the most important (meta) decision: "Who is the best decision maker for this decision?" (Hess & Bacigalupo, 2011, p. 714). SOA can enable managers to gain a more comprehensive understanding of the interconnections between themselves, their organizations, and the wider community (through Internal-External Reflection, as discussed later in this chapter). This gives the manager the ability to see how their behaviours affect other people, and how they can use their behaviour in a positive way to inform decisions. Wise managers always consider the internal and external worlds together and constantly evaluate and re-evaluate their decision-making position, knowledge, beliefs, values system, and attributes against both their internal world and the external world as well as the interconnection of both.

Cognitive-Emotional Mastery (CEM)

Wisdom is an amalgamation of cognition, affect (emotion), and conation (volition), and develops as a balance of these three qualities. Wise decisions are the result of this balance (Birren & Fisher, 1990). As Matthews (1998) puts it: "a wise person weighs the knowns and the unknowns, resists overwhelming emotion while maintaining interest, and carefully chooses when and where to take action" (p. 211). Wisdom requires a harmony between emotion and reason (Roca, 2007). Harmonization here means considering both reason and emotion when making a decision at a given time. Harmonization does not necessarily mean equal attention to either reason or emotion. Rather, the decision maker may rely more on reason than emotion on one occasion and vice versa on another. Recognizing that there is no confrontation or trade-off between emotion and cognition in decision making, a manager needs both cognitive and emotional competencies in order to make a wise management decision. Cognitive-Emotional Mastery (CEM) refers to the extent to which the decision maker's cognitive abilities and emotional skills and qualities are integrated throughout the decision-making process.

Making wise management decisions requires the manager to not only have intellectual, cognitive, and reasoning abilities, but also be able to consider and integrate emotions when making decisions. Wise people are able to apply what they know, cognitively and emotionally, and thus to take right actions towards right ends. This is why wisdom is more than just accumulated knowledge (Intezari & Pauleen, 2014). The importance of emotions in management strategic decision making is such that some neuroscientists such as Damasio (2005) have empirically demonstrated that, when emotion is absent in decision making, it is almost impossible to make any decisions at all. Similar findings are reported in wisdom studies. Baltes and Staudinger (2000), for example, argue that wisdom refers to the balanced and coordinated interplay of intellectual and motivational aspects of human functioning. Moreover Kramer (1990) presents a framework (of which the central tenet is integration) conceptualizing wisdom and emphasizes that cognition, affect, feelings, and emotions are integrated and interdependently involved in wisdom.

Accordingly, both rationality and non-rationality play important roles in strategic decision making (Calabretta, Gemser, & Wijnberg, 2017). They link analytics, which are mainly based on data and information, with insight and creativity. In the same vein, Simon (1987, 1978) emphasizes that a theory of decision making should give an account of both logical (rational) and non-logical (non-rational) decision-making processes. The manager needs to be able to understand the relationship between available knowledge and previous experiences and the decision situation. With this understanding, he then can apply the knowledge and experience in the most effective way to address the decision situation.

Wise management decision making requires the manager to think outside the square. A decision maker who can do this can consider a wider range of alternatives, and different ways to evaluate those alternatives by using creative thinking (Anderson, 2002). This aspect of cognitive mastery connected with emotional mastery is critically important in future thinking (one aspect of the MPC principle). When the decision maker is evaluating the possible consequences of different alternatives, being creative is important, as the decision maker can imagine both alternatives and their consequences (Jones, Frish, Yurak, & Kim, 1998).

Wisdom in both traditional and contemporary discussions is associated with "holistic cognitive processes that move beyond a fragmented and impassive relativity, toward a more 'universal' or metasystemic awareness of interrelated systems" (Csikszentmihalyi & Rathunde, 1990, p. 31).

Managers with cognitive mastery do not make decisions based on a superficial analysis of the decision situation. They are able to explore possible meaningful relationships between different elements of a decision situation, including their own condition(s) in the decision situation. To this end, wisdom does not mean knowing specific or fragmented facts. Wisdom is 'knowing' the whole picture, with a true and deep understanding of the multidimensionality of, as well as the interrelationship among, the numerous aspects of the decision situation. Managers who want to make a wise decision need to balance excessive confidence and excessive cautiousness (Intezari & Pauleen, 2014). They need to have some confidence in their own ability to apply information and knowledge to the decision situation. The decision maker who, for example, is not overly confident is more likely to realize and admit his own limits of knowledge and experience. Confidence is central to making effective decisions. Managers need to have a reasonable level of confidence about the decisions that they make. The confidence dimension of emotional mastery can be developed based on awareness and reflection ('reflection' is discussed in the following section). Confidence is based on the manager's awareness of their knowledge and abilities. Knowing facts is dealt with by cognitive mastery, whereas balancing confidence and cautiousness engages emotional mastery.

As discussed in the previous chapter, emotional mastery is concerned with the emotional involvement of the decision maker in the management decision-making process in a way that the manager is not completely ignorant of or overly reliant on emotion. This balance complements and can enhance cognitive processes and decision making by directing the focus of attention, facilitating certain kinds of cognitive processes, helping with choosing among alternatives and making decisions, as well as broadening perspectives on problems (George, 2000). The scientific consensus about the role of emotion in decision making is growing. More and more findings underline that "emotion not only colours our perceptions and decisions; it appears, at the level of neurological circuitry, to be deeply embedded in the machinery of thought" (Hall, 2010, p. 65).

Wise decision making requires contemplation, and the decision maker should be able to regulate overwhelming emotion when articulating the decision problem and while assessing alternatives. For example, the decision maker should deal properly with anger and fear when making decisions and resist the tendency towards making rash decisions. Emotional mastery helps the decision maker to gain a more accurate perception and understanding of the decision situation. People's immediate reactions to decision situations are typically self-interested (Murnighan, Cantelon, & Elyashiv, 2001). Because the automatic responses are not controlled by conscious awareness, the individual's decision making and judgement are influenced by the automatic response. In situations where self-interest and professional responsibilities clash, self-interest provokes automatic responses to situations (Moore & Loewenstein, 2004).

Contemplation and patience before making decisions is critical in making appropriate ones as they help the decision maker to integrate different aspects and issues of a particular situation, for example balancing economic considerations and personal values (Bazerman & Malhotra, 2006; Keeney & Raiffa, 1993). This concern confirms the entwined link between CEM and MPC. Considering multiple perspectives requires time and contemplation. Birren and Fisher (1990) go on to argue that since wise people are not completely detached from the situation, they maintain a reflective state of mind that enables them to generate solutions to problems and integrate emotions. Wisdom, therefore, begins with a balance between passion and detachment or emotional regulation (Hall, 2010).

Applying CEM in the decision situation allows the manager to incorporate their feelings about the issues at hand into their decisions, and integrate them with the logical aspects of their decision-making ability. Based on a study of Western philosophy of wisdom and contemporary psychological studies, McKenna, Rooney, and Liesch (2006) list principles that, they argue, identify wisdom in management. According to the principles, wisdom in management is "based on reason but specifically incorporates the non-rational; a humane and virtuous teleology; practical action; and articulate communication" (p. 287). McKenna et al. (2006) assert that based on reason, wisdom evaluates the truth-value of the logical propositions of the reason applied to decision making. They also argue that by incorporating non-rationality, wisdom has a metaphysical, even spiritual, quality that releases wisdom from the rules of reason.

The need for applying CEM in decision making accords with Aristotle's notion of the doctrine of the mean (2009, *1107a*, 1–10), which posits that "excess and deficiency destroy perfection" (*1106b*, 12). The mean is an appropriate middle between two vices (Kleimann, 2013). The mean is not universal, but it is determined by the wise person (Aristotle, 2009, *1107a*, 1). That is, wise people behave in a mean state, and this is true for all other virtues.

For instance, wise people are neither cowardly nor rash. Thus, the integration of cognitive mastery and emotional mastery does not mean that cognition and emotion are limited in wise management decisions, but that the wise manager relies on various proportions of cognition and emotion depending on the situation. In some circumstances, the manager may need to make more rational decisions, while in others more intuitive ones. The balance between the two qualities also may vary from one person to another, according to the context, and in the relationship between the internal and the external.

Internal-external reflection

Perhaps the most important principle of wise management decision making is Internal-External Reflection (IER). As defined in the previous chapter, reflection is an in-depth consideration of phenomena or events by which a person attempts to better understand a situation, and his thoughts and feelings about it, as well as of those who are involved (Bolton, 2010). To make wise decisions managers need to continuously evaluate and re-evaluate their own position in the decision-making process against the internal and external world. In particular, when dealing with wicked problems and complex decision situations, where multiple stakeholders are involved and the consequences of the decision influence others' lives, reflection on inner and outer dimensions plays a critical role.

IER links both internal and external worlds together through the wise manager's awareness of the close interrelationship between self and the surrounding environment. IER is questioning the status quo, one's interrelationship with the wider community and the social world, as well as the way an individual accounts for his experience (Cunliffe, 2003). In this sense, wise management decision making is based on questioning core assumptions, and ways of being and doing.

IER opens managers up to critically analyse what is taken for granted in their practices. Through reflection internally and externally, a person can learn and develop by examining what he thinks has happened at a given time, and how others perceived the event and the person (Bolton, 2010). In particular, IER helps the manager appreciate the impacts of one's decisions and actions on others by examining and critically questioning one's own core assumptions, values, interests, and habitual thinking process. The manager can see the decision situation from the wider perspective, and locate himself in relation to the internal world, the wider external environment, and the problem at hand. EIR helps the manager to learn from previous experiences, and be impartial in considering various stakeholders' perspectives. Through IER, the manager questions his own knowledge and actions. It is a questioning of *how* one's presence and perspectives influence decisions and actions.

Reflection is not limited to assessing one's own understanding, knowledge, beliefs, and value systems, but also includes reflecting on the dominant values and beliefs of the external world (external reflection). External reflection is reflecting on other people's decisions, values, interests, goals, knowledge, and abilities as well as society's values system and beliefs in relation to a particular decision at a particular time. Through external reflection, wise managers can acquire better understanding of their surrounding environment that in turn can help them overcome their possible internal shortcomings.

Reflection enhances one's awareness of self and others (Bergsma & Ardelt, 2012). Waddock (2010) emphasizes that reflective practice is fundamental for developing wisdom as it enhances one's awareness of self, others, and systems. She argues that wisdom comprises three main components: moral imagination (considering the consequences of one's actions), systems understanding (realistic assessment of situations), and aesthetic sensibility (which combines logic/reason with perception/imagination). Furthermore, she suggests that for one to be able to 'see' the world 'holistically' through these three components, one needs to have awareness of self, others, and systems. This implies that reflection enhances the wise manager's MPC. Correspondingly, Bergsma and Ardelt (2012) define the reflective dimension of wisdom as "a perception of phenomena and events from multiple perspectives" that requires self-insight, self-examination, and self-awareness (p. 484). They emphasize that the capacity for self-examination and reflectivity provides the impetus to escape from relativistic intellectualization.

By questioning core assumptions of being and doing, wise management decisions may be made based on and/or lead to fundamental changes to both internal and external worlds. Wise managers are intellectually courageous, which refers to the extent to which one is intrinsically motivated and willing to conceive and examine alternative perspectives and ideas not popularly held.

Through IER, managers can develop a better SOA by understanding how their decisions and subsequent actions contribute to and affect themselves and the wider environment. Managers can recognize that they are actively engaged in shaping their internal world and the surrounding environment. The manager may realize that his core assumptions about the decision situation, values, and interests must be altered.

Table 8.1 Wisdom principles description

Wisdom Principles	Description*
Multi-Perspective Consideration (MPC)	The extent to which the decision short- and long-term outcomes and ramifications are analysed, alternative points of view are represented as well as individual and communal interests and values are reconciled, and ethical codes are considered. Includes the following wisdom aspects: - Future Thinking - Perspective Taking (Considering alternative points of view) - Ethical Consideration
Cognitive-Emotional Mastery (CEM)	The extent to which the decision maker's cognitive abilities and emotional qualities are integrated throughout the decision-making process. Includes the following wisdom aspects: - Cognitive Mastery - Emotional Mastery
Self-Other Awareness (SOA)	The extent to which the decision maker's self-awareness (awareness of the internal world) is integrated with his/her Other-awareness (awareness of others, and the external world). Includes the following wisdom aspects: - Self-Awareness - Other-Awareness
Internal-External Reflection (IER)	A detailed consideration and critical (re-)evaluation of the decision-related facts and assumptions in order to gain a better understanding of the decision situation and how to address the decision problem. Includes the following wisdom aspects: - Internal Reflection - External Reflection

* The wisdom aspects listed in the table, have been discussed in detail in the previous chapter.

The change, however, is not limited to the internal world, as the external world may also need to be altered or transformed for the greater good (Baltes & Staudinger, 2000). Wisdom is balancing various elements (e.g. short and long term, intra-, inter-, and extra-personal interests) in order to *adapt, alter,* or *move* to a new environment (Sternberg, 1998, 2004). Making a wise decision may be based on an adoption of external belief frameworks. That is, the wise manager may adapt to the external belief systems rather than insisting on his own inner value system.

Biloslavo and McKenna (2013) refer to Nelson Mandela as a case in which the person's value system, the dominant social interests' values system, and attitudes are reformed towards good ends. In this sense, wisdom manifests as an other-regarding and unselfish quality (Prewitt, 2002), that generates pervasive positive effects (Küpers, 2007). Yang (2011) argues that wise people may influence the external world at the societal and organizational levels: "outstanding leaders may display wisdom if they are able to produce positive influences on themselves, on others around them, on their organizations, and on the larger community" (p. 628). As Arlin (1990) puts it "wise decisions, solutions, and judgments are often acknowledged as wise, because they push standards to their limit or create types of meta-standards that redefine the acceptable" (p. 237). Table 8.1 provides descriptions for each principle.

As we have emphasized in this and previous chapters, the wisdom principles are inter-related, and, therefore, must be considered as a whole during the decision-making process. Below we describe the relationship between the wisdom principles.

Wisdom Principles Relationships

IER connects and strengthens the other wisdom principles MPC, SOA, and CEM (Figure 8.3). As discussed earlier in this chapter, wise management decisions are effective decisions that are based on a consideration of multiple perspectives (MPC). The accuracy and development of MPC is highly dependent on the extent to which the decision maker is able and willing to incorporate both cognition and emotions into the decision-making process (CEM). A manager who lacks self-awareness or is unaware of what is going around him and the decision situation will not be able to achieve a high level of CEM. As Kramer (1990) asserts "one must be able to first become aware of and then transcend one's projections before one can develop both the empathic skills and the cognitive processes associated with wisdom" (p. 296). SOA helps the manager to acquire a better understanding of emotion-related characteristics in relation to one's decisions. The three principles are highly dependent on IER (Figure 8.3).

IER can lead to a better understanding of self and others (SOA), and help make decisions based on a critical assessment and (re-)evaluation of one's and others' pre-vious decisions (failures and successes), values, interests, goals, knowledge, and abilities. By enhancing the manager's SOA, IER may lead the manager to develop or fortify their attributes and values to match the environmental context. A manager who has a high level of SOA better understands what motivates him or others in relation to the deci-sion situation, and what is driving the decision that he makes. IER allows the manager to understand whether the motives are the right ones, and how to act accordingly. This accords with Sternberg's (1998) Balance Theory of wisdom, in that the wise manager may take one of three different responses to the environmental context: change, adap-tation, or adopting a new environment.

A decision cannot be wise if it is ego-centric; it needs to take a broader perspective, including self and others. Awareness, by and of itself, does not necessarily take the

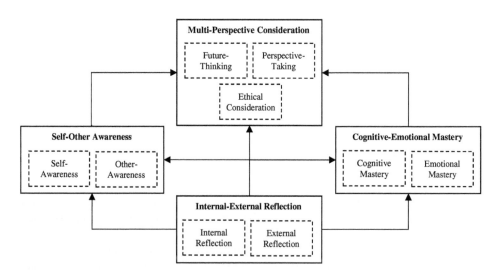

Figure 8.3 Wise management decision-making: wisdom principles relationships

decision maker beyond being self-centric. A reflective assessment of SOA can help the decision maker to gain a better understanding of the relationship between self and others. Awareness of one's own and others' attributes and characteristics as well as of the surrounding environment enables managers to interact empathically with others, make sound judgements and decisions, and effectively act in a given context by bearing in mind, and unifying, different points of view (MPC). As Stacey (2003) points out, people's awareness of self and others is important in individuals' interrelationships: "the nature of interaction between people depends upon the extent to which those people are aware of the nature of their own and each other's behaviour" (p. 134). Hess and Bacigalupo's (2011) understanding of self-awareness represents the interconnection of self-awareness, other-awareness, and empathy: "being self-aware also implies acknowledging one's weaknesses and having the confidence to recognize the strengths of others in decision making. Self-awareness also includes the skill of recognizing the impact of one's styles and behaviours on others" (p. 716).

MPC is also supported by CEM. A decision maker who balances his cognitive assessment of the decision situation by applying emotional mastery can have greater empathy towards those people who will be affected by the consequences of the decision. A decision maker's cognitive process and empathy requires awareness of both self and others. This awareness is enhanced through reflection. Reflection reduces self-centredness and, as a result, increases one's compassionate love and sympathy for others by leading one to have deeper understanding of the motives and behaviours of self and others (Bergsma & Ardelt, 2012). Accordingly, development of CEM requires SOA and IER. In order for the manager to be cognitively and emotionally competent, he needs to be aware of himself and the surrounding environment. CEM, on the other hand, helps a person enhance his SOA. For example, an insightful understanding of one's (in-)abilities, knowledge, and personality can lead to an unbiased and better awareness of self.

From Principles to Practice

How do the wisdom principles and wise management decisions manifest in the decision-making process? One of the key challenges in the information age that we live in is how to effectively use data and information in decision making (Figure 8.4). Allee (1997) argues that decision makers may be trapped in a 'data addiction' loop if they attempt to solve the problem by objectifying knowledge and information, and merely relying on data. The decision maker keeps collecting data and information (the Collection level in

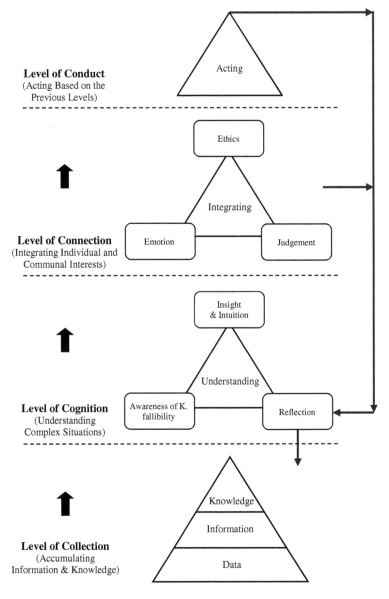

Figure 8.4 The meta-competencies theory of practical wisdom (adapted from Intezari & Pauleen, 2013, p. 165)

Figure 8.4) without critically reflecting on the application of the data and information, and without using his insight and intellect to apply them (Intezari & Pauleen, 2013). Allee (1997) suggests that "the only way to break this addictive cycle is by moving to a higher level of self-awareness, self-reflection, and creative choice" and that "the real solution for difficult decisions often is not more information, but more *reflection*. The ultimate solution for hard choices is not an *Information* solution, it is a *Wisdom* solution" (p. 14).

As discussed in Chapter 6, an effective decision is the one that goes beyond intention. A decision problem is not fully addressed until the selected alternative is put into practice (the level of Conduct in Figure 8.4). The effective decision is made based upon a correct and comprehensive understanding of the decision situation by reconciling insight and intuition, and refining one's knowledge regularly through reflection (the level of Cognition). The levels of Collection and Cognition enable the decision maker to gain a more correct understanding of the decision situation.

We have learnt that wisdom engages and enacts ethics and consideration of stakeholders' perspectives and interests. Once the decision maker gains an understanding of the decision situation, the wise manager articulates the decision goals, develops and assesses alternatives, and chooses the best possible solution. The alternatives are developed and selected based upon the criteria that the decision will lead not only to effective actions and consequences but also to *right actions* by *right means* (level of Conduct) (Intezari & Pauleen, 2013).

We reiterate here that wise management decision making is an integrated approach to meta decision making that applies wisdom principles. That is, the four principles should be present in the decision-making process to ensure wise decision making. This accords with psychological studies of wisdom where the unitary and synthetic nature of wisdom is emphasized (Wink & Helson, 1997). Achenbaum and Orwoll (1991) provide a model of wisdom and argue that the enhancement of wisdom requires the development of all the areas of personality. Orwoll and Perlmutter (1990) argue for the importance of a synthesis of cognition and affect with wisdom. Kunzmann (2004) emphasizes that wisdom is different from other personal characteristics, as wisdom is "integrative and involves cognitive, affective, and motivational elements" (p. 505). Similarly, Ardelt (2004) and Bergsma and Ardelt (2012) conceptualize wisdom as an integration of cognitive, reflective, and compassionate personality traits. König and Glück (2013) confirm the conceptualization of wisdom as an integrative quality of cognition, reflection, and affect. Likewise, Pascual-Leone (1990) stresses that the integration of one's affect, conation, cognition, and experience is important in wisdom. In addition, Kramer (1990, p. 296) argues for an "affective-cognitive integration" which is the integration of dialectical and relativistic suppositions about affect, thinking, and reflection. Even in some less secularized Asian traditions, as Baltes and Kunzmann (2004) mention, wisdom is treated as an integration of mind and virtue.

Chapter summary

In this chapter, we introduced a model of wise management decision making, which is an approach to meta decision making. According to the model, a wise management decision is based on four principles: Multi-Perspective Consideration (MPC), Cognitive-Emotional Mastery (CEM), Self-Other Awareness (SOA), and Internal-External Reflection (IER). It is worthwhile to review these principles.

The MPC principle is concerned with making decisions based on multiple perspectives including the consequences of the alternatives over the short and long term, others' ideas, individual and communal interests, as well as legal and ethical commitments. MPC requires the decision maker to transcend self-interest by engaging deliberately with the consequences of the managers' actions, especially in uncertain situations where making decisions may not be very easy due to the high likelihood of negative impacts on others.

MPC draws on the other wisdom principles. Without awareness of one's own strengths, weaknesses, (in-)abilities, knowledge, and personality, as well as what is happening around him in the decision situation, one will be unable to accurately consider others' perspectives or points of view. Another principle that is important in wise management decision making is the integration of cognition and emotions (CEM). While possessing and being able to apply appropriate knowledge and expertise in identifying and handling strategic decision situations is a prerequisite for effective management decision making, a wise management decision requires more than pure reliance on cognition. Strategic decisions potentially have profound and wide impacts on numerous stakeholders. For this reason, over-reliance on or complete ignorance of feelings and emotions may result in an over- or underestimation of the impacts of a decision. The CEM principle underpins the need for harmonizing cognition and emotions in the decision-making process.

The level of SOA and CEM in a management decision-making process depends upon the extent to which the manager continuously applies a critical assessment and (re-) evaluation of previous decisions, his and others' values systems, interests, and knowledge, as well as the core assumptions underlying people's understating of the decision situation. Wise management decision making draws on a combination of both internal and external reflection: IER. IER serves as a mirror for the manager to better understand his position in the decision-making process in relation to the internal and external world contexts.

We discussed in this chapter that a management strategic decision is made at three main stages: meta decision making, decision making, and sub decision making. Meta decision making refers to the decision maker's assumption and approach to the process of deciding as a whole. The main decision-making process, which directly deals with the problem at hand, represents the second level of decision making. This level of decision making engages sub-decisions that deal with different phases and functions of a decision. The model suggests that applying wise management decision making as meta decision making not only improves the quality of decisions at a given time, but also enables managers to improve their ability to make decisions and develop their practical wisdom over time. The decisions that the wise manager makes and puts into practice then become practices that are reflected on again and become part of new iterations of decision making. Throughout the process, the decision maker's MPC, CEM, SOA, and IER continuously evolve over time, which in turn leads to the development of the decision maker's own innate wisdom. The pathway to wisdom in management settings will be further discussed in the following chapter.

It is important to note that the quality and effectiveness of decisions are directly linked to the consequences of the decisions. That is, during the process of decision making, it is difficult to clearly assess and decisively announce that the decision is going to be effective or 'wise', until the consequences emerge. Accordingly, we do by no means assume that the incorporation of the wisdom principles into decisions and action will guarantee the outcomes of a particular decision will be wise. There are a number of other factors that might be unidentifiable prior to the decision being made or otherwise beyond the decision maker's control that might negatively affect the outcome of a decision. The model of wise management decision making proposes an integral approach to bring together the most important and relevant aspects of management wisdom in the strategic decision-making process. Applying the meta decision-making model can enhance the likelihood of the outcome of the decision being considered and qualified as wise.

References

Achenbaum, A. W., & Orwoll, L. (1991). Becoming wise: A psycho-gerontological interpretation of the book of Job. *The International Journal of Aging and Human Development*, 32(1), 21–39.

Ackoff, R. L. (1999). On learning and the systems that facilitate it. *Reflection*, 1(1), 14–29.

Allee, V. (1997). *The knowledge evolution: Expanding organizational intelligence.* London: Butterworth-Heinemann.

Anderson, B. F. (2002). *The three secrets of wise decision making.* Portland, OR: Single Reef Press.

Ardelt, M. (2004). Wisdom as expert knowledge system: A critical review of a contemporary operationalization of an ancient concept. *Human Development*, 47, 257–285.

Aristotle. (2009). *The Nicomachean Ethics.* (D. Ross, Trans.). Oxford: Oxford University Press.

Arlin, P. K. (1990). Wisdom: The art of problem finding. In R. J. Sternberg (Ed.), *Wisdom: Its nature, origins, and development* (pp. 230–243). New York: Cambridge University Press.

Baltes, P. B., & Kunzmann, U. (2004). The two faces of wisdom: Wisdom as a general theory of knowledge and judgment about excellence in mind and virtue vs. wisdom as everyday realization in people and products. *Human Development*, 47(5), 290–299.

Baltes, P. B., & Staudinger, U. M. (2000). Wisdom: A metaheuristic (pragmatic) to orchestrate mind and virtue toward excellence. *American Psychologist*, 55(1), 122–136.

Bazerman, M. H., & Chugh, D. (2006). Decisions without blinders. *Harvard Business Review*, 84(1), 88–97.

Bazerman, M. H., & Malhotra, D. (2006). It's not intuitive: Strategies for negotiating more rationally. *Negotiation*, 9(5), 3–5.

Bergsma, A., & Ardelt, M. (2012). Self-reported wisdom and happiness: An empirical investigation. *Journal of Happiness Studies2*, 13(3), 481–499.

Biloslavo, R., & McKenna, B. (2013). Testing a 4-dimensional model of wisdom on wise political leaders. In W. Küpers & D. J. Pauleen (Eds.), *A handbook of practical wisdom: Leadership, organization and integral business practice* (pp. 111–132). Aldershot, UK: Gower.

Birren, J. E., & Fisher, L. M. (1990). The elements of wisdom: Overview and integration. In R. J. Sternberg (Ed.), *Wisdom: Its nature, origins, and development* (pp. 317–332). Cambridge, UK: Cambridge University Press.

Bolton, G. (2010). *Reflective practice: Writing and professional development* (3rd ed.). London: Sage.

Calabretta, G., Gemser, G., & Wijnberg, N. M. (2017). The interplay between intuition and rationality in strategic decision making: A paradox perspective. *Organization Studies*, 38(3–4), 365–401.

Cammock, P. (2003). *The dance of leadership: The call for soul in 21st century leadership* (2nd ed.). Auckland, New Zealand: Prentice Hall.

Csikszentmihalyi, M., & Rathunde, K. (1990). The psychology of wisdom: An evolutionary interpretation. In R. J. Sternberg (Ed.), *Wisdom: Its nature, origins, and development* (pp. 25–51). New York: Cambridge.

Cunliffe, A. L. (2003). Reflexive inquiry in organizational research: Questions and possibilities. *Human Relations*, 56(8), 983–1003.

Cyert, R. M., Simon, H. A., & Trow, D. B. (1956). Observation of a business decision. *The Journal of Business*, 29(4), 237–248.

Damasio, A. R. (2005). *Descartes' error: Emotion, reason, and the human brain*. New York: Penguin Books.

Donaldson, L. (2007). Ethics problems and problems with ethics: Toward a pro-management theory. *Journal of Business Ethics*, 78(3), 299–311.

Drucker, P. F. (1967). The effective decision. *Harvard Business Review*, 45(1), 92–98.

Endsley, M. R. (2004). *Designing for situation awareness: An approach to user-centered design* (2nd ed.). Boca Raton, FL: CRC Press.

Erikson, M. (2009). Authentic leadership: Practical reflexivity, self-awareness, and self-authorship. *Journal of Management Education*, 33(5), 747–771.

George, J. M. (2000). Emotions and leadership: The roles of emotional intelligence. *Human Relations*, 53(8), 1027–1055.

Goede, M. (2011). The wise society: Beyond the knowledge economy. *Foresight*, 13(1), 36–45.

Grimm, S. R. (2015). Wisdom. *Australasian Journal of Philosophy,* 93(1), 139–154.

Grossmann, I., Karasawa, M., Izumi, S., Na, J., Varnum, M. E. W., Kitayama, S., & Nisbett, R. E. (2012). Aging and wisdom: Culture matters. *Psychological Science*, 23(10), 1059–1066.

Hall, S. (2010). *Wisdom: From philosophy to neuroscience*. New York: Alfred Knopf.

Hays, M. J. (2007). Dynamics of organizational wisdom. *Business*, 2(4), 77–122.

Hess, J. D., & Bacigalupo, A. C. (2011). Enhancing decisions and decision-making processes through the application of emotional intelligence skills. *Management Decision*, 49(5), 710–721.

Holliday, S. G., & Chandler, M. J. (1986). *Wisdom: Explorations in adult competence*. Basel, Switzerland: Karger.

Intezari, A., & Pauleen, D. J. (2013). Students of wisdom: An integral Meta-competencies theory of practical wisdom. In W. Küpers & D. J. Pauleen (Eds.), *A handbook of practical wisdom: Leadership, organization and integral business practice* (pp. 155–174). Aldershot, UK: Gower.

Intezari, A., & Pauleen, D. J. (2014). Management wisdom in perspective: Are you virtuous enough to succeed in volatile times? *Journal of Business Ethics*, 120(3), 393–404.

Jones, S. K., Frish, D., Yurak, T. J., & Kim, E. (1998). Choices and opportunities: Another effect of framing on decisions. *Journal of Behavioral Decision Making*, 11(3), 211–226.

Keeney, R. L., & Raiffa, H. (1993). *Decisions with multiple objectives: Preferences and value tradeoffs*. Cambridge, UK: Cambridge University Press.

Kitchener, K. S., & Brenner, H. G. (1990). Wisdom and reflective judgment: Knowing in the face of uncertainty. In R. J. Sternberg (Ed.), *Wisdom: Its nature, origins, and development* (pp. 212–229). New York: Cambridge University Press.

Kleimann, B. (2013). University presidents as wise leaders? Aristotle's phrónêsis and academic leadership in Germany. In W. Küpers & D. J. Pauleen (Eds.), *A handbook of practical wisdom: Leadership, organization and integral business practice* (pp. 175–195). Aldershot, UK: Gower.

König, S., & Glück, J. (2013). Individual differences in wisdom conceptions: Relationships to gratitude and wisdom. *International Journal of Aging and Human Development*, 77(2), 127–147.

Korac-Kakabadse, N., Korac-Kakabadse, A., & Kouzmin, A. (2001). Leadership renewal: Towards the philosophy of wisdom. *International Review of Administrative Sciences*, 67(2), 207–227.

Kramer, D. A. (1990). Conceptualizing wisdom: The primacy of affect-cognition relations. In R. J. Sternberg (Ed.), *Wisdom: Its nature, origins, and development* (pp. 279–313). New York: Cambridge University Press.

Kunzmann, U. (2004). Approaches to a good life: The emotional-motivational side of wisdom. In P. A. Linley, S. Joseph, & M. E. P. Seligman (Eds.), *Positive psychology in practice* (pp. 504–517). Hoboken, NJ: Wiley.

Küpers, W. (2007). Phenomenology and integral pheno-practice of wisdom in leadership and organization. *Social Epistemology: A Journal of Knowledge, Culture, and Policy*, 21(2), 169–193.

Lombardo, T. (2010). Wisdom facing forward: What it means to have heightened future consciousness. *The Futurist*, 44(5), 34–42.

Maddalena, V., & Canada, H. (2007). A practical approach to ethical decision-making. *Leadership in Health Services*, 20(2), 71–75.

MacMillan, H., & Tampoe, M. (2000). *Strategic management: Process, content, and implementation*. New York: Oxford University Press.

Matthews, P. (1998). What lies beyond knowledge management: Wisdom creation and versatility. *Journal of Knowledge Management*, 1(3), 207–214.

McKenna, R. J., & Martin-Smith, B. (2005). Decision making as a simplification process: New conceptual perspectives. *Management Decision*, 43(6), 821–836.

McKenna, B., Rooney, D., & Liesch, P. W. (2006). Beyond knowledge to wisdom in international business strategy. *Prometheus*, 24(3), 283–300.

Meacham, J. A. (1990). The loss of wisdom. In R. J. Sternberg (Ed.), *Wisdom: Its nature, origins, and development* (pp. 181–211). New York: Cambridge University Press.

Messick, D. M., & Bazerman, M. H. (2001). Ethical leadership and the psychology of decision making. In J. Dienhart, D. Moberg, & R. Duska (Eds.), *The next phase of business ethics: Integrating psychology and ethics* (pp. 213–238). Oxford, UK: JAI Elsevier.

Mintzberg, H., & Westley, F. (2001). Decision making: It's not what you think. *MIT Sloan Management Review*, 42(3), 89–94.

Mintzberg, H., Raisinghani, D., & Théorêt, A. (1976). The structure of "unstructured" decision processes. *Administrative Science Quarterly*, 21(2), 246–275.

Moore, D. A., & Loewenstein, G. (2004). Self-interest, atomaticity, and the psychology of conflict of interest. *Social Justice Research*, 17(2), 189–202.

Murnighan, K. J., Cantelon, D. A., & Elyashiv, T. (2001). Bounded personal ethics and the tap dance of real estate agency. In J. A. Wagner III, J. M. Bartunek, & K. D. Elsbach (Eds.), *Advances in qualitative organizational research Vol. 3* (pp. 1–40). New York: Elsevier.

Newell, A., & Simon, H. A. (1972). *Human problem solving*. Englewood Cliffs, NJ: Prentice-Hall.

Nonaka, I., & Takeuchi, H. (2011). The big idea: The wise leader. *Harvard Business Review*, 89(5), 58–67.

Northouse, P. G. (2016). *Leadership: Theory and practice* (7th ed.). Los Angeles, CA: Sage Publications.

Orwoll, L., & Perlmutter, M. (1990). The study of wise persons: Integrating a personality perspective. In R. J. Sternberg (Ed.), *Wisdom: Its nature, origins, and development* (pp. 160–177). New York: Cambridge University Press.

Pascual-Leone, J. (1990). An essay on wisdom: Toward organismic processes that make it possible. In R. J. Sternberg (Ed.), *Wisdom: Its nature, origins, and development* (pp. 244–278). New York: Cambridge University Press.

Prewitt, V. R. (2002). Wisdom in the workplace. *Performance Improvement Quarterly*, 15(1), 84–98.

Reznitskaya, A., & Sternberg, R. J. (2004). Teaching students to make wise judgments: The "teaching for wisdom" program. In A. Demetriou (Ed.), *Positive psychology in practice* (pp. 181–196). New York: Wiley.

Robinson, D. N. (1990). Wisdom through the ages. In R. J. Sternberg (Ed.), *Wisdom: Its nature, origins, and development* (pp. 13–24). New York: Cambridge University Press.

Roca, E. (2007). Intuitive practical wisdom in organizational life. *Social Epistemology*, 21(2), 195–207.

Sharp, A. M. (2007). Let's go visiting: Learning judgment-making in a classroom community of inquiry. *Gifted Education International*, 23(3), 301–312.

Simon, H. A. (1960). *The new science of management decision*. New York: Harper & Row.

Simon, H. A. (1978). *Administrative behavior* (2nd ed.). New York: Free Press.

Simon, H. A. (1987). Making management decisions: The role of intuition and emotion. *The Academy of Management Executive*, 1(1), 57–64.

Smyth, H. (2008). The credibility gap in stakeholder management: Ethics and evidence of relationship management. *Construction Management and Economics*, 26(6), 633–643.

Stacey, R. D. (2003). *Strategic management and organizational dynamics: The challenge of complexity* (4th ed.). Harlow, UK: Pearson Education.

Sternberg, R. J. (1986). Intelligence, wisdom, and creativity: Three is better than one. *Educational Psychologist*, 21(3), 175–190.

Sternberg, R. J. (2004). What is wisdom and how can we develop it? *The Annals of the American Academy of Political and Social Science*, 591(1), 164–174.

Sternberg, R. J. (1998). A balance theory of wisdom. *Review of General Psychology*, 2(4), 347–365.

Waddock, S. (2010). Finding wisdom within – The role of seeing and reflective practice in developing moral imagination, aesthetic sensibility, and systems understanding. *Journal of Business Ethics Education*, 7(1), 177–196.

Wink, P., & Helson, R. (1997). Practical and transcendent wisdom: Their nature and some longitudinal findings. *Journal of Adult Development*, 4(1), 1–15.

Yang, S. (2011). Wisdom displayed through leadership: Exploring leadership-related wisdom. *The Leadership Quarterly*, 22(4), 616–632.

9 The path to management wisdom

Introduction

The complexity and dynamism of many management decision situations require managers not only to be able to effectively handle a problem at hand, but also to continuously improve their decision-making skills so they are able to act more responsively and wisely in future situations. There is a growing call for developing wisdom in management (Rowley & Gibbs, 2008). Maxwell has argued for an intellectual revolution in academia to promote wisdom over the mere acquisition of knowledge (1984, 2007, 2013). These and other calls lead to an important question: how can a manager learn, develop, refine, and improve her wisdom?

Management education and training programmes are based on the premise of knowledge transmission from lecturers and textbooks to students or trainees. As stated in this book, being knowledgeable does not necessarily mean to be wise or that one's decisions are wise. In Chapter 4, we argued that while knowledge is an aspect of wisdom, wisdom is qualitatively different from data, information, and knowledge. Many conventional MBA programmes and management training programmes, which are focused on teaching and transferring information or conveying propositional knowledge, do not teach about or help to cultivate wisdom. However, developing management wisdom can help professional practitioners improve decision making, especially when dealing with complex and wicked problems.

The four wisdom principles and the wise management decision-making model, as discussed in previous chapters, suggest a way forward for managers who want to develop and nurture their own management wisdom. Deliberately implementing these principles – MPC, SOA, CEM, and IER – can help a manager to make wiser decisions when dealing with complex and wicked problems.

To review, MPC (Multi-Perspective Consideration) was defined as the extent to which decision outcomes and ramifications are analysed, both short- and long-term outcomes are considered, alternative points of view are represented, individual and communal interests are reconciled, and ethical codes are respected.

Furthermore, we defined CEM (Cognitive-Emotional Mastery) as the extent to which the decision maker's cognitive and emotional abilities or qualities are integrated throughout the decision-making process.

SOA (Self-Other Awareness) was defined as the extent to which the decision maker's awareness of self and the internal world is integrated with her awareness of others around her and the wider external world.

Finally, we defined IER (Internal-External Reflection) as continuous (re-)evaluation of one's own position in the decision-making process against the internal and external world.

Rooney, McKenna, and Liesch (2010) argue that wisdom exists in everyone to some degree, although most people may not become truly wise. We have argued that a manager can make wise(r) strategic decisions by applying the wisdom principles. Now, the point that we want to highlight in this chapter is that the conscientious practice of wise management decision making is itself a path to becoming wiser. By regularly and consistently incorporating the wisdom principles into the decision-making process, the principles become ingrained and embodied. Even more, they become a form of *habitus*, understood as a largely unconscious psychological-cultural system of dispositions, values, skills, and behaviours.

Wise decision making as habitus enhances the manager's responsiveness to complex decision situations, as the principles become part of the manager's character. This habitus of wise decision making is based on integrating the wisdom principles into the decision-making process. This requires a consistent and deep engagement in reflection on self and others. This is a form of reflective learning that is based on practice. Overall, such a recursive reflection-practice process of wise decision making itself becomes a pathway towards practical wisdom.

In this chapter, we introduce a developmental model of management-based wisdom and argue that wisdom development is a continual learning process that engages and integrates all the wisdom principles through an embodied reflective-practice cycle.

Wisdom development

Wisdom is developed through an iterative ongoing process that includes the recursive interaction of reflection and practice (as compared to Experiential Learning Theory).[1] There are two suppositions that underlie the discussion of this process of management-situated decision-based wisdom development. These suppositions draw on what we have learnt so far.

The way that managers' decisions appear in practice is critical in identifying wisdom. In our studies of wisdom in management and organization contexts over the last several years, we noticed that managers identify wise or unwise managers based on the decisions they make and how they make them. Biloslavo and McKenna (2013) argue that wisdom can be judged only based on one's enacting behaviour. A manager will not be considered to be wise unless her decisions and actions are considered to be wise over a period of time. The first supposition, therefore, is that wisdom is action-oriented in nature, and manifests itself in decisions and actions.

The second supposition is that wisdom is a quality that can be learnt and developed (Intezari & Pauleen, 2013; Küpers & Gunnlaugson, 2017; McKenna, 2013). Some psychologists, such as Ardelt (2004, 2010), may argue that wisdom is a personal quality that does not exist independent of wise individuals, and, therefore, must be reserved for wise people. However, we agree with Grimm (2015) that wisdom is an 'in-process state', rather than a settled state. Accordingly, a person who is wise in one decision situation may or may not be wise in another. For example, a manager who does not have the required knowledge and experience in a particular industry may fail to correctly and completely understand a given decision situation in another industry, and, as a result, fail to make a wise decision. For most people wisdom is not a quality that we are born with, but rather one that can be developed. Even if one is not wise, we believe that by using the wisdom principles one can make wise or at least wiser decisions. As we discuss in this chapter, practice is an essential aspect of the wisdom development process. Developing wisdom requires continuous practice and development. Therefore, the practice of decision making can serve as a conduit to wisdom development. What one learns from previous decisions can improve one's decision-making ability (Nutt, 1989). In this way, managers can learn to become wiser.

We have discussed in Chapter 8 that wisdom is applied to the management decision-making process as a meta decision-making approach. Below we introduce a model of management wisdom development.

Wisdom development model

As we learnt in Chapter 1, wisdom is a cardinal virtue consisting of moral and intellectual virtues. Virtue was interpreted as excellence in quality and practice in its broader meaning, and more specifically as a socially valued character trait. While intellectual virtue can be developed directly in the classroom, moral virtues need to be acquired through habituation (O'Toole, 1938). O'Toole (1938) justifies this claim by providing two reasons: first, a classroom is not a laboratory of morals, and second, the mean of virtue may not be the same in different places and times, and for different people. Moral virtue, by definition, is a relative entity defined according to place, time, and person.

We emphasize that management wisdom is fostered through 'learning by doing'. More specifically, management wisdom development is an iterative process of practice and reflection. According to Aristotle (2009), practice is central to wisdom development. The habituation of the wisdom principles happens through practical experiences, where the manager learns over time how to make wiser decisions. This learning takes place by putting the wisdom principles into practice in daily management decision-making situations. A critical component of wisdom development is the habit of reflection, i.e. reflecting on real-life decision situations.

We learnt in the previous chapters that reflection involves the (re-)evaluation of one's own or others' assumptions, values systems, and knowledge in relation to the decision situation, as well as learning from previous decisions. Reflection can be a process of learning and self-development. Reflection involves "learning and developing through examining what we think happened on any occasion, and how we think others perceived the event and us, opening our practice to scrutiny by others, and studying data and texts from the wider sphere" (Bolton, 2010, p. 13). Through reflection on a decision, the manager can see what has worked and what has not or what can or should be changed and improved the next time. In this sense, the decision-making process becomes a learning process that happens through refined practice and reflection.

Reflection and practice do not happen in a closed loop, but rather through stages in a progressive and recursive process. It is a continuous and iterative interaction between practice and reflection that leads to the development of the decision maker's practical wisdom (Figure 9.1).

The practice-reflection cycle addresses self-other awareness, multi-perspective consideration, and cognitive-emotional mastery in a process of moment-to-moment awareness as the elements of a situation come to a point in need of decision and action (Figure 9.2). The practice-reflection cycle is associated with reflecting (Internal and External Reflection), learning and open-mindedness (as part of MPC), creativity (the

Figure 9.1 Practice-reflection recursive process

ability to think outside the square, as part of CEM), deep understanding of the world (being insightfulness vs. superficial, as part of cognitive mastery), and far-sighted deliberation (as part of MPC). To gain a high level of multi-perspective consideration, the manager needs to have self-other awareness. Through self-other awareness, wisdom allows the manager to judge her position in relation to the decision situation in terms of whether or not she is the right person to make the decision, or even get involved in the process. The interaction between self-awareness and other-awareness is recursive too. For example, if the manager's knowledge or expertise is inadequate for making an effective decision, her self-awareness of this knowledge (in)adequacy accompanied by other-awareness helps her to locate the required knowledge or expertise within or outside the organization to assist her to make an effective decision.

By practising MPC, the manager takes into account the circumstances and exigencies that confront them at a particular moment and then, taking the broadest view of self and others as to what it is best to do, they act. Through IER, a manager will be able to bring into consideration multiple perspectives and also focus on the future consequences of the present actions for other people and groups (Figure 9.2). The manager becomes sensitized to the impacts of their practice and actions on and in relation to others including the wider community (e.g. stakeholders in society, and the environment). This implies that a wise management decision not only values the decision maker's personal values, knowledge, and feelings or thoughts, but also requires her at the core of the decision-making process to constantly (re-)define her position with regard to personal, organizational, and societal values and beliefs.

To achieve wisdom, one needs to know one's standing relative to what is good or important for well-being, and know how to achieve well-being (Grimm, 2015): in other words, knowing the difference between ends and means (Higgs, 2012). This distinction leads to our understanding of values and knowing where, when, and how to apply our effort. To this end, wisdom through wise management decision making is embedded in and exhibited by action involving ethical considerations (Rowley, 2006). Wisdom is morally committed action that in the organizational context is concerned with applying organizational knowledge in the process of planning, decision making, and implementation (Bierly, Kessler, & Christensen, 2000). This implies that being practically wise in the business world means that each and every course of action should take into account ethical considerations.

Accordingly, wisdom is more concerned with the use of knowledge than its accumulation. The knowledge must be applied, and applied ethically towards achieving the well-being of self and others as well as the common good. To this end, wisdom

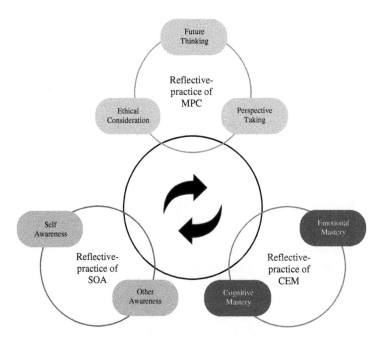

Figure 9.2 Reflection-practice as applied to all wisdom principles

through wise management decision making is embedded in and exhibited by actions that involve ethical considerations (Rowley, 2006). Wise leaders display wisdom by producing positive influences on themselves, on others within the organization, and in the larger community (Yang, 2011). Wise managers are able to create long-term well-being for stakeholders (Rooney, 2013). Wisdom is "the orchestration of human development toward excellence" (Baltes & Staudinger, 2000, p. 122). Wisdom requires deliberation about things that have good ends and can be brought about by action (Aristotle, 2009, *1141b*, 10–15). Thus, wisdom is concerned with learning and enhancing the capacity to learn (Hays, 2010), which evolves over time toward achieving well-being of self (internal world) and others (external world).

Wisdom development rests also on the iterative interaction of cognitive and affective development (Kramer, 1990). As explained in Chapter 7, mastery is not an end state. It is a process of continuous learning. Wise decisions are made based on an integration of cognition and emotion. This integration might be impossible to achieve if the manager fails to continuously reflect on the cognitive and emotional aspects of the decision situation. Cognitive mastery allows the manager to incorporate intellectual, cognitive, and reasoning abilities into the decision-making process. Complementing cognitive mastery, emotional mastery helps the manager to make more decisive and confident decisions in uncertain and turbulent decision situations by applying what they know about taking right actions towards right ends.

Deeper understanding is a result of the integration of internal and external reflection, i.e. IER. Integral reflection, done moment to moment, is known as *reflexivity*. This reflexivity has been defined in the literature as the continuous questioning of one's own perspectives and actions, including habitual experience processing, habitual ways of thinking and relating to other people, and the structures of understanding of self and

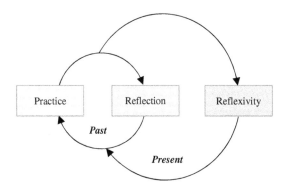

Figure 9.3 Practice, reflection, and reflexivity

their interrelation to the surrounding environment (Bolton, 2010). Reflexivity is more (complex) than just being reflective (Edwards & Küpers, 2014) as it questions one's interrelationship with the social world and the ways one accounts for one's experience (Cunliffe, 2003), presence, and perspectives (Fook, 2002). In essence, reflexivity is a habitus of real-time reflection on self and environment (Figure 9.3).

Thus, wisdom development in management requires moving from non-critical and individual reflection, post decision or action taking, on either the internal or external worlds, towards an ongoing reflective practice (IER) based on learning how to integrate MPC, SOA, and CEM. The manager needs to keep questioning her underlying assumptions, attitudes, thought processes, and habitual actions, by drawing on MPC. She then puts into practice the examined aspects, which will be re-evaluated prior to, during, and after the decision-making process. In this iterative integrated process of practice and reflection, wisdom is developed, exercised, and strengthened in decision making (Rowley, 2006).

Retrospective and prospective reflection

IER in wise management decision making as a reflective learning process will eventually evolve to include a moment-to-moment examination and awareness that focuses close attention upon one's own actions, thoughts, feelings, values, identity, and their effect upon other people, situations, and professional and social structures. Through reflection, the manager questions her management practice and her interrelationship with the social world. She accounts for her experience, presence, and perspectives, and how the management decisions contribute to the wider organizational and social environment. Moment-to-moment reflection (reflexivity) can be strengthened through the use of retrospective (backward-looking) and prospective (forward-looking) reflection (Figure 9.4). Wisdom development requires the manager to not only reflect on previous decisions, but also on the future possibilities and impacts on self and others of different alternatives. Prospective reflection can improve the manager's MPC ability by engaging the future-thinking aspect of wisdom. It involves the ability to locate oneself in the picture, in the moment, to appreciate how the manager's decisions and actions affect others.

On the management path to wisdom, reflective practice must persevere in the practices of management in general and decision making in particular. The manager

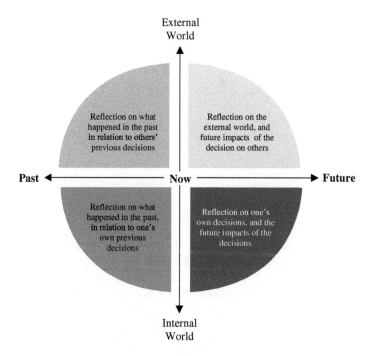

Figure 9.4 Retrospective and prospective reflection

needs to see wise decision-making practice as both an opportunity and a realization of reflective learning for acquiring a deeper understanding of the internal and external world (Chapter 8). Through wise decision making as a reflective practice, the managers are engaged, as a matter of *habit*, in thinking critically, responsibly, and ethically about what their action will mean and imply in the world.

This habitual reflective process needs to inform the manager how she actually practises decision making in the real world. As discussed throughout the book, wisdom is predisposed to act. The manifestation of wisdom in practice can be in the form of changes in the internal and/or external worlds. Through the reflective-learning process, the manager may make fundamental changes in her values system and assumptions. For example, when a manager learns that her values system does not reflect the society's values or ethics, the manager may change her internal world in order to reconstruct her values system to align it with that of society. The manager may also work to change the external world for the greater good, directing the belief and value systems, attitudes, and interests of others in the wider community (organization and business community). This happens when the manager realizes that the decision situation will not be effectively addressed unless the wider community's values, beliefs, and assumptions change. For example, in an organization where people do not consult with each other and do not share their knowledge and experiences, the manager cannot change the situation unless people accept that sharing their knowledge with others is a valuable practice and can improve individual and organizational performance.

The reflective-practice process in Figure 9.5 represents the interaction between the decision-making practice (as it engages MPC, CEM, and SOA) and the reflections of the manager over time.

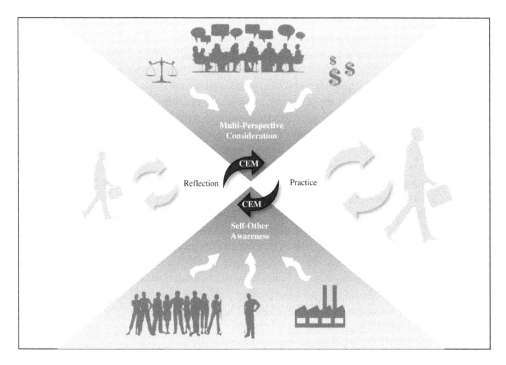

Figure 9.5 Managing a path to wisdom

The reflective-learning process can be self-directed learning. The development of wisdom takes time. It relies on an evolving understanding of self and others, and learning how to integrate such understanding to improve and further one's own (internal world) and others' (external world) well-being. The ability to engage in the depth and breadth of reflection required to initiate and maintain self-directed learning requires the development and habituation of wisdom principles. To master wise decision making, the wisdom principles must become increasingly entwined in the decision situation. The manager's wisdom develops as the 'causes and effects' of the wisdom principles gradually become embodied and habitus. Through the reflective practice of the wisdom principles, the manager's decisions move towards more morally committed and socially responsible right conduct. In this sense, wisdom serves as a predisposition to decision making. That is, wise decision making becomes a habitus more than an intentional implementation of the wisdom principles. If a manager is empathetic towards others, she then makes empathetic decisions. If the manager is self-centric, her decisions are then self-centric. Similarly, if the manager is wise, she makes wise decisions. The wise manager makes wise decisions as a matter of habit. Accordingly, for a manager to be able to make wise decisions, she needs to continuously practise wise decision making.

Chapter summary

Wise management can be understood as embodied management practice. As such it is multidimensional in that it engages, as discussed in Chapter 7, multiple qualities concerning individual and communal values and interests. The qualities constitute the four wisdom principles: MPC, CEM, SOA, and IER (Chapter 8). While we argue that the principles provide the fundamental skill set for making wise decisions, it is 'practice that makes perfect' when it comes to developing these decision-making skills and ultimately walking the path to wisdom. For wise managers, the wisdom principles are more than a set of principles; they are habituated and embodied skills.

Wisdom finds expression in how one behaves in dealing with others and complex decision situations. Wise management decisions are made by managers who learn by practice over time. In this chapter, we argued that a manager's wisdom develops through embodying the wisdom principles over time by continuously practising the principles. The manager's wisdom skills are gradually refined by the manager in the course of professional practice. This refinement of the wisdom skills is for both personal development and for the greater good of the organization and society.

Learning how to make wise decisions requires exposure to and active engagement in the real world. It is necessary to have practical experience with decision making in difficult situations. The learning takes place through a combination of learning and practical experience. The manager must be at the coalface implementing the wisdom principles in a variety of situations in order to learn how to make wise decisions. Embodying the principles requires a dedicated and deepening management practice and the ongoing development of awareness. It is foremost about learning about one's self and others and increasing one's capacity to learn.

The integration of the wisdom principles through the reflective-learning process leads the manager to the questioning of her perspectives, understanding, and actions, including the habitual processing of experience, ways of thinking and relating to other people, and the way self is understood as well as its relationship with the surrounding environment. Through practising wise management decision making, the manager learns to locate herself in the bigger picture, and consider the impact of her management on others in her decisions and actions. Learning wise decision making requires a reflexive (re) evaluation of the manager's decision-making position, which includes reflecting on and appraising one's personal attributes and one's decisions, while constantly monitoring, considering, and integrating the wider environment. The manager enhances her capacity and ability to critically and continuously question her management assumptions, approach, and practice, by improving her awareness about and responsiveness in her relationship with others and how her management practice (including various practices from decisions to actions) contribute to the surrounding environment. The surrounding environment encompasses the organization, business community, and society.

Developing one's wisdom requires the manager to initiate and maintain self-directed and reflective learning towards the 'habituation' and embodiment of wisdom principles. While at one level management decision making is an iterative process of practice and reflection, at a deeper level (wise) decision making can be understood as the embodied and habituated skills of Multi-Perspective Consideration, Self-Other Awareness, Cognitive-Emotional Mastery, and Internal-External Reflection.

The practice of wise decision making in the course of one's career and daily life will inevitably lead to wisdom itself. Wisdom development rests on wise decision making as well as taking an active role in improving self and the surrounding environment. The path to management wisdom is open to all, but like business success itself, requires perseverance and commitment: perseverance to practise and a commitment to deeply reflective learning.

Note

1 The process of developing wise decision-making capacity engages reflection. However, the approach we offer in this book as to reflection is different from the one suggested by Experiential Learning Theory (ELT). ELT has a respected place in management education (Frost & Wallingford, 2013). ELT defines learning as "the process whereby knowledge is created through the transformation of experience. Knowledge results from the combination of grasping and transforming experience" (Kolb & Kolb, 2005, p. 194; Kolb, 1984, p. 41). Although the wisdom development approach presented in this chapter may resemble the practice and reflection of ELT, we believe that the model of wise management decision making's overall focus on the development of practical wisdom expands on ELT in many important ways. For example, according to Holman, Pavlica, and Thorpe (1997), ELT values internal thinking over the role of human relatedness, and the social and historical position of the learner in learning. In contrast, the wise management decision-making model's emphasis on MPC, SOA, CEM, and EIR carries the recognition of the importance of selflessness (humility) and virtue/morality, as well as organizational context and the social and group relations approach in learning (Gould, Stapley, & Stein, 2004).

It is not just about learning how to make wise decisions, but doing so through exposure to the real world. Developing wisdom requires a critical (re)evaluation of one's decision-making position, which includes reflecting on and appraising one's personal attributes and one's decisions, while constantly monitoring, considering, and integrating the wider environment.

References

Ardelt, M. (2004). Wisdom as expert knowledge system: A critical review of a contemporary operationalization of an ancient concept. *Human Development*, 47(5), 257–285.

Ardelt, M. (2010). Are older adults wiser than college students? A comparison of two age cohorts. *Journal of Adult Development*, 17(4), 193–207.

Aristotle. (2009). *The Nicomachean Ethics*. (D. Ross, Trans.). Oxford, UK: Oxford University Press.

Baltes, P. B., & Staudinger, U. M. (2000). Wisdom: A metaheuristic (pragmatic) to orchestrate mind and virtue toward excellence. *American Psychologist*, 55(1), 122–136.

Bierly III, P. E., Kessler, E. H., & Christensen, E. W. (2000). Organizational learning, knowledge and wisdom. *Journal of Organizational Change Management*, 13(6), 595–618.

Biloslavo, R., & McKenna, B. (2013). Testing a 4-dimensional model of wisdom on wise political leaders. In W. Küpers & D. J. Pauleen (Eds.), *A handbook of practical wisdom: Leadership, organization and integral business practice* (pp. 111–132). Aldershot, UK: Gower.

Bolton, G. (2010). *Reflective practice: Writing & professional development* (3rd ed.). London: Sage.

Cunliffe, A. L. (2003). Reflexive inquiry in organizational research: Questions and possibilities. *Human Relations*, 56(8), 983–1003.

Edwards, M. G., & Küpers, W. (2014). *Integral science*. Albany, NY: The State University of New York Press.

Fook, J. (2002). *Social work: Critical theory and practice*. London: Sage.

Frost, D. E., & Wallingford, V. (2013). Experiential learning for developing managers: A practical model. *Journal of Management Development*, 32(7), 756–767.

Gould, L. J., Stapley, L. F., & Stein, M. (Eds.). (2004). *Experiential learning in organizations*. London: Karanac.

Grimm, S. R. (2015). Wisdom. *Australasian Journal of Philosophy*, 93(1), 139–155.

Hays, J. M. (2010). The ecology of wisdom. *Management & Marketing*, 5(1), 71–92.

Higgs, J. (2012). Realising practical wisdom from the pursuit of wise practice. In E. A. Kinsella & A. Pitman (Eds.), *Phronesis as professional knowledge* (pp. 73–85). Rotterdam, The Netherlands: Sense Publishers.

Holman, D., Pavlica, K., & Thorpe, R. (1997). Rethinking Kolb's theory of experiential learning in management education. *Management Learning*, 28(2), 135–148.

Intezari, A., & Pauleen, D. J. (2013). Students of wisdom: An integral meta-competencies theory of practical wisdom. In W. Küpers & D. J. Pauleen (Eds.), *A handbook of practical wisdom: Leadership, organization and integral business practice* (pp. 155–174). Aldershot, UK: Gower.

Kolb, D. A. (1984). *Experiential learning: Experience as the source of learning and development.* Englewood Cliffs, NJ: Prentice-Hall.

Kolb, A. Y., & Kolb, D. A. (2005). Learning styles and learning spaces: Enhancing experiential learning in higher education. *Academy of Management Learning & Education*, 4(2), 193–212.

Kramer, D. A. (1990). Conceptualizing wisdom: The primacy of affect-cognition relations. In R. J. Sternberg (Ed.), *Wisdom: Its nature, origins, and development* (pp. 279–313). New York: Cambridge University Press.

Küpers, W., & Gunnlaugson, O. (2017). *Wisdom learning: Perspectives on wising-up business and management education.* New York: Routledge.

Maxwell, N. (1984). *From knowledge to wisdom: A revolution in the aims & methods of science.* Oxford, UK: Basil Blackwell.

Maxwell, N. (2007). Can the world learn wisdom? *The E-Newsletter of Solidarity, Sustainability, and Non-Violence*, 3(4). Retrieved from www.pelicanweb.org/solisustv03n04maxwell.html.

Maxwell, N. (2013). From knowledge to wisdom: Assessment and prospects after three decades. *Integral Review*, 9(2), 76–112.

McKenna, B. (2013). Teaching for wisdom: Cross cultural perspectives on fostering wisdom. *Academy of Management Learning & Education*, 12(2), 319–320.

Nutt, P. C. (1989). *Making tough decisions.* San Francisco: Jossey-Bass.

O'Toole, C. J. (1938). The teaching of intellectual and moral virtues. *Ethics*, 49(1), 81–84.

Rooney, D. (2013). Being a wise organizational researcher: Ontology, epistemology and axiology. In W. Küpers & D. J. Pauleen (Eds.), *A handbook of practical wisdom: Leadership, organization and integral business practice* (pp. 79–98). Farnham, UK: Gower.

Rooney, D., McKenna, B., & Liesch, P. (2010). *Wisdom and management in the knowledge economy.* New York: Routledge.

Rowley, J. (2006). Where is the wisdom that we have lost in knowledge? *Journal of Documentation*, 62(2), 251–270.

Rowley, J., & Gibbs, J. (2008). From learning organization to practically wise organization. *The Learning Organization*, 15(5), 356–372.

Yang, S. (2011). Wisdom displayed through leadership: Exploring leadership-related wisdom. *The Leadership Quarterly*, 22(4), 616–632.

Index

Please note that page references to figures are in *italics* and reference to tables are in **bold**. Footnotes are denoted by the letter 'n' and the note number following the page number.

For Product Safety Concerns and Information please contact our EU
representative GPSR@taylorandfrancis.com
Taylor & Francis Verlag GmbH, Kaufingerstraße 24, 80331 München, Germany

www.ingramcontent.com/pod-product-compliance
Ingram Content Group UK Ltd.
Pitfield, Milton Keynes, MK11 3LW, UK
UKHW051835180425
457613UK00023B/1268